Attachment in Group Psychotherapy

Attachment in Group Psychotherapy

Cheri L. Marmarosh
Rayna D. Markin
Eric B. Spiegel

American Psychological Association

Washington, DC

Published by
American Psychological Association
750 First Street, NE
Washington, DC 20002
www.apa.org

To order
APA Order Department
P.O. Box 92984
Washington, DC 20090-2984
Tel: (800) 374-2721; Direct: (202) 336-5510
Fax: (202) 336-5502; TDD/TTY: (202) 336-6123
Online: www.apa.org/pubs/books
E-mail: order@apa.org

In the U.K., Europe, Africa, and the Middle East, copies may be ordered from
American Psychological Association
3 Henrietta Street
Covent Garden, London
WC2E 8LU England

Typeset in Goudy by Circle Graphics, Inc., Columbia, MD

Printer: Edwards Brothers, Inc., Lillington, NC
Cover Designer: Minker Design, Sarasota, FL

The opinions and statements published are the responsibility of the authors, and such opinions and statements do not necessarily represent the policies of the American Psychological Association.

Library of Congress Cataloging-in-Publication Data

Marmarosh, Cheri L.
 Attachment in group psychotherapy / Cheri L. Marmarosh, Rayna D. Markin, and Eric B. Spiegel. — First edition.
    pages cm
 Includes bibliographical references and index.
 ISBN-13: 978-1-4338-1321-4
 ISBN-10: 1-4338-1321-1
 1. Group psychotherapy. 2. Attachment behavior. 3. Object relations (Psychoanalysis) I. Markin, Rayna D. II. Spiegel, Eric B. III. Title.
 RC488.M342 2013
 616.89'152—dc23
                                   2013001883

British Library Cataloguing-in-Publication Data

A CIP record is available from the British Library.

Printed in the United States of America
First Edition

http://dx.doi.org/10.1037/14186-000

To my Secure Bases with much love and appreciation:

My parents, sister, beloved husband, Joel, stepdaughter, Hanna,
and my daughter, Audrey.

I dedicate this book, in loving memory, to the late Jack Corazzini, who
was a secure base to dozens of group therapists, myself included. I still often
recall his reassuring words when I am uncertain or fearful in a group.
"It's not what you do," he always said, "It's what you do about what you do,
that counts." Jack, you live on in all of those people whom you inspired.
—*Cheri Marmarosh*

To Lily, who teaches me more about attachment every single day.

I would like to thank the first group I was ever a part of, my family,
and my husband for their love and support. I would also like to thank
my mentor, Dennis Kivlighan, who taught me that, like life,
group therapy is essentially about taking risks and being oneself.
—*Rayna Markin*

Lily: Having the honor of being your parent has taught me what
it really means to be an attachment figure. Your happiness,
spirit, and curiosity inspire me daily.

Rayna: Your humor, intellect, passion and tenderness bring
a ray of sunshine to the cloudiest of days. Thanks for being the best
partner a husband could ask for.

Thanks also to my parents, Sharon and David, and brothers,
Alan and Jesse, for their love and support.
—*Eric Spiegel*

CONTENTS

ACKNOWLEDGMENTS

There are many to whom we would like to express thanks for their support, encouragement, and feedback in the writing of this book. We would like to thank Eric Chen, Wanda Collins, Bob Conyne, Wendy Fischer, Charles Gelso, Dennis M. Kivlighan, Jr., Joyce Lowenstein, Rosemary Segalla, and Gail Winston for their invaluable insights.

We would also like thank the 2012 Group Psychotherapy Class in the Professional Psychology Program at the George Washington University for their helpful feedback. What they lack in experience, they more than make up for in the passion to learn. We would also like to thank Eliza Behymer for her generous help and assistance in the preparation of the manuscript.

Lastly, we would like to thank Susan Reynolds for the confidence she showed in our idea and the enthusiasm with which she welcomed our manuscript. Her suggestions and feedback have been invaluable. Our editor, Beth Hatch, has also been extremely helpful, and her input has truly strengthened our work.

Attachment in Group Psychotherapy

INTRODUCTION

Almost all mental health issues can be effectively treated in group therapy (Burlingame & Krogel, 2005; Burlingame, MacKenzie, & Strauss, 2004), and most issues for which individuals seek treatment are related to interpersonal issues or influence interpersonal functioning (Yalom & Leszcz, 2005). For example, patients who have long histories of recurrent depression often complain of feeling isolated and disconnected from others. Their loneliness often perpetuates the depression, and the depression often leads to continued withdrawal, negativity, and the self-fulfilling expectations of rejection. Group therapists can offer diverse therapeutic interventions to help these members identify cognitive processes that maintain their symptoms and interpersonal difficulties, challenge maladaptive behaviors that interfere with their relationships, regulate emotions that are painful or uncomfortable to experience, and gain insight into their underlying motivations and conflicts that inhibit closeness (Rutan & Stone, 2001; White & Freeman, 2000; Yalom & Leszcz, 2005).

http://dx.doi.org/10.1037/14186-001
Attachment in Group Psychotherapy, by C. L. Marmarosh, R. D. Markin, and E. B. Spiegel
Copyright © 2013 by the American Psychological Association. All rights reserved.

Regardless of the issues with which group members present, the format of the group (i.e., structured, nonstructured, online), or the theory supporting the group interventions, leading groups is often challenging because there are many internal and interpersonal dynamics influencing the process at any one point in time. Some group members try to manage their fears of abandonment by seeking frequent reassurance and sympathy. Other members defend against weakness by trying to feel superior. Still other members outwardly withdraw from the group while quietly longing for closeness and connection. Each member enacts a different interpersonal dance that affects the overall group climate, and this requires the group leader to intervene in different ways. How can the leader determine which interventions are most palatable and will ultimately benefit each member and the group as a whole? According to attachment theorists, addressing this question requires an understanding of how members relate to others—in other words, their *attachment patterns*.

Our early bond with our primary caregiver (historically the mother) lays the foundation for adult attachment strategies and internal working models of the self and other (Bowlby, 1988; Sroufe, Egeland, Carlson, & Collins, 2005). If a caregiver is sensitive and responsive to the infant or child's needs, the infant or child learns that others are trustworthy and learns to form secure relationships, neither avoiding intimacy nor fearing abandonment. If the caregiver is insensitive, is unresponsive, or responds in inappropriate ways (e.g., by consistently neglecting the infant when he or she cries), the infant or child learns that others are unavailable, unreliable, or untrustworthy and learns to form insecure relationships—avoiding needs, splitting off emotional vulnerability, or fearing abandonment. These early attachment patterns influence future relationships and the attachment styles seen in adulthood (Sroufe et al., 2005). Adults with insecure attachment styles not only have less capacity for healthy intimacy, but they also are more prone to mental health problems such as depression, anxiety, and interpersonal difficulties (Mikulincer & Shaver, 2007b). These individuals will often benefit from group therapy.

As individuals interact in group therapy, they rely on their previous attachment experiences to manage group processes, meet internal needs, and cope with their emotions. Their internal representations of self and others and emotion-regulating strategies are automatically triggered in the group. The group leader must create a safe environment where individuals can explore these implicit attachment-based processes as they are activated in the group sessions. Through feedback from the group and the leader, members explore their current emotional and relationship difficulties in the here and now of the group process, allowing for corrective emotional experiences that contradict attachment failures and ultimately facilitate more attachment security.

This book applies attachment theory to group therapy, explaining how group therapists can work effectively with members who have different attachment histories and current interpersonal strategies. Indeed, an understanding of attachment theory will help group therapists even before the first session of therapy. Screening potential group members, determining who is appropriate for group therapy, and preparing new members before they begin group therapy are critical to successful outcomes. Some individuals are more at risk of dropping out of the group, are inclined to be a scapegoat in the group, struggle to remain engaged in the group process, and avoid emotional intimacy. This book explains why such individuals may have these problems, how to screen for them, whether to assign them to group therapy, and if they are assigned to group therapy, how to prepare them beforehand to maximize the likelihood of a successful outcome. The book also provides group leaders with a structure for ameliorating these problems in group sessions.

Because attachment theory is relevant to a wide variety of presenting problems, this book will appeal to all group therapists. It explains how the leader can facilitate emotional regulation and changes in maladaptive beliefs for those members who struggle with insecure attachment. The remainder of this introduction introduces the various attachment styles and dimensions, explains the relevance of these styles to group therapy, provides clinical examples, and provides an overview of the book's content and organization.

ADULT ATTACHMENT STYLES

The dimensional model of attachment (Brennan, Clark, & Shaver, 1998) posits that there are two underlying fundamental dimensions of adult attachment: anxiety and avoidance. *Anxiety* corresponds to how fearful a person is about relationships, and *avoidance* corresponds to how a person avoids emotional vulnerability in relationships. Depending on whether one is high or low on these two dimensions, his or her attachment style can be more secure (low anxiety and low avoidance), more preoccupied (high anxiety and low avoidance), more dismissing-avoidant (low anxiety and high avoidance), or more fearful-avoidant (high anxiety and high avoidance). Figure 1 depicts the two dimensions and how individuals can fall within four different quadrants based on their level of anxiety and avoidance.

Secure individuals, those low on both dimensions of avoidance and anxiety, neither avoid intimacy with others nor fear rejection or abandonment. They feel capable of seeking out support and trusting others, and they tend to report caring connections with attachment figures and compassion and empathy for romantic partners and family members. Even when there are

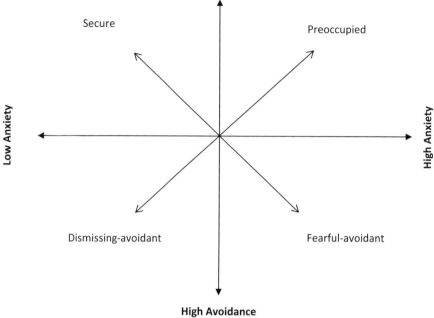

Low Avoidance

Secure

Preoccupied

Low Anxiety

High Anxiety

Dismissing-avoidant

Fearful-avoidant

High Avoidance

Figure 1. Dimensional model of adult attachment.

challenges within a relationship, these individuals tend to forgive others (Mikulincer & Shaver, 2007b).

Preoccupied individuals, those low on avoidance but high on anxiety, are often described as clingy or needy. They report more anxiety about relationships and are hypersensitive to signs of rejection or abandonment. These individuals engage in hyperactivating strategies—that is, they exert intense efforts to achieve and maintain intimate contact—and they are preoccupied with fears of being alone. These individuals tend to seek out others for comfort but are often dissatisfied with the support they receive (Mikulincer & Shaver, 2007b).

Dismissing-avoidant individuals, those high on avoidance but low on anxiety, often keep to themselves and can appear self-reliant. They deny fears of being alone or abandoned and do not generally seek out emotional support from others. They tend to use deactivating strategies—that is, they push others away—to deflect intimate contact, such as making a joke or changing the subject after someone shares something vulnerable. These individuals withdraw and minimize attachment-based needs, and they deny anxiety about rejection and abandonment (Mikulincer & Shaver, 2007b).

Fearful-avoidant individuals, those high on both dimensions of avoidance and anxiety, experience attachment-related anxiety yet avoid intimate contact with others. In essence, they alternate between deactivation (because of fears of rejection) and hyperactivation (because of fears of abandonment). Some theorists have referred to this style as *disorganized* because people with this style engage in both activating and deactivating strategies. Indeed, these individuals are uniquely conflicted because they may withdraw from therapy and avoid intimacy with others in relationships while simultaneously longing for closeness and connection. Their inconsistent behaviors make it particularly hard for them to maintain healthy relationships and regulate emotions under duress (Mikulincer & Shaver, 2007b).

Other commonly used categorical conceptualizations of adult attachment include Bartholomew and Horowitz's (1991) four category model and the Adult Attachment Interview (George, Kaplan, & Main, 1996). In this book, we rely primarily on the dimensional approach because it provides great utility to clinicians (Wallin, 2007) and researchers are moving toward a dimensional conceptualization of attachment (Fraley & Waller, 1998). Instead of focusing only on the two dimensions of anxiety and avoidance, we focus on the four quadrants representing interactions between anxiety and avoidance. However, when we report the work of researchers and theorists who use different attachment measures (both infant and adult) and rely on different conceptualizations of attachment, we use the terminology of the original authors. This occurs most frequently in Chapter 3, in which we review the empirical literature. The reader can consult Table 1 to see how common attachment terms are defined and roughly relate with one another.

Additionally, we often use the word *more* to qualify specific attachment patterns—for example, we may refer to "individuals with more preoccupied attachments." We do this to reflect the fact that individuals fall along a continuum. Their internal representations of self and others are much more complex than simple attachment categories, and not all insecurely attached members are the same even when they fall within the same spectrum of attachment insecurity. In addition, there are many factors that influence how these overall attachment styles are expressed within the therapy group, including the type of therapy group, the group member's diagnoses and level of functioning, and the attachment styles of the members and of the leaders.

ATTACHMENT AND GROUP THERAPY

Group members' attachment styles will always influence the group process. All people implicitly bring their internal working models (i.e., beliefs) of selves and others to new interactions (Andersen, Reznik, & Glassman, 2005;

TABLE 1
Infant and Adult Attachment Category Terms and Definitions

	Infant attachment categories	Adult attachment categories	Adult romantic attachment categories	Adult romantic attachment dimensions
Assessment use	Strange Situation: observation of infants and children briefly separated from and then reunited with their caregivers (Ainsworth, Blehar, Waters, & Wall, 1978)	Adult Attachment Interview: semistructured interview that focuses on the adult's experience of childhood attachment relationships and the effects of these childhood attachments on the adult being interviewed (Main, Goldwyn, & Hesse, 2003)	Self-report: measurement of adult attachment directly by asking people to report on how they feel and function in current relationships (Bartholomew & Horowitz, 1991)	Self-report: measurement of adult attachment directly by asking people to report on how they feel and function in current relationships (Brennan, Clark, & Shaver, 1998)
Attachment term and criteria	*Secure:* explores room, and when caregiver leaves, the child is distressed but able to resume play or exploration when caregiver returns	*Autonomous:* coherent, collaborative discourse; values attachment, and consistent evaluation of experience regardless of whether positive or negative	*Secure:* Endorse, "It is relatively easy for me to become emotionally close to others. I am comfortable depending on others and having others depend on me. I don't worry about being alone or having others not accept me."	*Secure:* these individuals fall in the low range for both dimensions of attachment anxiety and attachment avoidance. They endorse items that indicate ease with emotional closeness and desire for intimacy.
Attachment term and criteria	*Avoidant:* fails to cry or express distress when caregiver leaves; avoids caregiver at reunion, no comfort seeking; appears unemotional on outside but is experiencing stress internally	*Dismissing:* not coherent, dismissing of attachments; contradictory responses ("Mom was supportive," later reveals that she was never home and abandoned family); excessively brief responses	*Dismissive:* endorses "I am comfortable without close emotional relationships. It is very important to me to feel independent and self-sufficient, and I prefer not to depend on others or have others depend on me."	*Dismissing:* these individuals fall in the low range for attachment anxiety but in the high range for attachment avoidance. They endorse items that indicate no fears of abandonment but also no needs for closeness or dependency on others.

Attachment term and criteria	*Resistant/ambivalent:* distress before separation, little exploration, preoccupied with caregiver; not comforted by parent after separation; fails to return to play or exploration	*Preoccupied:* not coherent, preoccupied with past attachment experiences; appears angry, passive, or fearful; excessively long sentences with vague expressions	*Preoccupied:* Endorses "I want to be completely emotionally intimate with others, but I often find that others are reluctant to get as close as I would like. I am uncomfortable being without close relationships, but I sometimes worry that others don't value me as much as I value them."	*Preoccupied:* these individuals fall in the high range for attachment anxiety but in the lower range for attachment avoidance. They endorse items that indicate significant fears of rejection and abandonment but deny avoidance of dependency or desire for closeness in relationships.
Attachment term and criteria	*Disorganized:* disoriented behaviors when with caregiver; collapse of attachment strategy; frozen, paralyzed, clings to caregiver but averts eyes; when not with caregiver, can demonstrate other attachment styles	*Unresolved/disorganized:* lapses in reasoning when topics of loss or abuse are discussed; prolonged silence or detached speech; fits into other categories when not activated	*Fearful:* endorses "I am somewhat uncomfortable getting close to others. I want emotionally close relationships, but I find it difficult to trust others completely, or to depend on them. I sometimes worry that I will be hurt if I allow myself to become too close to others."	*Fearful:* these individuals fall in the high range for both attachment anxiety and avoidance. They endorse items that indicate intense desires for closeness, fears of rejection, and also avoidance of dependency.

Note. Data from Wallin (2007).

Berk & Andersen, 2000), including interactions in group therapy. Group members, like us all, often perceive group interactions on the basis of earlier interpersonal experiences with significant others. Members' attachment styles influence how they have learned to navigate relationships, and they influence the relationships within the group and group process as well. This is one reason group therapy is so helpful. Members engage the group in the same ways they engage people in their daily lives. Even the group member with more attachment security will rely on past relational experiences to interpret new relational experiences, and these interpretations will influence how the individual regulates emotions, empathizes with others, accepts nurturance, expresses and appreciates conflict, and reflects on interpersonal experiences with insight in the group.

For illustration purposes, the following clinical examples depict group members with different attachment styles.

A Secure Member

Juan[1] had never been in counseling before and reported a close relationship with his family. Being on the other side of the country while his family struggled to cope with his father's recent unemployment left him distracted and unable to focus on his classes. The intake coordinator felt that a group would be helpful to Juan because he felt alone and isolated and was struggling with issues other group members could relate to. Juan was quiet at first and then opened up about his feelings of anxiety about being in therapy. Although he expressed ambivalence about being in the group, he quickly developed rapport with the members and was able to talk openly about his feelings. When group members questioned him about his guilt, Juan shared that he felt ashamed that he intentionally avoided going home for the break because he was afraid to see his father. This led him to share information about his cultural background and how he struggled between maintaining his Latino family roots and fitting in with his college peers. Juan was not only able to open up to others in the group, he was able to empathize with them as well. He often reached out to members with compassion but was also able to disagree with members in an appropriate manner. He was well respected in the group and became a leader whom other members trusted and relied on for feedback and support.

Juan's experience of the group demonstrates how a securely attached group member can be both well suited for group and facilitate the group process. More secure individuals tend to model appropriate self-disclosure

---

[1]Throughout the book, names and identifying characteristics of patients have been changed or clinical composites have been used to protect the confidentiality of patients.

(Shechtman & Rybko, 2004) and are able to express negative feelings about the therapist or being in treatment (Woodhouse, Schlosser, Crook, Ligiéro, & Gelso, 2003). More secure individuals are also able to reach out to others with empathy. In addition to providing support, they are able to express a different opinion and tolerate conflict. They are able to navigate relationships without the ongoing fears of being abused, neglected, or abandoned (Mikulincer & Shaver, 2007b).

A Preoccupied Member

Although Linda never fails to attend a group therapy session, she never leaves the group completely satisfied and typically ends up feeling like, once again, she did not receive the support that she hoped for. She desires more: more time with the group, more understanding from her fellow group members, more attention from the group leaders, and more from herself, of whom she is constantly critical. Linda has a dramatic presentation in the group. When she enters the room, a whirlwind follows her. She is often in a state of crisis, is passionate and lively, and her emotions practically bubble over and out of her skin when she talks in the group. Linda requires frequent reassurance from others because she often anticipates rejection. When a new group member entered the group, Linda said, "I can tell by the look in your eyes that you don't really like me." At first, some group members worked especially hard to try and take care of and reassure Linda. However, eventually they grew frustrated with her, rolling their eyes at her, changing the topic when she began to talk, and even giving Linda feedback that she was "draining" the group.

Linda's experience of group therapy is characteristic of preoccupied patients, whose fear of abandonment and loss makes them distrustful of others and hypersensitive to rejection from personal others and groups (Bartholomew & Horowitz, 1991; Jurist & Meehan, 2008; Smith, Murphy, & Coats, 1999). These patients attempt to control their anxiety over abandonment and loss by minimizing emotional distance and soliciting displays of affection from others (Bartholomew & Horowitz, 1991; Feeney & Noller, 1990). As in Linda's case, preoccupied patients learn early on that to reach their self-preoccupied caregiver, they need to display their dependency needs intensely, escalating their sense of helplessness and emotionality (Dozier, Stovall, & Albus, 1999; Main, 1995; Wallin, 2007). These energetic attempts to meet at least some of their attachment needs for proximity, support, and love occur amid a lack of confidence that these needs will be met by others (Cassidy & Kobak, 1988). Sadly, although these hyperactivating strategies are meant to facilitate intimacy, they ultimately push others away because significant others in the patient's life, and eventually those in the therapy group, come to feel suffocated (Connors, 2011; Wallin, 2007).

A Dismissing-Avoidant Group Member

During the group sessions, Amy often avoided the members, gave out advice, and changed topics in the group without listening to others or considering their feelings. She rarely shared her own needs with the group, and to make matters worse, she managed to offend members with comments such as, "You need to have a thicker skin and not be so sensitive to what I say," "Feelings are just not that important," and "Sometimes talking about the relationships in here just seems like a waste of time to me." If not handled well, Amy is at risk of being a scapegoat, dropping out of treatment, and/or inhibiting group cohesion.

Attachment theory offers one lens to understand how Amy's past relationships influence her behaviors and interactions within the therapy group and what types of interventions will be helpful to her and the group (Brumbaugh & Fraley, 2007). Amy is a group member with more avoidance and less anxiety, falling within the dismissing-avoidant attachment style. This is evident in her dismissing attitude toward dependency, sense of superiority, lack of empathy for others, and lack of insight into her own interpersonal issues (Bartholomew & Horowitz, 1991; Mikulincer & Shaver, 2007b). Rather than seeing herself as needing treatment, she prefers to align herself with the leaders and is uncomfortable expressing her own vulnerability within the group.

A Fearful-Avoidant Group Member

Mike missed three consecutive group sessions, and the leader called him several times. He never returned the phone calls and came to the next session as if nothing had happened. When the leader asked him more about missing the group and not responding, he quickly apologized. His demeanor indicated that he felt badly about not responding, but he did not consider his absence to be of much significance to the group. When group members challenged him about his inconsistent attendance, Mike quickly promised he would be there in the future in order to avoid the attention he was receiving in the group. A fellow member was aware of Mike's history of depression and substance abuse, and he asked Mike whether he was abusing alcohol again. Mike admitted to binge drinking the previous weekend but explained that this was a "one-time event and not a real problem like before." Mike had a long history of physical and sexual abuse as a child and as an adult had turned to alcohol frequently to cope with his emotional pain. During the session, group members were becoming more anxious and frustrated with his outward expression that he was fine while obviously needing help. The group members were often left containing Mike's feelings because he managed to withdraw from the group while they ended up preoccupied with fears about his safety and well-being.

Unlike more dismissing-avoidant members, some group members, like Mike, come to group devaluing themselves as much as they devalue others. They do not feel superior to others, nor do they reject their longings for dependency. These more fearful-avoidant individuals are high on both the dimensions of anxiety and avoidance. Similar to more dismissing-avoidant individuals, fearful-avoidant individuals deactivate, avoid intimacy, and withdraw from relationships, but they do not deny the need for others or overemphasize self-sufficiency. At the same time, similar to more preoccupied individuals, more fearful-avoidant individuals are often concerned with rejection and abandonment, are ambivalent about relationships, and look outside themselves for comfort, security, and soothing. These individuals often vacillate between hyperactivating and deactivating strategies.

Unlike the individuals only high on attachment anxiety who mainly engage in hyperactivating strategies to connect with others, more fearful-avoidant members withdraw to protect themselves from the pain of disappointment and rejection. They do not seek out or cling to relationships the way more preoccupied individuals do. As a matter of fact, Bartholomew and Horowitz (1991) found that the fearful-avoidant attachment style is associated with a lack of assertiveness and increased tendency of being exploited in relationships. More fearful-avoidant individuals, often referred to as disorganized, have been linked to early trauma and later character pathology such as borderline personality disorder (Fonagy, Target, Gergely, Jurist, & Bateman, 2003).

According to Shaver and Clark (1994), more fearful-avoidant individuals tend to be more distrustful and have more difficulties compared with individuals who have other attachment styles. In a review of the attachment literature, fearful-avoidant individuals were found to have more negative internal images of romantic partners, more difficulties in relationships, the least empathy for others, and the poorest prognosis in treatment (Mikulincer & Shaver, 2007b).

TRAJECTORY OF THE BOOK

This book is organized into two parts. Part I (Chapters 1–3) reviews the theory and empirical research on attachment and group psychotherapy. Chapter 1 first presents the basic tenets of attachment theory, showing how early attachment experiences with caregivers influence adult relationship patterns and adult mental health status. The chapter then relates attachment theory to different group psychotherapy approaches, including our own approach, which we describe in Part II of this book. Chapter 2 reviews different measures of attachment, the research supporting these measures, and their strengths and weaknesses. These measures can be used in clinical practice and in research. Chapter 3 reviews the empirical literature on how patient attachment style influences the therapy process and treatment outcome (i.e., how different attachment styles are triggered in therapy). The chapter also reviews how therapist attachment patterns, and the interaction between therapist and patient attachment, influence therapy process and outcome. The growing body of empirical work that is applying attachment theory to group psychotherapy is emphasized.

Part II (Chapters 4–12) provides clinical guidance and case examples for working with different attachment styles in group therapy. Chapter 4 explains how to screen, place, and prepare group members of different attachment styles. The chapter notes red flags that signal when an individual may not be a good candidate for group therapy, as well as how group leaders can minimize potential damage if they decide to place such individuals in group therapy. Chapter 5 reviews the main techniques for facilitating a secure attachment style in group therapy. The chapter emphasizes empathy, emotion regulation, mentalization, insight, group cohesion, and group climate. Chapters 6 through 8 explain how to apply these techniques with specific insecure attachments: more preoccupied group members (Chapter 6), more dismissing-avoidant members (Chapter 7), and more fearful-avoidant members (Chapter 8). These chapters provide ample clinical examples of how group therapy can foster here-and-now emotional experiences that help group members move toward felt security and change.

Chapters 9 through 11 apply attachment theory to special populations and specific topics within group therapy. Specifically, Chapter 9 focuses on eating disorders, trauma, and addictions; Chapter 10 focuses on diversity within group psychotherapy; and Chapter 11 focuses on the experience of loss and the process of termination in group therapy. Finally, Chapter 12 includes two in-depth case vignettes that highlight how attachment styles within group therapy influence the acceptance of new members, conflict within the group, group cohesion, and the process of change. More important, the case vignettes underscore how the group leader can make mistakes that lead to ruptures in group cohesion, as well as how the leader can repair these ruptures. Ultimately, these cases demonstrate how to facilitate more secure attachments for members within the safe haven of the group.

I

THEORY AND EMPIRICAL RESEARCH ON ATTACHMENT AND GROUP PSYCHOTHERAPY

1

AN OVERVIEW OF ATTACHMENT THEORY AND ITS APPLICATION TO GROUP PSYCHOTHERAPY

This chapter highlights the major tenets of attachment theory, explaining how early attachment experiences influence affect regulation, the capacity to empathize and sustain intimate relationships, and the onset of diverse mental health issues often treated in group therapy. The chapter briefly reviews the application of attachment theory to diverse theories of group psychotherapy and sets the stage for how group leaders can best use attachment theory in their clinical work by describing the key attachment-based processes that foster change in group treatment.

ROOTS OF ATTACHMENT

Early Needs for Safety

John Bowlby (1969, 1973, 1980), who developed attachment theory, believed that most psychopathology has its origin in problems that occur

http://dx.doi.org/10.1037/14186-002
Attachment in Group Psychotherapy, by C. L. Marmarosh, R. D. Markin, and E. B. Spiegel

early in development when infants' basic needs for safety and felt security are not met. Although Bowlby was trained as a psychoanalyst and was supervised by Melanie Klein, he believed that many of the issues that children struggle with are based not on their aggressive drives or a paranoid state of mind but on their attempts to maintain ties to their caregivers. Bowlby, along with other object relational analysts (Fairbairn, 1952; Winnicott, 1971), believed that the attachments to the caregivers are the most significant contributors to the development of the self and of psychopathology.

According to Bowlby (1969, 1973, 1980), the infant's early attachment experiences with significant caregivers provide the foundation for what he called *internal working models* (or *internal representations*) of the self and others. In essence, internal working models are internalized sets of beliefs that guide behavior, emotion regulation, and future relationships (Bowlby, 1982). The infant (and, later, the child) starts to learn about who she is based on interactions with the caregiver. If an infant interacts with a loving caregiver who attends to her needs, is attuned to her emotions, and can provide felt security (e.g., soothing her when she cries in distress), the infant will internalize a sense that "I am loved," "I am cared for," and "My feelings are important." In addition, the infant starts to internalize perceptions of others. "People love me" and "People are trustworthy" become part of her working model of others. The individual develops a sense of felt security when with the caregiver and, over time, a more secure attachment in significant relationships.

If, on the other hand, the infant interacts with a caregiver who is overwhelmed by his or her emotions, unavailable, and unable to provide felt security (e.g., ignoring or yelling at her when she cries), the infant is more inclined to internalize a sense that "I am worthless," "I am hated," or "I am overwhelming," and these internal representations become part of his working model of self. In addition, the beliefs that "People are dangerous" or "People disappoint" become part of her working model of others.

Attachment Security

The infant or child not only internalizes mental representations of the self and of others but also learns how to cope with automatic fight–flight responses caused by the perception of threat or danger. It is critical for the infant to engage slowly in more exploration of the external world, and he or she does this by studying faces, looking at things, crawling, touching, tasting, hearing, and smelling things. During this exploration, the infant or child often experiences fear or distress that requires external emotion regulation via the caregiver. If the caregiver soothes the infant during these stressful experiences, the infant learns to turn toward the attachment figure for emotional regulation and felt security (Beebe & Lachmann, 2002). Once emotions are managed within the context of the relationship, the infant can resume exploration. For example, if a child is playing with toys and is frightened by a loud noise, the secure child can run to the caregiver and regain a sense of felt security. The caregiver facilitates a sense of safety, perhaps with a hug and some reassuring words. Once fear is regulated, the child can safely separate from the caregiver and resume play, a type of exploration. Over time, this leads to an ability to self-soothe and rely on others when needed, developing a more secure attachment style.

Attachment Insecurity

If the attachment figure is unavailable or inconsistent, the infant or child learns to deal with emotions the best way possible in the context of the relationship. For example, if a caregiver responds to the infant's needs only sometimes, the infant may learn to cling to the caregiver for fear that the caregiver will leave or not be available when the infant needs soothing. Instead of exploring the environment and engaging in play, the infant is preoccupied with maintaining proximity to the caregiver. The infant has learned to emphasize attachment over engagement with the world and is at risk of developing a sense of self that is needy, overwhelming, and weak while simultaneously developing a sense that others are rejecting and abandoning, yet strong. This infant is said to have a resistant attachment style—that is, what would be considered a preoccupied attachment in adults (Ainsworth, Blehar, Waters, & Wall, 1978).

Whereas the resistant infant typically receives inconsistent responses from the caregiver, the avoidant infant, what would be considered the dismissing-avoidant adult, tends to receive negative or no response (for example, the caregiver may ignore or punish the infant when the infant displays signs of distress). The avoidant infant has learned that the caregiver does not facilitate felt security when the infant is in emotional need. The dismissing-avoidant infant copes with feelings by focusing on the external world rather than seeking proximity to the caregiver. The avoidant infant is learning to cope with internal states independently and is likely to defend against dependency with self-sufficiency later in life.

An individual does not internalize a sense of self and others overnight. Internal working models develop over repeated interpersonal interactions with the caregiver, and they are influenced by the way the caregiver responds to the developing infant or child's needs for protection and stimulation, often before language is acquired (Beebe & Lachmann, 2002). Protection promotes survival and ensures the infant is safe from danger, and stimulation encourages curiosity, growth, and individuation. Bowlby (1969) described two behavioral systems that foster this safety and growth: proximity seeking and exploration. These systems are believed to be a function of evolution in which the infant or child seeks proximity to a more competent adult for safety and protection from predators, and at the same time, the infant or child explores his or her environment and becomes more autonomous.

Research on Proximity Seeking and Exploration

Bowlby's student and colleague Mary Ainsworth was the first to empirically study his theoretical assumptions about these two interacting systems by observing children's behavioral reactions to a stressful situation in which the child has the opportunity to engage in proximity seeking and exploration (Ainsworth et al., 1978). This study has become famous, and the methodology has been called the *Strange Situation*. Through observation of young children who were briefly separated from and then reunited with their caregivers, Ainsworth and her colleagues found that children with secure attachments were able to tolerate this stressful situation and recover quickly from separation after they were reunited with the caregiver, whereas insecurely attached children were more anxious, unable to resume exploration after reunion, denied distress, or were unable to recover from the separation from the caregiver, even after being reunited. Children with more secure relationships to their primary caregivers were able to regulate their distress with the help of their caregiver and explore new situations more freely. More important, they were able to rely on their primary caregivers for comfort when they felt distressed, and their caregivers were able to facilitate emotion regulation. Insecurely attached children either avoided comfort from their primary caregiver or clung to them without resuming exploration and play. In essence, the threat of separation elicited hyper–proximity seeking that failed to provide emotional regulation, the children remained distressed, or it did not elicit any proximity seeking, despite physiological arousal (Sroufe & Waters, 1977). The results revealed that these insecurely attached children had learned ways of interacting with their caregivers when under duress that influenced how they regulated their emotions and how they interacted in their environments.

Bowlby (1982) maintained that the importance of a certain type of caregiver was at the root of these children's behaviors. He argued that a *secure base*—a caregiver who provides emotional containment and soothes the child during distress and also promotes curiosity and exploration in the environment—is optimal for a child's development. Main, Kaplan, and Cassidy (1985) found empirical support for the link between behavior during the Strange Situation and the child's development of internal representations. Specifically, they found that the results of the infant's Strange Situation behaviors predicted corresponding results in the narratives that the same children when they were 6-year-olds and asked to describe pictures of parent–child separations. Furthermore, children who were asked to draw their families during the separations had drawings that were predictive of each child's first year attachment to his or her mother.

THE LIFELONG EFFECTS OF EARLY ATTACHMENT

Bowlby (1982) not only theorized that a secure base was critical during infancy and child development, he also argued that secure attachments influence us all our lives "from the cradle to the grave" (p. 163). Empirical researchers have found support for Bowlby's assumption and have tracked the influence of infant attachment to adulthood (Sroufe, Egeland, Carlson, & Collins, 2005). Sroufe (2005) described an incredible data set of infants who were tracked for 30 years to examine the impact of early attachment on later development. The Minnesota study (Sroufe et al., 2005) included 200 at-risk mothers and their infants who participated in Ainsworth's Strange Situation at 12 and 18 months of age. Following the early evaluations of infant attachment, children were assessed repeatedly throughout their childhood and into adulthood. As expected, they found that the caregiver's psychological unavailability was related to avoidant attachment and that all of the children with caregivers described as unavailable had toddlers who were classified as avoidant when assessed at 18 months of age. With regard to toddlers who developed disorganized attachments, they found that caregivers were more abusive and that maltreatment included physical abuse and emotional neglect.

The study demonstrated a link between secure infant attachment and ability to regulate emotions in preschool, taking on leadership roles in camps as adolescents, and later psychopathology. Although they are less at risk of mental health issues, Sroufe (2005) described how those with secure attachments in infancy still have difficulties later in life but appear to weather such stresses more effectively. Results also revealed that the most at-risk individuals were classified as disorganized during infancy. They found the most significant correlations between disorganization at infancy and psychiatric problems at age 17.5 years and marital hostility in adulthood. They also found that adults who engaged in cutting and self-destructive behaviors were more likely to have had disorganized infant attachments, histories of sexual abuse, and dissociation. All in all, Sroufe (2005) stated that attachment history was "clearly related to the growth of self-reliance, the capacity for emotional regulation, and the emergence and course of social competence, among other things. Moreover, specific patterns of attachment had implications for both normal development and pathology" (p. 349).

In addition to studying the impact of early attachment, Sroufe and colleagues (2005) also described how parents do many things for their children in addition to providing felt security when they are distressed. Parents set limits and boundaries, facilitate problem solving, engage in play, and expose children to different people and activities. One of those other things that Sroufe et al. (2005) considered important is sensitive caregiving, which they found to be a better predictor of competency and difficulties later in life than attachment alone. It appears that attachment is the foundation of the infant–caregiver relationship, a platform to begin the process of development, but caregiver emotional attunement is also critical.

The Mechanism of Lifelong Influence: Internalizing Emotion Regulation

Although Sroufe et al. (2005) considered caregiver sensitivity to be separate from attachment, Schore suggested otherwise. From his research on early neurobiology and attachments, Schore (1994) concluded that the secure attachment to an attuned caregiver facilitates the transfer of emotion-regulating capacities from the caregiver to the infant. In essence, the infant first depends on the other for regulation and then eventually internalizes the other and develops the capacity to self-soothe (Behrends & Blatt, 1985). One way the caregiver facilitates this transfer is by knowing what is intolerable for the infant and what is within the infant's capacities for coping. This ensures that the infant's arousal is within a moderate range, or optimal arousal. According to Schore, optimal arousal incorporates a balance between sympathetic activation and parasympathetic activation.

The sympathetic nervous system is responsible for mobilizing the body's resources under stress, often called the *fight–flight response*. The parasympathetic nervous system is complementary to the sympathetic system and is responsible for facilitating rest and the decrease of the fight–flight response. For example, the infant cries when the caregiver leaves, initiating the sympathetic system. Then the caregiver returns, bends down, looks into the child's eyes, and embraces the child, thereby soothing the child and initiating the child's parasympathetic system. In early development, the child needs to rely on the caregiver for parasympathetic activation and is learning to self-soothe via the caregiver.

The Mechanism of Change in Therapy: Fostering Secure Attachment

Neuroscientists and clinicians are now arguing that for change to occur in psychotherapy, the therapist must maintain a role that is similar to a sensitive, responsive caregiver. The therapist must facilitate both interpersonal experiences that integrate emotions (the right brain) with intellectual understanding (the left brain) to foster changes in emotion regulation (Cozolino, 2002; Fonagy & Target, 2008; Schore, 2002; Siegel, 2007). The therapist provides the secure base from which patients can explore their beliefs about themselves and others (i.e., their internal working models) and helps the patient regulate her emotions when she encounters something threatening or painful. The patient internalizes the self-regulating ability and learns to self-soothe.

The mechanism is the same for group psychotherapy. In 2010, the *International Journal of Group Psychotherapy* published a volume dedicated to neurobiology, interpersonal systems, and group psychotherapy. In this volume, Flores (2010) noted, "From a psychobiological standpoint, group psychotherapy can be thought of as a delicate establishment of a regulatory attachment relationship aimed at stabilizing physiology and emotions, and revising the emotional memory of attachment patterns" (p. 559). The leader, group members, and group as a whole facilitate emotion regulation and changes in internal representations for those members who struggle with insecure attachments.

Before discussing how therapists can foster the ability to regulate emotions in an adaptive way, it is important to understand how insecurely attached individuals already cope with negative emotions.

COPING WITH SUBOPTIMAL CAREGIVING

Insecurely attached infants and children use deactivation and hyperactivation to cope with a lack of sensitive, responsive caregiver. Although these behaviors effectively allow the individual to cope during infancy and childhood, they become maladaptive strategies in adulthood.

Deactivation: The Root of Dismissing-Avoidant Attachment

According to Schore (1994, 2002), mothers of more avoidant children are unable to facilitate optimal arousal and instead have aversive reactions to their infants' dependency on them and block their infants' proximity-seeking behaviors. In other words, they do not respond optimally and end up responding in ways that keep the infant in overwhelmingly distressing situations for too long. The caregiver may let the infant cry for hours before picking the child up and trying to soothe the child (Beebe & Lachmann, 2002). Even while trying to soothe the child, the caregiver may be averse to the physical contact and may display frustration and annoyance, even disgust (Main & Weston, 1982). During this experience, the infant learns that proximity seeking does not facilitate soothing or modulate the stress. Even more tragic is that the proximity seeking adds another emotionally painful stressor because the infant's needs for comfort are then rejected (Schore, 1994). The repeated experience of need and rejection leads to the formation of a defensive process in which the infant turns off the proximity-seeking behaviors by shifting the attention away from the caregiver during distress and therefore reducing the emotional rejection and shame.

When the mother pushes her infant away and fails to engage in proximity seeking, the infant ends up in a hyperaroused situation evidenced by increased heart rate and negative affect—what is called sympathetic activation. The caregiver copes with the emotional stress by shutting down and failing to engage in mutual gazing with the infant, inhibiting the infant from benefitting from the caregiver's ability to soothe. According to Schore (1994), the infant may learn to avoid gazing into the caregiver's eyes to prevent further distress generated by the caregiver, who may look angry or unexpressive during a time of emotional need. Schore argued that the infant must find some way to down-regulate this sympathetic system activation alone and therefore shifts from a sympathetic-dominant distress state to a parasympathetic despair state. The infant learns to be defensively independent or self-reliant, and the attachment needs are sublimated (Sroufe, Fox, & Pancake, 1983). The infant then no longer suffers in sympathetic activation. Fosha (2000) described this as "dealing but not feeling" (p. 43), because the dismissing-avoidant individual sacrifices an emotional life to maintain cohesion and the ability to function.

Hyperactivation: The Root of Preoccupied Attachment

More resistant infants do not turn off proximity seeking but instead experience unregulated hyperactivation of the sympathetic nervous system. These infants increase proximity seeking and appear to struggle to rely on the emotion regulating capacities of the caregiver. For example, these infants display anger and clinginess when the caregiver returns after the Strange Situation, and they do not easily resume exploration. According to Schore (1994), caregivers of resistant infants are often inconsistent caregivers and therefore are not able to facilitate the infants' trust in the caregiver's responsiveness. Again, the caregiver is not able to maintain an optimal level of arousal and is more inclined to be inconsistent when responding to the infant.

Tronick (1989) and Beebe and Lachmann (1988, 2002) described mothers who are constantly activating the infant or trying to stimulate the infant despite the infant's desire to look away. In essence, the mother is not able to read the infant's need for less stimulation and is more likely motivated by her own needs for closeness than the infant's needs. The infant learns to submit to the caregiver and is so absorbed in emotion regulation that he or she sacrifices exploration. The result of this overstimulation leads to a bias for the predominance of the sympathetic nervous system over the parasympathetic system, the opposite of what happens to the avoidant infant (Schore, 1994). Fosha (2000) called this "feeling but not dealing" (p. 43) because the individual is overly focused on the emotional needs of the self and the other at the expense of exploration and independence.

Traumatic Emotion: The Root of Fearful-Avoidant–Disorganized Attachment

In the Strange Situation experiment, some infants demonstrated a set of unusual behaviors that were not indicative of a resistant or avoidant attachment. The observers noticed that some infants would engage in odd behaviors when the caregiver returned after separation, such as falling to the ground, spinning in a circle, dissociating, or freezing. These children appeared to be unable to decide what to do when the caregiver returned. They did not demonstrate a desire for closeness or comfort, nor did they ignore the caregiver and resume play. They appeared paralyzed. These responses are thought to develop when an infant experiences the parent as too frightening. Instead of immediately seeking proximity, the infant is faced with a horrible dilemma. The infant is naturally drawn to seek proximity from the caregiver when distressed, but in this case, the caregiver also triggers terror. In essence, the safe haven is also the source of the trauma. These children had a disorganized attachment style, which corresponds to the fearful-avoidant attachment style in adults. Disorganized children's drawings of their families depict the horror they experience. They draw dismembered body parts, skeletons, and people who are then scratched out of the pictures (Main, 1995; Main et al., 1985). Main's work showed that parents of disorganized children had experienced some type of trauma or unresolved losses. Most important was the unresolved nature of the past trauma that left these caregivers unable to cope with and move past it. The caregivers were unable to regulate the emotions of their infants, were emotionally or physically abusive to the infants, or were paralyzed in fear toward the infant. The infant either feels fearful of the caregiver or perceives the caregiver as fearful of the infant; either reaction inhibits a sense of felt security that is necessary for emotion regulation. Fosha (2000) described this experience as "not dealing and not feeling" (p. 44). Individuals with a disorganized attachment must escape the terror and isolation that come with having a threatening attachment figure. They are not able to feel or address feelings because there is no caregiver available to help them cope with these emotional states. Dissociation alleviates the dilemma and facilitates the maintenance of self-cohesion.

ATTACHMENT AND ADULT RELATIONSHIPS

Healthy Adult Relationships and Mentalization

Although we can see how early caregiver experiences influence adult attachments, how do secure attachments influence our ability to sustain healthy intimacy? According to Fonagy (2000), one of the most important qualities humans learn during development, which influences all future relationships, is how to understand each other's thoughts, feelings, beliefs, and desires. According to Fonagy (2000), mentalization is the capacity to understand and interpret human behaviors in terms of underlying mental states that exist within the individual. We learn, in the context of secure relationships, to expect that others have intentions separate from our own (i.e., we acquire an *intentional stance*), and we learn to navigate each other's needs and actions. Fonagy argued that the intentional stance is learned from the experiences with the caregiver, and it goes hand in hand with having a secure attachment that allows one to conceive of another's mind.

Fonagy, Gergely, Jurist, and Target (2002) described how a caregiver who is attuned to the infant facilitates the infant's experience of reflecting on the infant's internal state. The secure caregiver is curious about the infant's feelings, needs, and intentions, and a reflective caregiver is able to comprehend accurately that the child is crying because he or she might be hungry. The caregiver is then able to express to the infant, "You must be hungry," and is able to respond in an attuned fashion, such as getting a bottle to feed the infant. This sequence initiates a process of linking an internal state, hunger, with an emotional state, crying, and the intentions of the other, getting the bottle when the infant is in need. This repeated experience allows the infant (and, later, the child) to develop into a secure adult who can empathize with others, provide support to others in times of need, manage emotional stress effectively, and seek out own support during times of duress (Mikulincer & Shaver, 2007b).

A caregiver who is unable to reflect on the infant's internal states may perceive the infant's cries as pleas for attention or excessive neediness. Or the caregiver may perceive the infant's cries as a reflection of an inability to care for the infant and be paralyzed with self-defeating thoughts. Beebe (2005), in her studies of mother and infant interactions and insecure attachments, observed that if an infant felt overaroused when the caregiver maintained eye contact, he or she coped with this stimulation by looking away and breaking contact. If the caregiver could tolerate this separation and empathize with the infant's need to self-regulate, the mother could allow the child to disengage and then reengage when ready. If, on the other hand, the caregiver had a more preoccupied attachment style and could not tolerate the separation, interpreted the break in eye contact as rejection, then withdrew from the child, or continued to stimulate the infant despite the infant's need to break contact, the child was either abandoned or left in a highly emotional state of arousal without the ability to regulate.

The ability of the caregiver to accurately translate the child's crying into an indicator of an internal need or hunger within the infant, as well as the ability to be optimally responsive to the infant, influences the infant's development of emotion regulation and secure attachment. As a matter of fact, parents who are rated higher on the capacity to reflect on the other were 3 to 4 times more likely to have secure children compared with children whose parents had poor reflective capacities (Fonagy, Steele, Steele, Moran, & Higgitt, 1991).

Not only does the caregiver's capacity to mentalize influence the development of the infant's attachment, the infant's attachment influences the development of his or her reflective capacities as he or she evolves into an adult caregiver (Fonagy, 2000). The cycle repeats itself, and secure infants become caregivers who are able to read the intentions of others, including their children (Mikulincer & Shaver, 2007b). In essence, security begets security. Reflective capacity is one of the key elements of a secure attachment and is intimately related to our ability to empathize with others and our ability to share our internal experiences with them, sustaining intimacy. Social psychologists studying adult attachment have found support for Fonagy's assertions and have empirically demonstrated that insecurely attached adults have more difficulty empathizing with others, providing support during emotional distress, forgiving others, and maintaining intimacy (for a review, see Mikulincer & Shaver, 2007b). We can imagine that adult insecure attachments and compromised reflective capacities are major contributors to a wide range of emotional struggles and mental illnesses.

Problematic Adult Relationships and Psychopathology

Bowlby (1973) described how attachment insecurity could lead to struggles with anxiety because the infant does not have the buffer of a secure base. Later, Bowlby (1980) described how the death or loss of the caregiver early in development could lead to hopelessness and despair. According to Mikulincer and Shaver (2007b), more than 100 studies have now explored the relationship between adult attachment and symptoms of anxiety and depression. Specifically, clinical researchers have reported links between adult attachment and chronic depression (Cyranowski et al., 2002), dysthymia (West & George, 2002), bipolar depression (Fonagy et al., 1996), and anxiety disorders (Manassis, Bradley, Goldberg, Hood, & Swinson, 1994). Overall, the findings indicate that the more secure the attachment, the less severe the symptoms of depression and anxiety. The research also indicates that more preoccupied individuals have greater ratings of both depression and anxiety, whereas these symptoms are reported less frequently by more dismissing-avoidant individuals. Chapter 9 of this volume reviews in more depth the application of attachment to substance abuse, eating disorders, and trauma.

Attachment and Personality Disorders

A great deal of research has focused on early attachments and the development of borderline personality disorder (BPD; Fonagy et al., 2002). BPD is a chronic and common psychiatric disorder characterized by recurrent patterns of interpersonal difficulties, fears of abandonment, feelings of emptiness, emotional lability, angry outbursts, poor impulse control, self-mutilation (i.e., cutting), and suicidal ideation and behaviors (American Psychiatric Association, 2000). Many theorists argue that the majority of symptoms presented by patients with BPD stem from insecure attachments (Diamond et al., 1999; Fonagy et al., 2002; Holmes, 2004; Levy, 2005). Chapter 8 of this volume reviews the fearful-avoidant–disorganized attachment in more depth, and Chapter 4 reviews mentalization-based group treatments designed specifically for patients with a history of trauma.

Attachment and Adjustment Issues

Not all difficulties that individuals struggle with have a diagnosis. Many people who seek psychotherapy treatment struggle with loneliness, family issues, marital difficulties, and interpersonal issues that interfere with friendships. They may have secure attachments to their caregivers but still struggle adjusting to life issues such as grief, career transitions, and parenting concerns, to name a few. Thus, even individuals with secure attachment patterns can benefit from psychotherapy. As a matter of fact, psychotherapy researchers have found that client attachment security is related to the development of the therapy alliance and positive outcome from therapy (Daniel, 2006). Both social psychologists and clinical psychologists have applied attachment theory to understand how internal representations of self and other affect these relationships.

Social psychologists have amassed an enormous literature supporting the link between attachment styles and functioning within friendships and couples (see Mikulincer & Shaver, 2007b, for a review). Rigorous empirical studies have found that secure adults have more success dating, are perceived as more attractive, and have increased marital satisfaction compared with insecurely attached adults. In addition, secure individuals have more intimate friendships, are able to seek out the support of others during times of need, and are able to offer support to others when they are distressed. They still struggle with issues, but they are able to get help and benefit from support when they receive it (Sroufe et al., 2005). They are able to empathize, demonstrate compassion, and forgive others when they do something that is hurtful, whereas insecurely attached adults struggle to remain engaged when they are injured. Insecurely attached individuals have less tolerance for frustration, are less successful at offering support, are worse at managing conflict, and struggle to repair ruptures in relationships (Mikulincer & Shaver, 2007b). It is no wonder that clinicians rely on attachment theory to understand the underlying complex issues that bring people to psychotherapy.

ATTACHMENT AND PSYCHOTHERAPY TREATMENTS

Bowlby (1988) believed that to achieve positive therapeutic outcomes, clinicians need to facilitate felt security within the treatment, explore how the individual relates to people based on inaccurate working models of self and others, link current relationship difficulties to previous attachment failures, and facilitate a corrective emotional experience for the patient. Bowlby emphasized the curative impact of the relationship to facilitate an understanding of maladaptive patterns and to facilitate change.

Since Bowlby's (1988) original work, *A Secure Base,* many clinicians have written books that have applied his theory to individual psychotherapy (Fosha, 2000; Holmes, 1996; Sable, 2001; Wallin, 2007), psychoanalytic treatment (Bowlby, 1988; Cortina & Marrone, 2003; Fonagy 2001), couple psychotherapy (Clulow, 2001; S. M. Johnson & Whiffen, 2003), family psychotherapy (Hughes, 2007), and substance abuse treatment (Flores, 2004). These books emphasize the importance of the therapist identifying patient attachment organizations and exploring how these attachments relate to symptoms, emotion regulation, interpersonal relationships, and the therapy process. Like Bowlby, the authors of these books view the therapist as a secure base that provides the patient (individual, couple, or family) a new relational experience that contradicts earlier attachment failures. The clinicians almost always emphasize empathy, attunement to deep emotional experiences in the here and now, active listening and engagement, openness, and curiosity. Clinicians focus on both verbal and nonverbal interactions, the tracking of core emotions, and enactments of attachment related issues.

Although there have been empirically supported group therapy treatments for specific issues related to attachment difficulties, such as group treatment for eating disorders (Tasca, Ritchie, et al., 2006), BPD (Bateman & Fonagy, 2003; Ogrodniczuk & Piper, 2001; Wilberg et al., 2003), depression (MacKenzie & Grabovac, 2001), and posttraumatic stress disorder (Schnurr et al., 2003), less has been written about the application of attachment theory to group psychotherapy in general. Before we describe our own model of attachment in group therapy, we first review other group approaches that include attachment-based processes.

GROUP PSYCHOTHERAPY THEORIES: BRIDGES TO ATTACHMENT THEORY

It would be unfair to review the application of attachment theory to group therapy without acknowledging the many theories already applied to group therapy that endorses attachment-based interventions. These theories and approaches to group therapy have much in common with attachment theory. For example, object relations theories, self psychological theories, and interpersonal theories of group therapy incorporate attachment-related concepts. More recent cognitive behavioral approaches such as cognitive appraisal therapy (Wessler & Hankin Wessler, 1997) have also been applied to group therapy and integrate Bowlby's theory.

Bowlby's "recognition of the importance of attachment in human development has become widely accepted within object relations theory" (Rice, 1992, p. 35), and Bowlby was not alone in his movement toward an emphasis on the impact of the caregiver on the infant's emotional regulation and development. Winnicott (1971) also emphasized the importance of the mother–infant relationship and coined the term *good enough mother* to emphasize the importance of sensitive caregiving during infant development. Fairbairn (1952), like Bowlby, asserted that infants were motivated to seek relationships not for pleasure but to reduce internal tension. These theorists share the importance they give to early environmental failures and how these failures influence psychopathology and treatment (Fonagy, 2001).

Object Relations Theory and Group Therapy

Although few have applied attachment theory to group psychotherapy, many have applied object relations theory to group psychotherapy (Alonso & Rutan, 1984; Bion, 1961; Ganzarain, 1989; Schermer & Pines, 1994). These theorists emphasize the importance of exploring early relationships as they naturally unfold in the group process. Inevitably, group members respond to each other, the leaders, and the group in the context of their earlier, internalized relational experiences. The hope is that these internal representations will emerge in the group where they can be experienced, explored, and understood. The leaders attempt to be emotionally available within the group, look for members' projections and transference reactions within the group, and explore their own countertransference reactions to fully understand the group process and determine what interventions will best facilitate both emotion regulation and insight. Similar to attachment-oriented clinicians, these group therapists hope to foster healthier internal representations of self and other based on the group experience.

Self Psychological Theory and Group Psychotherapy

In addition to object relations theorists, self psychologists have noted similarities between self psychological theory and attachment theory (Fonagy, 2001). Self psychological theorists (Kohut, 1971; Kohut & Wolf, 1978) emphasize the importance of the caregiver in facilitating emotion regulation and the development of a cohesive self. Self psychological theory also focuses on how the early experience with the caregiver fosters adult relationships and intimacy. Much as Bowlby described a secure base, Kohut (1971) described a healthy selfobject experience. According to Kohut, a child relies on self-objects (i.e., a caregiver), to provide, maintain, and foster the development of a cohesive self. Much like a secure base, this intrapsychic experience of the caregiver facilitates regulation within the self, promotes the achievement of goals, and contributes to future intimate relationships.

Many self psychologists have applied self psychological theory to group psychotherapy (Ashbach & Schermer, 1992; Segalla, 1998; Stone, 1992). Harwood (1983) described how the group process elicits the members' experience of previous selfobjects. The group leaders focus on how the group process may stir up past interpersonal injuries and are sensitive to the members' needs to protect themselves from repeated trauma. The leaders focus on the current group relationship interactions and look for how the members relate to each other, the leader, and the group based on their needs to avoid the painful injuries they endured in childhood. Much like Bowlby emphasized the importance of an attuned caregiver, self psychological group therapists emphasize the importance of empathic attunement and the opportunities to repair injuries that occur within the group because this process strengthens the member's core sense of self. The process of rupture and repair in the here and now is critical to these group therapists and parallels the emphasis attachment-oriented therapists place on restoring emotion regulation and repairing attachment injuries in the group.

Interpersonal Theory and Group Psychotherapy

Probably the most familiar theory of group therapy is Yalom's (1995) interpersonal process theory of group treatment. Yalom argued that there are many curative mechanisms within the group, and he suggested that interpersonal problems are often the root of psychological pain and symptoms. Although Yalom agreed that the origins of the interpersonal difficulties members come to treatment with may stem in childhood and that transference reactions, what he calls parataxic distortions, influence the group process, he does not focus on delving into the deeper roots to these issues in the group. Unlike self psychological or object relational group therapists, he has advocated focusing the treatment on the current ways that these distortions influence here-and-now interactions in the group because, according to Yalom, these current interactions are the ones that have the power to change internal representations that come with members to the group. He has argued that authentic feedback and the connections within the group challenge and revise past assumptions and facilitate new ways of coping with conflict and fears of closeness.

Yalom and Leszcz (2005) noted, "It is the affective sharing of one's inner world and *then the acceptance by others* that seem of paramount importance. To be accepted by others challenges the client's belief that he or she is basically repugnant, unacceptable, or unlovable" (p. 56, italics in original). This description of a corrective emotional experience sounds much like Bowlby's notion of the revision of internal working models of self and other that occurs during therapy when the patient shares an emotionally meaningful experience and is understood and accepted in ways that contradict earlier attachment experiences.

Yalom and Leszcz (2005) went on to state that for a corrective emotional experience to take place, members must experience the group as safe, and there must be significant engagement and genuineness in the group to allow members to rely on the authenticity of the experience. They offered an example of a group member who risked expressing her anger in the group after feeling unable to express this emotion due to fear of abandonment, and they went on to describe how she felt accepted by the group and had a different experience from the one she dreaded. Yalom and Leszcz did not apply attachment theory but described how the group functioned as a secure base for this member and facilitated her expression of emotions without the dreaded consequence of abandonment.

This example highlights how insight into the group process is important, and it is critical for members to be able to reflect on their group experience. Yalom and Leszcz (2005) stated that "this reflecting back, this self-reflective loop, is crucial if an emotional experience is to be transformed into a therapeutic one" (p. 30). Yalom and Leszcz described what Fonagy called *mentalization* and the importance of linking emotional experience with the cognitive understanding of internal needs, intentions, and the perceptions of others.

Yalom (1995) stated that successful group members relied on a cognitive map, "some intellectual system that framed the experience and made sense of the emotions evoked in the group" (p. 31). Attachment theorists would argue that the map group members can rely on is a system of self-understanding that bridges automatic and implicit reactions in the present to emotionally vulnerable experiences in the past. Attachment theory is one map that facilitates not only the members' experiences but also guides the leaders' understanding of what is happening in the group as well. Although these approaches incorporate attachment-based interventions, there are specific group treatments that have been designed with attachment theory in mind.

APPROACHES TO GROUP PSYCHOTHERAPY BASED ON ATTACHMENT THEORY

Several researchers and clinicians have applied attachment theory to a specific model of group therapy. For example, McCluskey (2008) developed a group approach focused mainly on attachment theory, what she called a *theory of attachment-based interest sharing*. Her approach includes distinct phases of treatment that focus on group members' exploration of themselves from an attachment perspective. Sessions address the motivation underlying caregiving, the experience of affection and sexuality, and the understanding of defenses. She described the leaders' role as facilitators of the group process, functioning as secure bases, to help members identify their attachment-related assumptions and develop new ways of engaging with others that is different from the way they engaged in their pasts.

More recently, Kahn and Feldman (2011) described their relationship-focused group therapy, which combines couple and group psychotherapy to address attachment-related themes of affect regulation and "neuropsychophysiological integration" (p. 519). This approach emphasizes the identification of transference in the group, the use of twinship (i.e., joining with a member with whom you identify and share a similar experience) to facilitate emotion regulation, and the internalization of new relationship experiences.

Even cognitive behavioral group treatments are integrating attachment theory. J. Stern (2010) described the application of cognitive appraisal therapy (Wessler & Hankin Wessler, 1997) to parent training groups. He argued that to help parents in the group, the group must facilitate the members' emotions that are triggered from their childhoods and are being reenacted in the present. This approach is based on Bowlby's theory and integrates attachment theory to cognitive behavioral interventions.

Kilmann et al. (1999) developed a 17-hour manualized attachment-focused group intervention that targets attachment concerns of insecure individuals. Attachment-focused group interventions have been shown to improve interpersonal style, increase satisfaction with family relationships, decrease agreement with dysfunctional relationship beliefs, and increase secure attachment patterns compared with a control group of insecure group members (Kilmann et al., 1999). These are not the only clinicians applying attachment theory to group therapy. We argue that the basic facilitators of change in group therapy, regardless of model or orientation, are supported by attachment theory.

APPLYING ATTACHMENT THEORY TO ALL TYPES OF GROUP THERAPY: OUR MODEL OF CHANGE

We have reviewed a variety of theories that describe how and why group therapy is effective and how attachment-based principles apply to all of them. We believe that these curative factors cut across all types of groups, ranging from psychoanalytic groups to cognitive behavioral groups. What facilitates changes in group members is not based mainly on the type of group treatment per se but on what happens between members across group treatments. Expression of emotion (Castonguay, Pincus, Agras, & Hines, 1998), cohesion (Budman, Soldz, Demby, Davis, & Merry, 1993; Burlingame, Fuhriman, & Johnson, 2001), relational climate (Dierick & Lietaer, 2008), interpersonal learning (Yalom & Leszcz, 2005), and empathy (J. E. Johnson, Burlingame, Olsen, Davies, & Gleave, 2005) have consistently emerged as critical group-therapeutic factors that facilitate change across theoretical approaches. Even more structured groups that focus on addressing maladaptive cognitions, such as cognitive behavioral group therapy, emphasize the importance of group cohesion, trust, and empathy (White & Freeman, 2000). Although empirical studies support these curative mechanisms, there has been no overarching theory explaining exactly why group cohesion, empathy, emotional expression, and safety continue to be such crucial elements of successful group psychotherapy practices.

We argue that the emotional experience in the here and now, the presence of a responsive group that allows for a corrective emotional experience, and the ability to reflect on oneself and others are all important aspects of group therapy, regardless of the group leader orientation, because they revise internal representations of self and other. We agree with Bowlby (1988), who argued that the psychotherapy endeavor re-creates the opportunity for patients to (a) explore previous injuries (in the here and now) that have left them unable to maintain closeness or tolerate distance, (b) develop internal capacities to cope with emotions that have been overwhelming or inaccessible and that have a negative impact on relationships, and (c) facilitate their ability to create a cohesive narrative that helps explain their avoidance, dissociation, or anxiety. In group treatment, not only do members experience current relationships in the group, they also revisit the internal representations of previous attachments and injuries, implicitly and explicitly, that have left them struggling to maintain intimacy and coping with challenging symptoms. The members are able to reengage each other in a process of restructuring automatic implicit relational processes, bringing emotion, insight, and a narrative into current relational experiences. All group therapies emphasize the importance of addressing maladaptive cognitions of self and other, addressing over- or underregulation of emotion, and facilitating genuine interpersonal interactions that foster the capacity for intimacy.

In addition, group therapy offers something that individual therapy does not: the opportunity to explore a wider range of attachment-based problems. Because different members bring different attachment dimensions to group therapy, they will push the group to explore a variety of issues. Yalom and Leszcz (2005) described group therapy as a "hall of mirrors" (p. 1162) in which group members can see in others things that they personally struggle with. Having multiple people in the group with different issues, attachments, and ways of regulating emotions is likely to activate members in multiple ways. This can promote enormous opportunity for growth.

More important, group fosters not only dyadic attachments but also attachments to the group as a whole. Although we know relatively little about group attachments, social psychologists are arguing that the attachments we have to important groups we belong to have the power to enhance self-esteem and positively influence our perceptions of others (Mikulincer & Shaver, 2007b). Preliminary research findings by Keating et al. (in press) have revealed that these two aspects of the self are related and that reducing attachment avoidance to the therapy group predicts decreases in attachment insecurity outside of the group at 12 months after group treatment. In essence, facilitating group attachment security in group therapy influences dyadic attachments outside of therapy. Chapter 5 of this volume reviews the specific curative mechanisms that facilitate more secure attachments in group therapy.

THE GROUP AS A SECURE BASE: GROUP ATTACHMENTS

In our book, we emphasize group attachments and the impact they have on group therapy; however, many attachment researchers believe that one's attachment is exclusively derived from the early interaction with the caregiver. Although attachments can be influenced over time by many relationships, these developmental psychologists would argue that attachment to the group is not the same as the attachments one develops early in life to the caregiver. We agree that they are different but disagree that attachments to groups are less important to survival. We believe that just as we are inherently seeking caregivers to provide safety and security, we seek out groups to do the same. As a matter of fact, there is new biological evidence that the hormone oxytocin not only causes one to engage in more maternal behaviors toward a child and love toward a romantic partner, it also promotes ingroup trust and cooperation and defensive aggression toward competing outgroups (De Dreu et al., 2010). In essence, not only are we biologically hardwired to seek individual relationships to promote our survival, we are also driven to seek out and protect our clan.

In addition to this biological evidence, Ornstein (2012) described the tragic, yet inspiring, situation of a group of young children in a concentration camp during the Holocaust that relied on each other, the group, because they had lost their caregivers. She said that they were extremely attached to one another and could not be separated from each other for even brief amounts of time. Ornstein suggested that they developed an intense attachment to one another to cope with the loss of secure adult caregivers. Later, the children were able to develop attachments to their new caretakers. She believed that "what saved these children's sanity and what explains the absence of severe psychopathology was their attachment to each other" (p. 18).

CONCLUSION

Ornstein recognized the power of the group, yet many clinicians have yet to recognize the importance of groups to facilitate change (Piper, 2008). Multiple authors have applied attachment theory to different forms of psychotherapy but little to group therapy. We hope that our book encourages clinicians not only to practice group therapy but also to examine how their attitudes about group treatment and their experience within groups are always influenced by their past significant relationships. More important, we hope to demonstrate how group therapy, above and beyond other forms of treatment, can facilitate long-term changes in members who come to group alone, unable to trust or depend on others, and struggling to make sense of their symptoms and how they hinder their capacity for intimacy.

Group therapy can provide a safe environment in which members are able to reveal their genuine perceptions of one another and the group that are often influenced by past relational experiences. Group members' interpersonal feedback, insight, empathy, and compassion foster corrective emotional experiences that eventually help members take risks and develop intimate relationships, knowing they always have the secure base of the group to rely on. We believe that through the lens of attachment theory, we are better able to empathize with our group members and help them begin to address the implicit way they cope within relationships, regardless of our theoretical orientation or the type of group we are running.

2

MEASURING GROUP AND DYADIC ADULT ATTACHMENT STYLES

Have you heard the story about the blind men and the elephant? There were several blind men all touching different parts of an elephant, from its rough tusks to its smooth skin. The men ardently disagreed on the nature of this beast until they realized that they were merely touching different parts of the same animal. Akin to these blind men, attachment researchers are faced with an array of attachment measures, each of which conceptualizes and assesses attachment somewhat differently. The question thus arises: Are these various measures that supposedly all assess attachment capturing different aspects of attachment, or are they measuring different constructs?

To apply attachment theory to group therapy, it is important first to understand how one assesses attachment. The measurement of attachment has been controversial, with no single agreed-on method of assessment. Although many measures of adult dyadic attachment have evolved since the 1980s, only recently have researchers begun to assess group attachment styles with a single measure. In this chapter, we review measures of group and dyadic attachment,

http://dx.doi.org/10.1037/14186-003
Attachment in Group Psychotherapy, by C. L. Marmarosh, R. D. Markin, and E. B. Spiegel

focusing in on the advantages and disadvantages of each approach to measuring attachment, and conclude with a discussion of what we believe is the "best" way to assess attachment based on what aspect of attachment one wishes to measure. We begin this chapter by focusing on measures of group attachments and then address measures of dyadic attachments.

MEASURING ADULT GROUP ATTACHMENT STYLES

Historically, researchers and clinicians have considered attachment within dyadic relationships. However, more recently, social and clinical psychologists have expanded the theory of attachment to include attachment to groups. Broadly speaking, *group attachment* can be defined as an internal representation of groups based on early family (or other social or cultural groups) experiences that generally predict expectations about a new or previously unknown group (see Markin & Marmarosh, 2010; Smith, Murphy, & Coats, 1999). Group attachment theory posits that individuals develop internal working model of groups from early personal experiences with groups and that these internal working models guide individuals' expectations and behaviors in subsequent groups, similar to dyadic relationships. According to group attachment theory, groups provide individuals with a sense of self and security. Individuals develop a regulatory system for managing group relationships and the anxiety that arises in relation to them (Smith, Murphy, & Coats, 1999).

Development of the Social Group Attachment Scale

Smith et al. (1999) have been the only researchers to create a measure of group attachment styles. The Social Group Attachment Scale (SGAS; Smith et al., 1999) is a 25-item measure of an individual's attachment style to groups. Items on the SGAS were adapted from items found in Collins and Read's (1990) and Bartholomew and Horowitz's (1991) measures of dyadic attachment. Individuals are asked to consider their membership to a specific target group that is "most important to you." Factor analysis of the SGAS revealed two orthogonal (i.e., not related) dimensions: Avoidance and Anxiety (Smith et al., 1999). Individuals with greater group attachment Avoidance tend to dismiss groups and are more likely to consider withdrawing from the groups they are in. These individuals avoid closeness to groups, do not identify with groups, and do not seek social support from them and, similar to the case of dyadic attachment, seem to experience less positive affect (Rom & Mikulincer, 2003; Smith et al., 1999). Items on the SGAS that tap into rejection of intimacy (Avoidance) include "I am nervous when my group gets too close."

In contrast, individuals with greater group attachment Anxiety report fewer and less satisfying social supports within a group and tend to be preoccupied with acceptance and rejection from the group. Group attachment Anxiety has been found to be related to experiencing group interactions as threatening and, similar to dyadic attachment, more negative and intense affective states. These individuals experience groups as rejecting and need to cope with negative feelings that arise while in the group, which typically include anxiety, fear, and disappointment (Rom & Mikulincer, 2003; Smith et al., 1999). Items on the SGAS that tap into anxiety and concern about acceptance (Anxiety) include "I often worry that my group doesn't really accept me" (Smith et al., 1999). Smith et al. conducted three separate studies to assess the reliability and validity of their measure of group attachment. Overall, they found that the two dimensions of group attachment (Anxiety and Avoidance) can be assessed with good reliability and validity and stability over time (ranging from .75 to .91).

Research Using the SGAS

Although the SGAS was first developed and validated by social psychologists, there is some evidence that it is also valid in a clinical sample of group psychotherapy patients (Holtz, 2005). The SGAS has been used in empirical studies on adjustment to college and therapists' expectations of patients' attitude about group therapy. More specifically, Marmarosh and Markin (2007) found that group attachment style predicted college students' initial adjustment to college over and above dyadic attachment, lending support to the theory that group attachment is distinct from dyadic attachment. Marmarosh et al. (2006) found that therapists' group attachment anxiety was correlated with their belief that their patients would have negative expectations about group therapy. Specifically, the greater the therapists' group attachment anxiety, the more they expected their patients to worry that group therapy is the place you get dumped if individual therapy is not available and that it is an inferior treatment. Although no empirical data were given, Marmarosh (2009) argued that many current assessment instruments used in college counseling centers can be supported by attachment theory, and many group therapy interventions are aimed at facilitating secure working models.

Advantages and Disadvantages

The SGAS represents a significant contribution to the study of group attachment theory, as it is the first attempt to empirically measure an individual's attachment to groups. As measured by the SGAS, group attachment is considered to be dimensional, which is consistent with recent research on dyadic attachment that suggests that self-report attachment is dimensional rather than categorical. The survey has good psychometric properties and appears to be a reliable and valid measure of group attachment. Although the advantages to the SGAS are that it is an easy and quick measure to administer and score that demonstrates adequate psychometric properties, the measure also has significant disadvantages or limitations.

The first and primary possible limitation is theoretical as well as empirical. Specifically, can an individual really have a different dyadic and group attachment style, or is the SGAS just measuring dyadic attachment? Although the correlations between dyadic and group avoidance and anxiety have not been found to be identical, they have been found to be positive and significant (ranging from $r = .41$ to .70; Smith et al., 1999). These correlations suggest at least some overlap between group and dyadic attachment constructs. Yet it is also important to keep in mind that to derive these correlations between dyadic and group attachment avoidance and anxiety, Smith et al. (1999) correlated scores on the SGAS Anxiety and Avoidance scales with scores on the Romantic Partner Attachment Avoidance and Anxiety scales. Because these two measures have the same subscales, correlations were easy to interpret. However, because both measures were completed through the same person's self-report, correlations may have been artificially inflated. Thus, in reality, the two attachment constructs may be more distinct than the initial correlations suggest. The conceptual issue of whether group attachment is a separate construct from dyadic attachment is complicated to sort out theoretically and empirically. Finding a meaningful distinction between dyadic and group attachment in the research may depend on the development of a group attachment measure that is clinically sensitive enough to pick up on small yet meaningful differences. A separate limitation of the SGAS is that it does not assess a group member's internal representation of the group, which is implicit and cannot be easily measured using self-report. A measure of how group members internally represent groups may be relatively more clinically meaningful to group leaders, working from an attachment perspective, who strive to help their members develop more secure internal working models.

MEASURES OF ADULT DYADIC ATTACHMENT

Although one can find a plethora of adult dyadic attachment measures in the literature, in this section, we focus on those measures most commonly used in the attachment research or those measures with the strongest psychometric properties. We begin with a discussion of the Adult Attachment Interview (AAI) because it is often considered the gold standard of adult dyadic attachment measures, against which other dyadic attachment measures are frequently compared. We then present a summary of information about the various self-report measures of dyadic attachment in Table 2.1. Finally, we discuss general advantages and disadvantages of measuring dyadic attachment using a self-report measure that can be used in group therapy.

The Adult Attachment Interview

The AAI (George, Kaplan, & Main, 1996) is perhaps the most recognized method for assessing attachment and was also the first adult attachment measure. This semistructured interview focuses on the adult's experience of childhood attachment relationships and the effects of these childhood attachments on the adult being interviewed. These interviews are scored using subscales that relate to the participant's *experience* of caregiving (e.g., mother or father as loving or rejecting) and their *discourse style*, or the participant's state of mind with respect to these childhood experiences (e.g., overall coherence of transcript and of mind and idealization).

The major strength of the AAI is that, in theory, it assesses aspects of attachment that are assumed to be at least partially out of conscious awareness and, by doing so, taps into the individual's internal working model of attachment. This is a unique advantage of the AAI that is not present in other measures of attachment, at least not to the same degree. The interview does this by focusing in on how interviewees talk about their childhood experiences more than what they say about them (Hesse, 1999). For example, the autonomous interview is characterized by coherence, collaboration with the interview process, and balance in describing favorable as well as unfavorable circumstances. Another important advantage to the AAI is that it has been found to have excellent psychometric properties. It is stable over time (Bakermans-Kranenburg & van IJzendoorn, 1993; Benoit & Parker, 1994; Crowell & Treboux, 1995; Fonagy, Steele, & Steele, 1992), has good interrater reliability (Allen, Hauser, & Borman-Spurrell, 1996; Pianta, Egeland, & Adam, 1996), and appears to be a valid measure of attachment (Bakermans-Kranenburg & van IJzendoorn, 1993; Sagi et al., 1994).

Still, there are disadvantages to the AAI. Most important, administering and scoring the AAI requires in-depth training and is a time-consuming process. In addition to the sophisticated training needed to administer and score the AAI, the interview itself is time consuming and expensive to administer, transcribe, and rate, making it difficult to use in research and practice. Second, because the AAI focuses on past caregiving relationships, rather than current peer or romantic relationships, the interview does not examine feelings and behaviors that arise from separation in current dyadic relationships. Thus, it is possible that adults demonstrate a different attachment style in

TABLE 2.1
Self-Report Dyadic Attachment Measures: Format and Psychometric Properties

Measure	Format	Attachment dimensions	Category scales	Reliability	Advantages and disadvantages
Adult Attachment Questionnaire (Hazan & Shaver, 1987)	Single-item, forced-choice self-report Participants choose which of three attachment proto-types best fits them in romantic relationships Revised version includes Likert scale (Shaver & Hazan, 1993)	Not applicable	Three-category system: Secure, Ambivalent, and Avoidant	Internal consistency for the measure cannot be calculated, and the test–retest reliability is uncertain (Daniels, 2006). Some have reported it to be unstable—70% over 5 months to 4 years (reported in Cromwell & Treboux, 1995)	Advantages ■ First self-report measure of attachment, inspiring subsequent self-report measures Disadvantages ■ Probably does not capture dismissing-avoidant style (Stein et al., 1998) ■ Relatively poor psycho-metric properties (see Daniel, 2006)
Revised Adult Attachment Scale (Collins & Read, 1990)	Participants rate 18 Likert-type items on a 5-point scale regarding feelings about "romantic relationships"	Comfort with closeness (Close), ability to depend on others (Depend), and fear of abandonment (Anxiety)	Three Clusters: Secure = high scores on Close and Depend Anxious-Ambivalent = high scores on Anxiety and moderate scores on Close and Depend Avoidant = low scores on all 3 dimensions.	Adequate test–retest reliability; .71 for Depend, .52 for Anxiety, and .68 for Close over 2 months (Collins & Read, 1990); adequate internal consistency, Cronbach's α; .75–.84 for Depend, .70–.72 for Anxiety, .69–.73 for Close (Collins & Read, 1990; Wilson & Costanzo, 1996)	Advantages ■ Superior internal consistency to Hazan and Shaver's (1987) measure ■ Can be used as a dimensional scale or yield prototypes or clusters Disadvantages ■ Scores might be more reflective of the qual-ity of current romantic relationships

| The Simpson Questionnaire (also called the Adult Attachment Scale; Simpson, 1990; Simpson, Rholes, & Nelligan, 1992) | Participants rate 13 Likert-type items based on how they feel toward romantic partners in general on a 7-point scale; revised version has 17 items | Attachment Avoidance and Anxiety | Dimensional scores can be converted into Hazan and Shaver's three styles or prototypes | Cronbach's α coefficients for 13-item version; .42–.51 for Secure, .79–.80 for Avoidant, and .59–.79 for Anxious (Simpson, 1990; Sperling et al., 1996); 17-item measure; .70 (men), .74 (women) for Avoidance, .72 (men), .76 (women) for ambivalence (Sperling et al., 1996); no test–retest reliability available | Advantages:
 ■ Yields dimensional scores that also can be converted into Hazan and Shaver's (1987) prototypes and can be converted to Ainsworth's original infant attachment categories
 Disadvantages:
 ■ α coefficients are relatively low, which may make it difficult to detect significant findings
 ■ Asks participants about romantic relationships in general, rather than a specific romantic relationship, which may elicit idealized or wished for versions of one's relationships (Stein et al., 1998)
 (continues) |

Measure	Format	Attachment dimensions	Category scales	Reliability	Advantages and disadvantages
Relationship Questionnaire (Bartholomew & Horowitz, 1991)	Participants rate four prototypes on a 7-point Likert scale for "general relationship style"; can be used for relationships in general or a specific relationship; used to rate self and other	Dimensions can be derived	Four-category system of self and other: Secure, Preoccupied, Dismissing, and Fearful	Test–retest reliability over an 8-month period varied from .49 to .71 (Scharfe & Bartholomew, 1994)	Advantages: ■ Distinguishes between fearful and dismissing individuals ■ Allows for participants to be classified as two simultaneous attachment types Disadvantages: ■ Pools various conceptualizations of attachment together, making measure conceptually confusing (Stein et al., 1998)

Measure	Description	Scoring	Classification	Reliability	Advantages/Disadvantages
Relationship Scale Questionnaire (Griffin & Bartholomew, 1994)	Participants rate 30-items on a 5-point Likert scale about feelings in "close relationships"	Dimensions can be derived	Scores can be used to derive the three attachment scales developed by Collins & Read (1990) and the four-prototype classification system	Test–retest correlations for the four attachment styles over an 8-month period; .53 for female and .49 for male respondents (Scharfe & Bartholomew, 1994); average Cronbach's α coefficients for prototype scores range from .41 for Secure to .70 for Dismissing (Griffin & Bartholomew, 1994)	Advantages: ■ Scores can be derived a number of ways dimensionally and categorically ■ Can be filled out based on close relationships or romantic relationships Disadvantages: ■ Studies of external validity needed (Stein et al., 1998).
Experiences in Close Relationship Scale (Brennan, Clark, & Shaver, 1998)	Likert scale (1–7), 36-items measure that asks participants to rate how they experience the items in general in romantic relationships	Attachment Avoidance (reflects thoughts about others) and Anxiety (reflects thoughts about self)	Four-category system: Secure = low anxiety and low avoidance, Preoccupied = high anxiety and low avoidance, Dismissive Avoidant = low anxiety and high avoidance, and Fearful Avoidant = high anxiety and high avoidance	High reliability found in a sample of college undergraduates (Brennan et al., 1998) as well as in a clinical sample, although differences between men and women were found in the clinical sample (Parker, Johnson, & Ketring, 2011)	Advantages: ■ Conceptualize attachment along two orthogonal dimensions ■ Excellent reliability

current romantic and peer relationships than to caregivers (Daniel, 2006). Third, the AAI has demonstrated validity, but some have questioned whether it is truly a measure of attachment or a measure of the impact of caregiving (Stein, Jacobs, Ferguson, Allen, & Fonagy, 1998). Last, although the classification system is categorical rather than dimensional, Main (1991) suggested that certain classifications imply the existence of multiple and contradictory models of attachment. Because the system is categorical, the AAI may oversimplify the attachment style of adults who possess more than one attachment style.

Self-Report Instruments of Adult Dyadic Attachment

Although the AAI evolved from developmental psychology and infant attachment studies, self-report measures of adult attachment in romantic relationships grew out of social psychology. As one may expect, there are a number of important differences between attachment measures created by social psychologists versus those created by developmental psychologists. First, whereas social psychologists see attachment as an interpersonal process, developmental psychologists view attachment as an intrapsychic process. From this, attachment measures from social psychology examine attachment in current social relationships and assume that attachment style is consistent across these current relationships. Second, unlike developmental psychologists who assess adults' unconscious state of mind regarding attachment experiences, social psychologists approach the measurement of adult attachment directly by asking people to report on how they feel and function in current relationships. Here, we discuss advantages and disadvantages that cut across all self-report dyadic attachment measures. Table 2.1 presents advantages and disadvantages specific to each self-report measure.

All self-report measures of attachment share certain underlying advantages and disadvantages. In contrast to the AAI, which seeks to assess attachment internal working models by accessing one's unconscious state of mind regarding attachment, self-report measures of attachment locate attachment solely in one's conscious mind. Thus, scores on self-report attachment measures depend on one's awareness and self-insight, and perhaps on aspects of social desirability (see Kobak & Hazan, 1991). A popular criticism of these measures is that they may be too simplistic because they limit attachment to romantic relationships and to aspects of attachment that are conscious to the individual (Daniel, 2006). Another major issue with self-report measures of attachment is whether they are a valid measure of attachment or rather a measure of the quality of romantic relationships. One indication that a self-report measure assesses the traitlike variable of attachment, rather than the quality of a particular relationship, at one particular time, is if scores are stable over time (i.e., test–retest reliability). However, overall, studies on the stability of scores on various self-report measures are conflicting and vary depending on the particular measure (see Table 2.1). For example, the test–retest reliability of the Adult Attachment Questionnaire has ranged anywhere from no stability to 70% (Crowell & Treboux, 1995). Finally, whether a certain attachment measure yields dimensional or categorical attachment scores can be seen as an advantage or disadvantage depending on one's perspective. Researchers increasingly agree that self-report measures of attachment are more appropriately conceptualized as dimensional rather than categorical (Fraley & Waller, 1998). However, although the dimensional approach permits more nuanced comparisons within an attachment type (Stein et al., 1998) and allows for the possibility that an individual may have more than one attachment style (Simpson, Rholes, & Nelligan, 1992), some researchers argue that the dimensional approach does not adequately capture the fearful-avoidant attachment category. At the same time, self-report measures of attachment are relatively quick and inexpensive to administer, and no special training or clinical judgment is needed to score them. The ease with which these measures can be used in research and practice makes them more practical and more frequently used, especially compared with the AAI.

WHAT IS THE "BEST" WAY TO MEASURE ADULT DYADIC ATTACHMENT?

There has been much debate over what is the "right" way to measure adult attachment (see Steele, 2002). Some have argued that interview methods (particularly the AAI) are the "true" measures of attachment, but others have protested that self-report measures of attachment also yield important attachment-related information. However, because both the AAI and self-report measures have been extensively used in the research and produce interesting and theoretically consistent findings, there seem to be many credible ways of measuring adult dyadic attachment (see Daniel, 2006). However, when interpreting the array of attachment studies out there, it is important for the reader to understand that although the various measures of adult attachment are generally well validated and reliable, they each assess something slightly different and correlate only partially with each other (Crowell, Fraley, & Shaver, 1999; Shaver, Belsky, & Brennan, 2000; Stein et al., 2002).

Specifically, self-report attachment measures that focus on romantic relationships have been found to correlate with one another (Brennan, Clark, & Shaver, 1998; Sperling, Foelsch, & Grace, 1996), suggesting that these various measures are assessing a similar phenomenon. However, interview-based assessment methods for attachment, such as the AAI, seem to tap into different aspects of attachment than do self-reported attachment scales

(Sperling, Foelsch, & Grace, 1996). Furthermore, measures that assess attachment as a style do not correlate with measures that assess attachment as a set of behaviors (Crowell, Treboux, & Waters, 1993; Kobak & Hazan, 1992). Overall, studies that use more than one attachment measure tend to demonstrate important differences, rather than similarities, again suggesting that various measures of adult attachment assess different dimensions of attachment (Crowell & Treboux, 1995).

FUTURE DEVELOPMENTS IN MEASURING GROUP AND DYADIC ATTACHMENT

Methods for assessing adult dyadic attachment have evolved and expanded since the original AAI classification system was introduced in 1996, whereas methods for assessing group attachment styles are still new and just beginning to evolve. From the vantage point of group psychotherapy researchers and clinicians, measures of dyadic and group attachment are relevant in that they predict important group process and outcome variables and how group leaders can effectively work with group members with different attachment styles. Future research on dyadic attachment should explore how various measures of group member and leader attachment style predict different process and outcome variables. Because measures of attachment only partially correlate with each other, it may be that all measures of dyadic attachment are useful to understanding group phenomenon but in different ways. For example, self-report measures of attachment may correlate with group members' self-report of their experiences of the group, like group cohesion, whereas attachment as assessed by the AAI may correlate with more objective group member variables such as diagnosis. Moreover, a measure that assesses group member dyadic attachment specifically to other members and the group leaders would be helpful for researchers to develop in the future, rather than assuming that attachment styles are the same inside and outside of group therapy. Mallinckrodt, Gantt, and Coble (1995) developed the Client Attachment to Therapist Scale (CATS), which specifically assesses client dyadic attachment to the therapist in individual therapy. Future research could validate this scale, or develop a similar scale, to specifically assess group member attachment to the group and group leader.

CONCLUSION

This chapter sought not only to review the relevant measures of dyadic and group attachment but also to underscore the complexity of measuring a multifaceted construct like attachment by focusing on the advantages and disadvantages of each measure. Looking forward, future research on measures of dyadic attachment needs to focus on what measure of attachment is helpful, when, and under what circumstances. In contrast, future research on the measurement of group attachment needs to focus on developing and expanding on the existing measure of group attachment and perhaps creating an interview-based measure. More research is needed to distinguish dyadic and group attachment, but this research would require the development of alternative and more sophisticated measures of group attachment.

Returning to the story of the three blind men and the elephant, told at the start of this chapter, it appears that different measures of attachment merely touch on different parts of the same elephant, and more research is needed. The fact that so many measures of attachment have arisen in the literature that all predict important process and outcome variables, but only partly relate to one another, points to the complexity of attachment theory and the difficulties in capturing all the different parts of the elephant in one measure.

3

ATTACHMENT IN INDIVIDUAL AND GROUP PSYCHOTHERAPY: EMPIRICAL FINDINGS

In this chapter, we review the empirical research on the role of patient adult attachment patterns in the process and outcome of individual and group therapies. We conclude with a section on how therapist attachment patterns, and the interaction between therapist and patient attachment, influence therapy process and outcome. Although we integrate empirical research throughout the book, we believe it is important to summarize, in one chapter, the robust empirical evidence supporting the application of attachment theory to therapy. The overall purpose of this chapter is to present empirical studies on how attachment is enacted in therapy, laying the foundation for the clinical material presented in Chapters 6 through 11.

http://dx.doi.org/10.1037/14186-004
Attachment in Group Psychotherapy, by C. L. Marmarosh, R. D. Markin, and E. B. Spiegel
Copyright © 2013 by the American Psychological Association. All rights reserved.

EFFECTS OF PATIENT ATTACHMENT STYLE
ON THE PROCESS OF INDIVIDUAL PSYCHOTHERAPY

Most of the empirical studies on the role of attachment patterns in individual adult psychotherapy have looked at the ways in which patient attachment patterns affect the therapy process. It is frequently hypothesized that patients with different attachment styles will behave differently in therapy, affecting the therapist–patient relationship, as well as the therapy process and outcome. In this section, we discuss how attachment style appears to influence how patients behave in therapy and the type of relationship they form with their therapist.

Attachment and Patient In-Treatment Behavior

The studies presented in Table 3.1 used the Adult Attachment Interview (AAI; George, Kaplan, & Main, 1996) to measure attachment state of mind and suggest that patient attachment representations and tendencies relate to certain patient behaviors during the process of individual therapy, such as

TABLE 3.1
Studies of Attachment and Patient In-Treatment Behaviors

Study	Attachment measure used	Main findings
Dozier (1990)	AAI (George, Kaplan, & Main, 1996) using Kobak (1989) Q-set	■ Greater security was associated with more compliance with treatment. ■ Stronger avoidant tendencies (i.e., more deactivating tendencies) were associated with greater rejection of treatment providers, less self-disclosure, and poorer use of treatment.
Korfmacher, Adam, Ogawa, & Egeland (1997)	AAI (George et al., 1996)	■ Patients with a secure (autonomous) state of mind were more emotionally committed to treatment and accepted more help. ■ Patients with a dismissing state of mind were less emotionally committed to treatment than those with a secure state of mind and preferred simple companionship over therapeutic interventions. ■ Patients with an unresolved state of mind were less emotionally committed to treatment than secure patients and more likely to require crisis intervention.

Note. AAI = Adult Attachment Interview.

self-disclosure, treatment compliance, and help-seeking behaviors. Specifically, these studies suggest that patients with a secure state of mind with regard to attachment engage more in behaviors that make better use of the therapy (e.g., they are more likely to seek help and self-disclose) than patients with insecure attachment representations. Some might wonder why patients with a secure attachment representation seek treatment, but having a more secure attachment does not necessarily inoculate individuals from loss, depression, anxiety, discrimination, or career and family struggles. As a matter of fact, having a more secure attachment representation facilitates the ability to seek treatment and receive support when issues present themselves. Patients with more dismissing tendencies, in contrast, seem to show the most difficulty making use of the therapy, self-disclosing little and rejecting help, compared with patients who have more preoccupied tendencies. Research is needed that identifies helpful interventions for engaging more dismissive patients and therapeutic strategies for working with more preoccupied patients' resistance. Furthermore, in her review on attachment and the therapy process, Daniel (2006) argued that the empirical study of systematic differences in in-treatment behavior and attachment is still limited. She suggested that it is often assumed that a patient's attachment-based behaviors toward the therapist mirror the patient's behaviors with others outside of the therapy. Yet there may be important differences in how a patient expresses and seeks out attachment needs within and outside of the therapy context. For example, a patient classified as dismissing-avoidant may be less likely to seek out help from the therapist but not from others in his or her life. More research is needed on how patients with different attachment patterns engage in therapy and whether these behaviors mirror the patient's attachment behaviors outside of treatment.

Attachment and the Therapy Relationship

In the following subsections, we consider two aspects of the therapy relationship that relate to patient attachment in individual psychotherapy: alliance and transference.

Alliance and Attachment

Identifying patient individual difference variables that predict the quality and course of the therapeutic alliance is an important area of study because the alliance is a consistent predictor of therapy outcome (Horvath & Bedi, 2002). Together, the studies presented in Table 3.2 suggest that patients with a secure attachment style form better alliances with their therapists than patients with a more insecure attachment, when assessed at one point in time in the therapy (Diener, Hilsenroth, & Weinberger, 2009; Kivlighan, Patton, &

TABLE 3.2

Studies of Patient Attachment and Alliance

Study	Attachment measure used	Main findings
Mallinckrodt, Coble, & Gantt (1995)	AAS (Collins & Read, 1990)	■ Comfort with intimacy positively correlated with alliance. ■ Fear of abandonment correlated negatively with alliance. ■ Ability to depend on others positively correlated with alliance scores.
Satterfield & Lyddon (1995)	AAS (Collins & Read, 1990)	
Kivlighan, Patton, & Foote (1998)	AAS (Collins & Read, 1990)	■ Comfort with intimacy and ability to depend on others positively correlated with alliance scores.
Eames & Roth (2000)	RSQ (Bartholomew & Horowitz, 1991)	■ Fearful attachment was associated with lower alliance ratings and secure attachment with higher alliance ratings. ■ Preoccupied attachment and dismissing attachment were associated with improvement in alliance ratings over time, although there was some question about the reliability of these findings. ■ Preoccupied attachment was associated with more frequent reports of ruptures and dismissing attachment was associated with fewer reports of ruptures, according to therapist report.
Kanninen, Salo, & Punamaki (2000)	Paper and pencil version of the AAI; divided patients into three clusters: autonomous, dismissing, and preoccupied	■ No differences were found between the three groups on initial ratings of the working alliance. ■ When looking at alliance over time; high-low-high pattern for alliance scores for both the secure and the preoccupied patients, with the fall in the middle of treatment and the rise in alliance toward the end of treatment steeper for the preoccupied patients than for the secure ones; for dismissing patients, the alliance was stable from the beginning of therapy to the middle of therapy and decreased toward the end of therapy.
Sauer, Lopez, & Gormley (2003)	Simpson's Adult Attachment Scale (Simpson, 1990)	■ No effect of patient avoidance or anxiety on the working alliance as rated by the patient or therapist in the initial phase of therapy.
Diener, Hilsenroth, & Weinberger (2009)	Meta-analysis of 12 studies that all examined patient-reported alliance and patient attachment style in individual psychotherapy	■ Secure attachment related to more positive therapeutic alliance, whereas insecure attachment related to more negative alliance, as reported by patients.

Note. AAI = Adult Attachment Interview; AAS = Adult Attachment Scale; RSQ = Relationship Scale Questionnaire.

Foote, 1998; Mallinckrodt, Gantt, & Coble, 1995; Satterfield & Lyddon, 1995). Other studies have looked at the relationship between patient attachment and alliance scores over time. From the limited research in this area, it appears that alliance scores may not vary by patient attachment in the beginning of therapy; however, toward the middle and end phases of therapy, important differences in the quality of the alliance may exist for patients with difference attachment styles (Kanninen, Salo, & Punamaki, 2000; Sauer, Lopez, & Gormley, 2003). Overall, these studies suggest that securely attached patients form better alliances than insecurely attached patients, as one may expect, and important differences in the change in alliance over time may exist among patients with different attachment styles. Last, research on attachment and alliance ruptures suggests that although alliance scores go up for preoccupied and dismissive patients over the first few sessions of therapy, preoccupied patients experience more ruptures with their therapists than do dismissive patients. Perhaps preoccupied patients become disappointed with their therapist or come to feel that their therapist is unavailable or rejecting as therapy progresses, whereas dismissive patients may invest just enough in the therapist–patient relationship to maintain a positive relationship at the beginning of therapy but not enough for an actual rupture to occur (Eames & Roth, 2000; Safran, Muran, Samstag, & Stevens, 2002).

Transference and Attachment

Although there are many definitions of the term, Gelso and Hayes (1998) defined *transference* as "the patient's experience of the therapist that is shaped by the patient's own psychological structures and past and involves displacement, on to the therapist, of feelings, attitudes, and behaviors belonging rightfully in earlier relationships" (p. 51). Viewed from the perspective of attachment theory, transference may be conceptualized as a misperception of another person on the basis of a patient's use of long-established internal working models, used to anticipate the motives and behaviors of a new attachment figure (Mallinckrodt et al., 1995). However, although it has been written about theoretically (Cortina & Marrone, 2003), little empirical research has looked at attachment and transference in the same study.

As a rare exception, Woodhouse, Schlosser, Crook, Ligiero, and Gelso (2003) studied patients' attachments to their therapists, transference reactions, and patients' conscious memories of parental caregiving in 51 patient–therapist dyads after one session in ongoing therapy. They found that more preoccupied or secure attachment to the therapist was related to therapist ratings of more negative and overall amount of transference. However, level of avoidant-fearful attachment to the therapist was not related to any type of transference. Some of these results were surprising, given that the authors did not find evidence to support their predictions that patients with more secure attachment to their therapists would have less transference and patients with more avoidant-fearful attachment toward their therapists would have higher levels of negative transference. One interpretation of these results is that patients with more secure attachments to their therapists felt safer to express their transference and patients with more avoidant-fearful attachments avoided forming intimate attachments to their therapists in which the transference would be activated.

Attachment and Psychotherapy Outcome

Attachment theorists have argued that the therapist should strive to provide the patient with attachment needs not adequately experienced in childhood (Bowlby, 1988; Pistole, 1989). According to attachment theory, if patients establish a more secure attachment to the therapist, this will lead to change in the patient's attachment style in close relationships (Bernier & Dozier, 2002; Davila & Levy, 2006; Jones, 1983; Mallinckrodt et al., 1995; Sperling & Lyons, 1994). Accordingly, preliminary research suggests that patient attachment style in close relationships is, in certain circumstances, related to the patient's attachment to the therapist and that change in attachment to the therapist predicts change in attachment in close relationships (Janzen, Fitzpatrick, & Drapeau, 2008; Mallinckrodt, Porter, & Kivlighan, 2005). In particular, several studies suggest that certain psychodynamic treatments are effective in facilitating more secure internal working models for patients (see Table 3.3). In her review, Daniel (2006) suggested two caveats to the research on attachment and outcome. First, she suggested the test–retest reliability of attachment measures may be low because adult attachment patterns naturally change over time, especially in high-risk clinical populations (Waters, Hamilton, & Weinfeld, 2000). Thus, without a control group, changes in attachment patterns may not be attributable to the treatment but to time and circumstance. Yet the existing studies show a consistent shift toward a secure attachment over the course of therapy, rather than random change, as would be the case if change was solely due to random effects. Furthermore, because secure attachment in clinical populations is arguably rare, this documented shift toward secure attachment is promising and merits future investigation.

EFFECTS OF PATIENT ATTACHMENT STYLE ON THE PROCESS OF GROUP PSYCHOTHERAPY

Group therapy provides a context in which a member's need for affiliation and closeness is likely to surface and play a central role in treatment (Yalom & Leszcz, 2005). Past experiences with individuals and groups affect

TABLE 3.3
Studies of Patient Attachment and Therapy Outcome

Study	Sample	Measure and when administered	Main findings
Fonagy et al. (1995, 1996)	35 psychiatric patients in psychoanalytically oriented in-patient treatment	AAI; before and after 1 year of treatment	40% of the 35 patients were classified as insecure at admissions but as autonomous upon discharge.
Travis, Bliwise, Binder, & Horne Moyer (2001)	29 clients in time-limited dynamic psychotherapy	The Relationship Questionnaire, pre- and posttherapy	Significant increase in number of secure patients and a significant decrease in number of fearful patients over the course of therapy. Changes in attachment related to General Assessment Scale scores and symptom levels, suggesting that changes in attachment may reduce symptoms.
Diamond, Clarkin, et al. (2003); Diamond, Stovall-McClough, et al. (2003)	10 patients in TFP	AAI; beginning of TFP and after 1 year of therapy	Three patients changed from insecure to secure, four did not show much change, and three changed from insecure to a category that could not be classified. Four patients initially classified as unresolved were not classified as such following treatment.
Levy et al. (2006)	90 patients diagnosed with borderline personality disorder randomized to TFP, dialectical behavior therapy, or a modified psychodynamic supportive psychotherapy	AAI and the Reflective Functioning (Fonagy et al., 1998) coding scale; at Time 1 and after 12 months of treatment	Participants showed a significant increase in the number classified as secure for TFP but not for the other two treatments.

Note. AAI = Adult Attachment Interview; TFP = transference-focused psychotherapy.

patients' attitudes toward group therapy, how they make use of group therapy, and the relationships they form within the group. This section reviews relevant research on the impact of group member attachment on the group therapy process and how member attachments are enacted in group therapy.

Attachment and Group Therapy Expectations and Attitudes

Despite empirical support showing that the effectiveness of group therapy is no different from that of individual therapy (Burlingame, Fuhriman, & Mosier, 2003; Burlingame & Krogel, 2005; McRoberts, Burlingame, & Hoag, 1998), people continue to express attitudes that minimize group therapy as a viable form of psychotherapy (Piper, 2008). Expectations and attitudes are important because they influence one's willingness to seek treatment (Vogel, Wade, & Hackler, 2007). Bowden (2002) found that at the time of intake, 77% of patients preferred individual therapy, whereas only 2.8% favored group. The question then becomes, why do some people hold negative expectations or attitudes about group therapy and others do not?

A patient is likely to approach the group therapy situation similarly to how he or she approaches other groups in his or her life and consistent with his or her internal working model about personal others and groups. Accordingly, research suggests that attachment style predicts one's expectations about group therapy. Specifically, individuals with more attachment avoidance in adult romantic relationships are more likely to fear being humiliated or shamed in group therapy (Marmarosh, Whipple, et al., 2009). Furthermore, individuals with more of an insecure group attachment are less engaged in group activities, hold more negative evaluations of groups, and perceive less support from groups (Smith, Murphy, & Coats, 1999). In contrast, individuals with a more secure attachment generally reveal more positive attitudes toward groups, positive memories of group interactions, and function better within team work (Rom & Mikulincer, 2003). In essence, these studies suggest that attachment style to dyads and groups may help to provide a deeper understanding of patients' expectations and attitudes toward group therapy.

Self-Disclosure and Attachment

Yalom and Leszcz (2005) argued that self-disclosure alleviates group members' feeling of isolation and underlies all other therapeutic factors in a group. Thus, it seems important to identify group member individual difference variables that predict the amount and quality of group member self-disclosures. Shechtman and Dvir (2006) found that adolescents classified as secure self-disclosed the most, used the most productive group behaviors, and were the most responsive to others in counseling groups, whereas avoidant adolescent group members scored the lowest on these measures. These authors suggested that because secure group members hold positive views of others and desire intimacy, they are more likely not only to self-disclose more but also to use self-disclosure more appropriately in group and to respond sensitively to other members' disclosures. In another study, Shechtman and Rybko (2004) found that members classified with avoidant attachments, both avoidant-dismissing and avoidant-fearful, tended to self-disclose the least, and members with ambivalent attachment had a moderate amount of self-disclosure. Because of their lack of self-disclosure, particularly for members with avoidant attachments, members with insecure attachment are more likely to feel isolated from the group and less connected to it. In general, group members with insecure attachments may be less likely than members with secure attachments to engage in behaviors that make good use of group therapy, such as self-disclosure, cognitive exploration, insight, and openness (Shechtman & Dvir, 2006; Shechtman & Rybko, 2004).

Attachment and Group Member–Leader Relationships

In the following subsections, we consider two aspects of group member–leader relationships that relate to group member attachment in group psychotherapy: alliance and transference.

Attachment and Alliance

Twenty-five years of research on alliance suggests that it is related to therapeutic outcome not only in individual therapy but also in group therapy (Abouguendia, Joyce, Piper, & Ogrodniczuk, 2004; Martin, Garske, & Davis, 2000). The group therapy alliance consists of a group member's perception of his or her emotional bond to the group and agreement on the goals and tasks for group therapy among group members and with the group therapist (Gaston & Marmar, 1993). A group member's experience of the group therapy alliance is likely to be affected by his or her attachment internal working models that guide his or her expectations of new individuals and groups. Yet few studies have examined the development of the alliance over the course of group therapy and its relationship to attachment. As an exception, one study found that for members with a more secure attachment, alliance ratings remained similar in the beginning and later stages of therapy. However, more preoccupied individuals rated the alliance more positively toward the end of therapy, whereas more dismissing-avoidant individuals rated the alliance more negatively toward the end of therapy (Kanninen, Salo, & Punamaki, 2000). Furthermore, Tasca and colleagues found evidence to suggest that the relationship between group member attachment and alliance ratings over time depends on the type of group therapy, with those with higher attachment anxiety rating the alliance higher over time in interpersonal-dynamic type groups but not in cognitive behavioral–type groups (Tasca, Balfour, Ritchie, & Bissada, 2007b). Clearly, more research is needed on group member attachment and the group therapy alliance, particularly looking at the alliance rupture–repair process.

Attachment and Transference

Yalom and Leszcz (2005) and G. Corey (2008) view transference as an important component of member-to-member and member-to-leader relationships. Although it has been written about theoretically (Cortina & Marrone, 2003; Markin & Marmarosh, 2010), little empirical research with groups has examined attachment and transference in the same study. Mallinckrodt and Chen (2004) are the only researchers we found who directly studied transference and attachment in group. Their sample consisted of 76 graduate students in 12 training groups. Group members reported memories of emotional bonds with parental caregivers and attachment anxiety and avoidance, as well as Impact Message Inventory Ratings of other group members. The authors conducted a social relations analysis and found that group members tended to view other members similarly, in terms of their Impact Message Inventory ratings, but differently from one another. These discrepancies were interpreted as indicators of transference and were significantly associated with negative memories of parental caregivers and attachment avoidance. This finding would suggest that internal working models of early parental caregivers shape a group member's perception of other members' behaviors, especially when early experiences with caregivers are negative and avoidant.

Attachment and Group Outcome

Overall, research investigating the relationship between attachment patterns and group therapy outcome is confusing. When looking at the attachment–outcome literature overall, Kirchmann et al. (2009) stated that several studies have a slightly positive influence of patient attachment security on outcome (e.g., Meredith, Strong, & Feeney, 2007; Meyer, Pilkonis, Proitetti, Heape, & Egan, 2001; Mosheim et al., 2000; Strauss, Lobo-Drost, & Pilkonis, 1999). Contrary to this, other studies have actually found advantages for avoidant (Fonagy et al., 1996) or ambivalent (Sachse & Strauss, 2002) patients. Kirchmann et al. (2009) suggested that these inconsistent results can be explained by differences in patient and treatment characteristics (e.g., composition of the group in terms of attachment status, diagnosis of the patients, gender, experience level of group leaders) or different operationalizations of attachment constructs (cf. Strauss et al., 2006). More sophisticated studies reveal that the relationship between group member attachment and group therapy outcome is complex, and one must consider different mediating variables and the type of group therapy. For example, group climate seems to be particularly important for group members who were classified as ambivalently attached (preoccupied group members), interpersonal learning for group members classified as having secure attachments, and therapists' acceptance and emotional availability for those classified as avoidant members in predicting a favorable group outcome (Kirchmann et al., 2009). Moreover, some evidence suggests that at a 1-year follow-up, members with more attachment anxiety may have better outcomes in group psychodynamic interpersonal therapy, whereas members with lower attachment anxiety may do better in group cognitive behavioral therapy (Tasca, Ritchie, et al., 2006). Table 3.4 renews the findings of several studies that have focused on how group members' attachments influence treatment process and outcome.

CONCLUSION

Empirical studies suggest that in certain circumstances, attachment patterns of patients and therapists relate to the therapeutic relationship, patient in-session behavior, and therapy outcome. Much of the attachment research highlights the merits of patients with a secure attachment, which is especially helpful for group therapists considering membership in their groups. At the same time, the research illuminating the relationship between insecure attachments and the therapy process and outcome can help group leaders with the various stages of group development, from preparing and screening more insecurely attached group members to providing a facilitative group therapy process and outcome for these group members. Overall, more research on both group leader and group member attachment is needed. Specifically, future studies on the relationship between group member attachment and group therapy outcome that take into account mediating and moderating variables is needed, along with studies on how to effectively engage more insecurely attached group members in productive group processes such as engaging in effective self-disclosures and building positive alliances.

TABLE 3.4
Attachment and Group Psychotherapy Process and Outcome

Attachment and Groups	Main Findings
	Group therapy process
Shechtman & Rybko (2004)	More insecurely attached adolescent group members were rated by observers as sharing less intimate personal information during a first group counseling session. More avoidant participants scored lower than secure people on self-disclosure, intimacy, and empathy at the end of the counseling process. Counselors rated anxiously attached participants as working less constructively than secure ones during group sessions.
Tasca, Taylor, et al. (2004)	Attachment predicted treatment completion in an eating disorders partial hospital treatment. More avoidant members were more likely to drop out of group therapy.
Shechtman & Dvir (2006)	The more avoidant members had the lowest rates of self-disclosure, the least effective work, and were most negative toward others in the group.
Tasca, Balfour, et al. (2007b)	For group members with binge eating disorder who received group psychodynamic interpersonal therapy, higher attachment anxiety and lower avoidance related to greater alliance growth. This was not found in cognitive behavioral group therapy.
Illing, Tasca, et al. (2011)	Higher attachment avoidance at pre-treatment was related to lower Engaged group climate at week 1, and was related to a greater impact of the group on the individual's experience of group engagement.
Harel et al. (2011)	Those with more attachment anxiety perceive the group climate as being more avoidant and having more conflict. The higher the scores on attachment avoidance, the lower the gains in perceived social support.
Kivlighan, Lo Coco, & Gullo (2012)	Actor-partner interdependence modeling (APIM) found that aggregated perceptions of attachment anxiety and avoidance were positively related to a member's perception of group conflict and aggregated perceptions of attachment anxiety and avoidance were negatively related to a member's perception of group engagement.
Gallagher et al. (2013)	Interpersonal learning in groups was associated with positive outcomes for those with greater attachment anxiety but not avoidance.

Group therapy outcome

Kilmann et al. (1999)	Attachment-Focused Group Treatment facilitated changes in attachment and interpersonal functioning for group members. Those receiving the group intervention reported less fearful and more secure attachment patterns up to 6 months post intervention.
Kilmann et al. (2006)	College students with insecure adult attachment patterns were randomly assigned into either an attachment-focused group or into a relationship skills focused (RS) group. AF and RS participants reported decreased agreement with dysfunctional relationship beliefs. AF participants also reported higher self-esteem, decreased angry reaction, and increased control of anger.
Tasca, Ritchie, et al. (2006)	More anxious group members in group therapy for eating disorders did better in group treatments that fostered cohesion, were more relational, and focused on emotion regulation compared to more structured groups such as CBT groups.
Tasca, Balfour, Ritchie, & Bissada (2007a)	Changes in attachment anxiety were associated with improved depression after group therapy.
Kirchmann et al. (2009)	Group psychotherapy for 289 inpatients revealed that the relationship between attachment and outcome was mediated/moderated by group factors such as group climate.
Kirchmann et al. (2012)	One out of five patients moved from an insecure to secure attachment category at the end of group treatment, and showed even more improvement 1 year following the end of group treatment.
Kinley & Rayno (2012)	Results indicated that increases in secure attachment and decreases in fearful attachment and, to a lesser degree, preoccupied attachment styles were found after 6 weeks of intensive group therapy. Change was not found in the dismissive attachment style. Changes in Secure and/or Fearful (but not Preoccupied) attachment styles were related to changes in interpersonal functioning.
Keating et al. (in press)	Attachment anxiety and avoidance regarding the therapy group attachment did improve during the group. This improvement generalized to more secure individual attachment up to 1 year post group therapy.
Maxwell et al. (in press)	102 women with binge eating disorder evidenced changes in attachment anxiety and avoidance following group treatment and these decreases were associated with greater interpersonal functioning. Decreased anxiety was related to decreased depression. There were no relationships between decreases in attachment anxiety or avoidance and binging behavior.

II

APPLICATIONS OF ATTACHMENT TO GROUP PRACTICE

4

ASSEMBLING THE GROUP: SCREENING, PLACING, AND PREPARING GROUP MEMBERS

In this chapter, we consider the role that attachment plays in the selection, placement, and preparation of potential new group members. Although there are several methods for assessing potential group candidates, including using group screening instruments, there is little existing literature on how attachment styles factor into group screening or how advance consideration of attachment styles can help group leaders recruit group members who are less likely to drop out of treatment.

This chapter also examines how attachment can be an important factor in placing group candidates into groups that are an appropriate match for their needs. Are there certain types of groups that are best for a potential group candidate with particular attachment dimensions? Would the other group members benefit from the placement of that candidate into the group? Considering how group composition influences and is influenced by attachment can help guide difficult placement choices.

http://dx.doi.org/10.1037/14186-005

Attachment in Group Psychotherapy, by C. L. Marmarosh, R. D. Markin, and E. B. Spiegel

Last, we review how a thorough preparation process can play a significant role in ensuring a successful group experience for group members who have high levels of attachment anxiety or avoidance.

WHY IS GROUP SCREENING NECESSARY?

Advance screening of potential group members is an important part of the group psychotherapy process. Because group members share personal life details, disclose emotional reactions, and receive spontaneous feedback from previously unknown comembers, the potential exists for emotional withdrawal in the group, conflict within the group process, inconsistent membership among group members, and, perhaps most significant, premature termination. Although withdrawal and conflict within the group setting may be upsetting to other group members, they have the potential to be processed because they happen in the "here and now" (Yalom & Leszcz, 2005). Premature group drop-outs, however, create emotional instability among the other group members and influence other group terminations as well (MacNair & Corazzini, 1994; MacNair-Semands, 2002; Yalom & Leszcz, 2005). MacNair-Semands (2002) noted that one reason pregroup screening sessions have become popular among group leaders is that they are associated with higher rates of attendance and decreased premature terminations. She observed that because pregroup screening assesses the interpersonal skills that group members need to develop to be successful, the leaders can select group members who are appropriate for the group. Thus, it is important to focus on the patient variables associated with group success or failure.

Starting in the 1980s, the American Group Psychotherapy Association formed a task force to develop a CORE (Clinical Outcome Results Standardized Measures) battery to provide group therapists with the information they would need to select appropriate patients for group treatment and to facilitate the assessment of change in group therapy. The CORE battery includes assessing the working alliance, group climate, empathy, and cohesion. The authors of the CORE and the CORE–Revised developed selection guidelines based on the empirical literature and determined that client behaviors, personalities, and interpersonal histories are important determinants of group attrition and outcome (Burlingame et al., 2006; Yalom & Leszcz, 2005).

On the basis of these guidelines, screening should consider factors such as capacity for insight, ability to regulate emotions, coping strategies, and previous experience with therapy when evaluating whether a potential group member can tolerate the anxiety that group may elicit (Burlingame et al., 2006). These factors also predict how well a group member will navigate the interpersonal challenges that evolve within a group therapy modality. Burlingame et al. (2006) argued that suitable candidates for group include clients who have difficulties in relationships but have insight into how their family issues influence their current relationships, have the capacity to discuss feelings, have the ability to form relationships, are able to commit to the meetings and duration of the group, have formed relationships with individual therapists, or who have complied with prior therapy obligations—in essence, individuals with more secure attachments.

These authors suggested that clients may not be suitable for group therapy if they endorse the following: "many interpersonal conflicts," "intensely avoidant," "frequently engage in self-defeating behaviors," "strong denial of issues," "describe issues in vague manner," "are certain they will not feel comfortable in group," "are prone to deviate from the group task," or "will affect the group safety in some way" (Burlingame et al., 2006, pp. 12–13). Although the authors based the exclusion factors on the empirical literature, they did not provide a theoretical rationale that explains why these factors lead to poor outcome in group therapy (Marmarosh, 2009). Attachment theory provides a more integrated understanding of these criteria and explains why some patients may not be suitable for certain types of group treatment.

GROUP SCREENING FROM AN ATTACHMENT PERSPECTIVE

In this section, we review several methods that group leaders can use to gain an understanding of a potential group member's attachment style as part of a group screening assessment. Although these methods are not designed to determine a definitive attachment style, they are geared toward helping the leader make a decision about an individual's readiness to join a group. The most common useful screening instrument is the group leader's reaction to the potential member and the group interview process. In addition to relying on the clinical interview, the group leader can provide self-report assessment instruments to determine the individual's dyadic or group attachments.

Interview: Exploring Attachment Styles and Readiness for Group

Because dyadic attachments develop in early relationship experiences with a primary caregiver, the individual intake interview itself is likely to evoke internal representations from the past in a vivid and experiential way. As an authority figure, the leader is likely to trigger attachment-based reactions during the interview and can look for both nonverbal and verbal indicators of attachment anxiety and avoidance.

Body Cues and Eye Contact

A clinician can learn a great deal about potential group members' attachment by observing their nonverbal reactions. More avoidant individuals (both fearful-avoidant and dismissing-avoidant) are more likely to demonstrate disinterest or avoidance in their body language (Wallin, 2007). For example, their arms are more likely to be folded, their bodies closed off. They might avoid eye contact. Yet despite this avoidance, they would not seem particularly activated. The overall impression would be coolness or aloofness. In contrast, more preoccupied individuals would be more likely to demonstrate physical agitation (e.g., flushed faces, sweating, open posture) when discussing their sense of worthiness, unresolved relationships, or wishes for increased interpersonal contact. More fearful-avoidant individuals would most likely display a mixture of these responses, perhaps first becoming agitated and then shutting down, as indicated through their body language. It is important to note the role of cultural factors in interpreting nonverbal cues, and a screening clinician should not reach any attachment or screening conclusions based on nonverbal cues alone. (See Chapter 10 of this volume for a review of attachment and diversity in group therapy.)

I Versus You Statements

How do individuals refer to themselves? First- versus second-person language, particularly when referring to experienced affect, can serve as indicator of comfort level with interpersonal interactions. More preoccupied individuals frequently use first-person language to describe feelings in interpersonal relationships, whereas dismissing-avoidant individuals may be more likely to use second-person language as a method of creating distance.

Verbal Specificity

How detailed or vague are the individual's responses to questions about relationships? Individuals with more dismissing-avoidant attachment styles tend to minimize and suppress emotions in interviews (Bartholomew & Horowitz, 1991; Main, 1991). This is often demonstrated with responses such as "I had a good childhood. It was very normal." When asked for more details, these individuals tend to be vague and evasive, and often many follow-up questions are needed to obtain basic qualitative relational information. In contrast, more preoccupied individuals have difficulty regulating affect and tend to become flooded with attachment-based memories, which lead them to become more verbose answering questions about relationship issues (Tasca, Ritchie, & Balfour, 2011; Wallin, 2007). We tend to see response patterns that are overflowing, undifferentiated, and confusing, characterized by a devalued sense of self and ambivalent, unresolved feelings toward other close relationships.

Level of Expressed Affect

Does the expressed affect appear restricted, balanced (e.g., appropriate), or overflowing? As with level of verbal specificity, dismissing-avoidant individuals tend to restrict emotion. An individual with a more dismissing-avoidant attachment is likely to give an intellectualized, emotionally devoid response to a question about his or her relationships. Preoccupied individuals tend to be overly emotionally expressive, particularly with regard to worry about relationship rejection and loss. More fearful-avoidant individuals, because they are experiencing high attachment anxiety and avoidance, often display strong, ambivalent emotions regarding the desire for and fear of intimate relationships.

Group Relational Goals

Does the individual enter the screening session with specific relational goals in mind for group? Although it is true that many individuals may not know exactly what they are looking to get out of group (particularly if they lack group experience), the absence of goals may also be defensive in nature. For example, in the interview, an individual may immediately say "I don't know" when asked about goals and display a lack of curiosity. This defensive lack of inquisitiveness is often seen with more dismissive-avoidant individuals who rely on deactivation and avoidance of vulnerability. In contrast, when discussing group relational goals, an individual may become emotionally activated and respond, "I don't know!" in a frustrated tone. Or they might have detailed goals for group involving a wish to become close with others. Both of these responses are more common with group members who are easily activated emotionally and engage in hyperactivating strategies, consistent with a more preoccupied attachment.

Response to "Here and Now" Process Comments

In every group screening appointment, at some point the group leader will make a process comment to the potential group member. Perhaps it will be an observation of a nonverbal behavior, tone of voice, or affective response. In some cases, it might be a simple question that turns the attention back to the process, such as "So as we discuss these issues, what reactions are coming up for you in this moment?" or "Let's turn our attention to our interaction. What are you experiencing as we talk about joining the group?" Regardless of the type of process intervention used, the potential group member's reaction to this shift from content to process can be an illuminating indication of how he or she will respond to the "here and now" of the group (provided that the group in question is an interpersonal process group). A preoccupied individual may become emotionally dysregulated at such a shift and may become concerned that he or she is not "doing something right" or that "you [the clinician] don't like me." A more dismissing-avoidant member is more likely to minimize or evade the question entirely. This individual might claim that he or she is "just answering the questions" or that "this isn't a big deal." A more fearful-avoidant member would probably become anxious, perhaps answering "it's never fun to talk about these feelings" and then most likely shut down when asked follow-up questions, saying he or she doesn't know the answers to the questions. Given the relationship between fearful-avoidance and relational trauma (Sroufe, Egeland, Carlson, & Collins, 2005), it is also possible that this individual would dissociate when under emotional duress within the group.

Screening for the Preoccupied Group Member

During a screening interview, an individual with a preoccupied attachment would most likely respond to questions regarding close relationships (e.g., family, romantic relationships) by becoming flooded with attachment memories during the interview and appearing anxious. This hyperactivation of the attachment system would be apparent in several ways. First, answers would most likely be lengthy, and the individual would remain focused on the primary attachment relationship even upon receiving prompts from the screening clinician to shift focus to other areas. Second, the person's answers would likely be affect-laden, tinged with strong and potentially ambivalent emotions. The individual would most likely become so lost in emotions that he or she would be poorly attuned to the interpersonal signals of the screening clinician (e.g., not noticing the clinician, missing nonverbal cues that it might be time to move on). Such an individual could become physiologically agitated during such moments, with matching symptoms, such as facial flushing, sweating, elevated heart rate, and muscle tension. The person might have some difficulty attending to questions or discussion about the group process, particularly if emotions have already been triggered by questions about attachment relationships. This is seen in the brief example that follows.

After spending 20 minutes in the screening interview exasperatingly sharing with the clinician how angry she was at her mother, Ava, a 28-year-old group referral, frequently answered "I don't know" to questions about her expectations for group treatment. As soon as she said "I don't know," she started complaining again about her mother. She didn't seem able to answer the question because she was flooded with attachment-based memories that did not allow her to process anything about the therapy group.

Preoccupied individuals may also overly attend to any perceived disruptions in the alliance with the screening clinician during the interview. It is not uncommon for the client to ask repeatedly about rapport, fit, and self-worth, for example. Common questions might include "Do you think I'm a good fit for the group?" "Do you think I can be helped?" and "What do you think?" This type of hypervigilant insecurity might also be seen in over-attending to the screening clinician's nonverbal cues.

Jamie, a 30-year-old woman, provides an example of this. During a screening interview, the leader frequently felt as if Jamie was scrutinizing his every movement or word. There were several junctures during the interview when she said, "What . . . were you about to say something?" Fitting the mold of high attachment anxiety, Jamie had an emotionally ambivalent relationship with her mother. She never felt that she was good enough for her boyfriends and engaged in chameleon-like behavior to adapt to each boyfriend. This "as-if" persona presented itself in the initial interview in that she seemed to be searching for what the leader was looking for so that she could meet his criteria.

Although much of this section has focused on individuals with pre-occupied attachment, many of the aforementioned criteria could be applied to group attachment as well. For example, one might recognize a more pre-occupied group attachment if the individual appeared emotionally fixated on past instances of group rejection or conflict. This might also be apparent in a strong desire to be a part of future groups, coupled with a fear of being rejected by them.

Screening for the More Dismissive-Avoidant Group Member

During a screening interview, someone with a dismissing-avoidant attachment would most likely present with a deactivated attachment system. The very context of the interview, much like group therapy, would increase the individual's avoidance and accompanying restrictive affect. Questions about close relationships (e.g., "How did your parents show affection?" "How long have you struggled with difficulties in relationships?") would certainly prompt avoidance, detachment, and defensiveness (e.g., intellectualization, isolation of affect, denial).

Although it is likely that more dismissing-avoidant individuals would answer personal questions in a superficial and positive manner, the process (e.g., content vs. process; Yalom & Leszcz, 2005) would tell the real story. As Main (1991) observed, on the Adult Attachment Interview (AAI; George, Kaplan, & Main, 1996), positive answers would be brief and vague. The interviewer's attempts to obtain additional information would be met with more vagueness and avoidance. It would be difficult for the interviewer to obtain meaningful information, and any stated responses would most likely be intellectualized and devoid of emotion. An example of this intellectualization would be individuals' use of second-person language to refer to themselves (e.g., "You work hard and stay focused on what you have to do; there's no time for you to get all emotional about things"). Nonverbal signals of restricted affect might include closed posture (e.g., crossed arms, leaning back as opposed to leaning forward) and avoidance of eye contact.

Individuals with a dismissing-avoidant group attachment would most likely display similar features at the group level. Just as it might be difficult to obtain meaningful information regarding close relationships with a more dismissing-avoidant dyadic attachment, individuals with a more dismissing-avoidant group attachment would most likely be brief and vague in their responses to questions about group relational goals. Any answers to these group goal questions would most likely be about the "doing" rather than "feeling" functions of the group. For example, an individual might say that her goal in the group is to "learn skills to be successful in group settings." If the interviewer followed-up with a request for clarification on what a successful outcome would be, the dismissing-avoidant individual might reply with vague statements such as "perform well," "do a good job," "accomplish a lot," or "I don't know . . . I'm not sure if I need to be in the group." These responses are possibly problematic because they indicate that the individual has trouble identifying more internal motivations and lacks insight into his or her interpersonal struggles. It is possible this individual would also resist efforts made by the group leader and other group members to expression emotions, be vulnerable, and/or take risks within the group. If pushed too hard, he or she might pull away from the group. Another indication of a dismissing-avoidant group attachment would be a reported history of detachment or isolation in group settings. Individuals might report being "loners" or not close to others in groups of which they are a part.

In general, individuals with more dismissing-avoidant attachment styles usually fall between the narcissistic and the obsessive style on a diagnostic continuum (Wallin, 2007). With individuals who are more narcissistic, there may be more idealizing (in an insincere way to further the person's narcissistic needs) and/or devaluing that occurs with the group leader and other group members. With more obsessive individuals, there may be more of an effort to exert control over the activities and discussion of the group (Wallin, 2007). Screening clinicians should be aware of this distinction and look for these discerning characteristics during the interview process.

Following is an example of defensive idealization. Al, a 37-year-old lawyer, idealized the psychiatrist who referred him to group. When asked about his reasons for wanting to join, he was quick to defer to the psychiatrist's judgment ("He said he thought it could help me improve my relationships with others"). When asked a follow-up question about whether group could be helpful to him, he agreed but did so in a casual, deflective manner: "I guess it couldn't hurt. Sure, why not."

Al's answers were short and to the point, clearly indicating that he did not want to share more about his need for the group. By answering in this manner, it appeared that he was also exerting some control over the flow of the interview, signaling that this was as far as he was willing to answer the question. These types of verbal and nonverbal behaviors are helpful in allowing a group leader to identify a potential group candidate with high attachment avoidance.

Screening the Fearful-Avoidant Group Member

For the purposes of an initial group screening, it is important to be aware of several interpersonal cues that a fearful-avoidant individual, a member with elevated anxiety and avoidance, is likely to display. First, a screening clinician may notice a pronounced sense of anxiety, which the individual may verbalize in some way. Second, compared with those with other attachment styles, they are more likely to seek physical distance (e.g., sitting farther away), more likely to take longer to respond to questions, and less able to generate sustained conversation (Collins & Feeney, 2004). Bartholomew and Horowitz (1991) found higher levels of coldness and passivity for these individuals than those with other attachment styles. According to Mikulincer and Shaver (2007b), of all the attachment types, fearful-avoidant individuals tend to have the least empathy for others. They are also most likely to have a fearful-avoidant attachment style and can fall within the healthier to borderline spectrum (Mikulincer & Shaver, 2007b).

The group therapist can assess for reflective functioning and empathy skills by asking follow-up questions that serve to explore the fearful-avoidant individual's mental world. For example, if the person answered the question "How did you know that you were cared for by your mother?" with "I don't know . . . it was confusing," the therapist might begin follow-up with "Can you think of a time she behaved in a caring way toward you?" This question would at least initially work with any defensiveness or inability to consider mental states beneath behaviors. After the person provided an example (e.g., "Sometimes she gave me and my sister candy when we were good"), the therapist might then ask, "How did you know she thought you were good?" "What do you imagine she was feeling toward you in that moment?" or "What were you feeling toward her in that moment?" to probe for awareness of underlying mental states. Alternatively, if during the screening the person often focused on a parent or romantic interest's frequent anger, the clinician might ask, "Why do you think he was angry so often?" to assess attention to underlying mental states or "Have you noticed any changes in this person's anger toward you across time?" to assess understanding of developmental components to mental states. The purpose of such follow-up questions is to assess the individual's capacity or willingness to engage in a reflective process.

Screening for the Secure Group Member

In a screening interview, individuals with a secure attachment, one with low anxiety and avoidance, present with an open, engaged, and nondefensive manner. They are comfortable and familiar with intimate relationships and value having them, in contrast to a person with high attachment avoidance. They also have appropriately high self-esteem and perceive themselves as worthy of care and love from others, in contrast to a person with high attachment anxiety (Bartholomew & Horowitz, 1991; Collins & Feeney, 2004).

Securely attached individuals demonstrate high reflective functioning and strong mentalizing capacities, as seen through their ability both to have an experience in the moment and reflect on that experience as it is happening. Additionally, they can internally reflect on their experience from their own vantage point as well as accurately imagine how another person might feel, think, and respond to them (Fonagy, Gergely, Jurist, & Target, 2002; Mikulincer & Florian, 2001; Wallin, 2007). Naturally, these are valuable skills for a group member to have, a subject covered in the section on group composition later in this chapter. The following case example from a screening session provides a clear illustration of the positive characteristics associated with secure attachment.

In the midst of describing his childhood to the group leader during the screening session, Marlon noted that when he was 13, his parents divorced. The therapist asked, "Tell me about being a 13-year-old boy and finding out your parents were getting divorced. What was that like for you?" As he began to describe the impact of the divorce on his family, Marlon looked at the therapist and slowly started to cry. "I was close with both of my parents, and I missed the time we all spent together as a family," he said. "My sister and I lived with my mother, and my father moved to an apartment nearby. He had custody of us on the weekend. It was really hard not being able to see my dad as much . . . not being able to throw the ball with him in the yard after school. Man, after all these years, I never stop being surprised at how much it still hurts . . . realizing that there were limits to how often I could choose to be around my parents. Learning at such an impressionable age that families don't always stay together. That parents don't always keep loving each other. That was a tough lesson for me to learn at the time, right when I was starting to take an interest in girls and dream of falling in love myself."

"What do you notice about your feelings as they come up in here right now?" the therapist asked.

Marlon replied, "Well, I've learned to trust them [his feelings] . . . it's part of being real with myself and others. Sometimes, I'm surprised when they come up in such a strong way, like right now. But even though it happened a long time ago, and I'm happily married with kids now, I guess the loss is still there. I feel it has helped me be a more present and available husband and father. But even though the meaning and magnitude of my parents' divorce has changed to me as I've grown up, the loss will always remain with me on some level."

In this example, there is a natural and spontaneous quality to Marlon's affect. It flows in connection to and appropriately with the biographical material he is discussing with the group leader. He is able to both fully experience his affect and then reflect on it in the presence of another person. Despite the lingering feelings of vulnerability from this childhood loss, he trusts in the therapeutic process enough to share these feelings with the group leader. He is responsive to the group leader's process questions, using first-person language, and links the past relational event (his parents' divorce) to his current internal and relationship experiences. In addition, there is a coherent quality to his narrative, and despite the intensity of the affect, he is able to pull together and summarize his reflections about his experience in the face of that affect.

One noticeable aspect of the case example is Marlon's ease with self-disclosure. Secure group members tend to show the highest rates of self-disclosure in group therapy compared with other attachment types (Shechtman & Dvir, 2006), and they also do so in the initial meeting (Shechtman & Rybko, 2004). This is impressive given that an initial group meeting tends to be stressful for most people (Shechtman & Rybko, 2004). Individuals with secure attachment are both more comfortable with self-disclosure and more open to receiving it from others (Collins & Feeney, 2004) because they have experienced the sensitive attunement responsiveness from their parents as young children (Wallin, 2007). Thus, they have experienced open and flexible states of mind from attachment caregivers that they have internalized and readily display in their interactions with others.

Although more secure members will most likely not be in group to work on attachment issues, they can still benefit greatly from the group experience. More secure members may join group to work through relationship losses (e.g., breakups, divorces), adjustment issues (e.g., new career, geographic move), and mood disorders (e.g., anxiety, depression), among other issues. The group as a social microcosm offers a rich here-and-now environment to process these issues and grow (Bernard et al., 2008; Yalom & Leszcz, 2005). As we explain in the section on group composition, the presence of enough members with secure attachment increases the likelihood of a successful group outcome, which therapeutically benefits all of the group members, including the secure members.

Assessment: A Valuable Complement to Interviews in Measuring Attachment

Using assessment as part of a comprehensive screening process can help group leaders identify attachment information that was not readily observable during the interview, or elaborate on attachment dynamics that emerged in the interview. If the group leader is interested in a quick assessment of dyadic and group attachment, several relatively brief measures are reviewed in Chapter 2 of this volume.

In addition, the Group Therapy Questionnaire (GTQ; MacNair-Semands & Corazzini, 1998, see the Appendix for a copy of this measure) is a measure that is frequently used to screen and prepare group members. It is based on existing principles of group therapy and allows the clinician to assess the client's personal history and group motivation, goals, and roles in a format that is easily accessible. The authors of the GTQ suggested using this assessment instrument to assess the readiness of an individual to join a therapy group. Taking approximately 35 to 45 minutes to complete, this measure can easily be used as part of the overall screening or preparation process. Although not directly assessing attachment style, the GTQ parallels adult attachment assessment with its questions on relationship intimacy and conflict. Marmarosh (2009) found the measure to be highly relevant to attachment assessment in group therapy screenings and compared the GTQ with the AAI (George et al., 1996). The extended case example of Carla later in this chapter features an application of the GTQ in the group screening.

GROUP PLACEMENT: USING ATTACHMENT AS A GUIDE

Thus far, this chapter has focused on screening and identifying potential group candidates on the basis of attachment dimensions and associated characteristics (e.g., mentalization, coherence of narrative, level of affect). We now move into using the information gleaned from the screening for the purpose of placing candidates into appropriate groups. Here it becomes important to consider how these attachment dimensions and characteristics will affect a potential group member's ability to use the group for therapeutic growth.

Placing the More Preoccupied Group Member

When deciding the appropriate group placement for a preoccupied individual, the leader needs to first identify the level and nature of the attachment anxiety. Individuals who display moderate, or even moderate to high, levels of attachment anxiety during the interview but are still able to at least partially attend to interpersonal cues may be able to function well in a less structured group, such as an interpersonal or psychodynamic group. As a matter of fact, common features of preoccupied people (e.g., personal devaluing, idealizing others) may be a fit for such groups. Personal devaluing can quickly surface in an interpersonal group, and the group offers multiple opportunities to receive interpersonal feedback. The interpersonal group format also invites members to share wishes for intimacy and explore how in-group behaviors inhibit these goals for closeness (Yalom & Leszcz, 2005).

When considering the nature of the attachment anxiety, Fonagy's concept of mentalization is an important factor to consider. Information about the reflective capacities of potential group members can help group therapists determine what type of group is best for individuals with high attachment anxiety. Wallin (2007) described the preoccupied diagnostic spectrum as ranging from higher functioning individuals to those in the borderline range. One can imagine that higher functioning individuals, although flooded by their attachment anxiety (e.g., perseverating on developmental attachment ruptures, obsessing over peer acceptance), might also have the reflective capacity to be aware of how they come across to others, be able to tolerate different opinions, and know that their reactions are a product of their own mental states versus being reality. These individuals may be able to tolerate the lack of structure and emotional intimacy that are descriptive of different types of groups, such as interpersonal or psychodynamic groups.

However, a dialectical behavior therapy (DBT) group may be more appropriate for individuals with high attachment anxiety who also display poor mentalizing abilities (Wallin, 2007). This combination of high attachment anxiety and low reflective functioning brings to mind the clinical presentation of borderline personality disorder (BPD). DBT groups were originally designed primarily for individuals with BPD or people with borderline features. These structured groups combine standard cognitive behavioral therapy (CBT) techniques, such as emotion regulation, with meditative techniques, such as mindfulness awareness, distress tolerance, and acceptance. The groups meet weekly for approximately 2 hours and feature psychoeducational skill-building tasks that are divided into four modules: emotion regulation skills, core mindfulness skills, distress tolerance skills, and interpersonal effectiveness skills. DBT groups seek to help members identify and label emotions, including positive emotions; develop nonjudgmental attention to the present moment through sensory awareness; increase tolerance of distressing emotions through acceptance, focusing, distraction, and self-soothing; and assert needs constructively and effectively in interpersonal interactions (Linehan, 1993; Linehan, Tutek, Heard, & Armstrong, 1994). One can imagine that these groups foster secure attachments to the group because they use mindfulness principles that facilitate mentalization. Yet at the same time, unlike more unstructured groups, these groups teach specific strategies for coping with the emotional lability that frequently accompanies BPD and preoccupied attachment.

Another structured group approach that may be a good fit for group candidates with more preoccupied attachment and borderline features is mentalization-based group therapy. Mentalization-based treatment (MBT), of which MBT group therapy is a component, is a specific attachment-based approach that focuses on enhancing mentalization and was originally developed with BPD in mind (Bateman & Fonagy, 2003; Fonagy & Bateman, 2006; Karterud & Bateman, 2011). The major curative mechanism of MBT group therapy is the process of working through problems in mentalization in the here and now. The group serves to identify, explore, and understand mentalization problems and then restore reflective thinking and feeling mental functions (Karterud & Bateman, 2011). MBT groups feature active leader intervention at any juncture in which mentalization processes are involved. This stands in contrast to unstructured process groups, which despite also emphasizing here-and-now process, might overestimate group members' ability to manage group process on their own and underestimate the mentalization deficits among the group members. An MBT group leader, by contrast, would pause the group process any time an opportunity to explore mentalization in the here and now was missed. The leader would bring the group back to the identified inter-personal interaction and carefully explore the intersubjective experiences of the group members (Karterud & Bateman, 2011). MBT groups also encourage affective mirroring and marking functions among their group members, critical elements in developing a secure attachment (Bateman & Fonagy, 2003; Gergely & Unoka, 2008; Wallin, 2007).

A final placement option for individuals on the preoccupied-borderline spectrum is individual therapy before or in conjunction with group treatment. As discussed earlier in the chapter, previous individual therapy experience is associated with greater continuation in group (MacNair & Corazzini, 1994; MacNair-Semands, 2002). Having a secure base such as an individual therapist can potentially help set the stage for subsequent group participation and help more preoccupied individuals tolerate the group therapy process.

Placing the Dismissing-Avoidant Group Member

Group leaders should carefully consider placement of potential group members who appear to display dismissing-avoidant attachments during the group intake. There is some evidence that high levels of attachment avoidance may be difficult to change in group, regardless of treatment type. For example, Tasca, Balfour, Ritchie, and Bissada (2007a) found no relationship between change in attachment avoidance and symptom improvement for either CBT or interpersonal-psychodynamic group therapy. For members with high attachment avoidance, groups that do not directly address or stimulate attachment, such as structured CBT groups, may be helpful in facilitating symptom improvement, assuming that the member does not drop out. If the group is more structured, the avoidant responses may be triggered less, increasing the chance of the individual becoming a consistent group member (Tasca et al., 2007a). In contrast, less structured groups, such as psychodynamic or interpersonal groups, may also be appropriate for a dismissing-avoidant type with the right pregroup preparation (see the subsequent discussion on group preparation). In addition, more mature groups (e.g., existing open-ended groups) may be better equipped to incorporate new dismissing members because advanced group members are less likely to be reactive to the avoidant behavior.

Placing the More Fearful-Avoidant Group Member

If a person with a more fearful-avoidant style has consistent difficulties mentalizing, then it may be more appropriate to refer the individual to a DBT or MBT group rather than an interpersonal process group. The efficacy of DBT groups for individuals who struggle to tolerate affect (i.e., those with borderline personality disorder; Linehan, 1993; Linehan et al., 1994) makes them a good fit for these types of groups that integrate mindfulness and cognitive strategies to cope with emotions. When seen from an attachment perspective, the emphasis of these groups on distress tolerance and emotion regulation is helpful in addressing the oscillation between hyperactivating and deactivating strategies. Furthermore, the structured group frame and skill-building focus could help temper the anxiety that a group modality would elicit.

In the extended case example that follows, we illustrate the screening and placement process for a person with a more fearful-avoidant attachment. The clinical example was selected because it addresses the group leader's struggle to determine the best type of group treatment for a specific individual who was referred to an interpersonal process group. The example highlights how the leader screened the individual and how the screening process led to an appropriate referral to group, but not to the referred interpersonal group.

Case Example: When Interpersonal Group Psychotherapy Is Not Recommended

Carla was a 30-year-old Latin-American woman referred to group by her former psychiatrist. The leader briefly spoke with Carla by phone to set up the initial screening appointment. When the leader asked her about her reasons for having an interest in the group, Carla said that her psychiatrist thought it was a good idea. She did not reveal any personal reasons for seeking group therapy at the time.

Upon meeting Carla in person, the leader noted that she appeared tense. Carla avoided making eye contact, and her body had a rigid, guarded appearance. The group leader mentally noted her anxiety and opened the screening session with an open-ended question: "What makes you interested in group therapy?" Although Carla stated that she didn't know what her main interest in group therapy was, she immediately started to describe her childhood in depth. Her parents were from Venezuela and immigrated to the United States, where she was born. She said she was an only child and had "abandonment issues" that stemmed from her relationship with her deceased father, who had passed away when she was 20 years old. She added that her father worked long hours throughout her childhood, and she felt he always chose his work over her. "He left me all the time," she said. "He was never there for me while he was alive." She described the culminating abandonment when her father left midway through her high school graduation for work. In addition to her father's abandonment, she also described his controlling nature. Carla remembered "unrelenting pressure" from him to pursue his academic choices (e.g., her college major). The group therapist noted that Carla quickly became immersed in her painful past when the leader had only asked one question about the reason she sought group treatment. She easily became flooded with emotions and was unable to stay focused.

The leader wanted to assess other attachments and asked about her relationships with her mother and friends. In contrast to her father, Carla described her relationship with her mother as "really close, a good relationship." When the leader asked for more details regarding the closeness, Carla hesitated and revealed feeling frustrated with her mother's dependency on her but then quickly added that she loved her mother very much. It became clear that Carla was ambivalent about her mother and anxious about revealing complex feelings about her. She would describe the relationship as close but then would share resentment she felt for feeling controlled by her. It was clear that Carla was uncomfortable setting boundaries with her mother and felt guilty for saying anything negative about her. Her extended family encouraged Carla to be "loyal" to her family by living nearby. This was a common dynamic in the families of others in her Venezuelan American community. By expressing a desire to live farther away from her family, Carla felt like she was abandoning her family.

The leader intuited that Carla was struggling with both her Latina cultural upbringing and her attachment to her caregivers and family. He wanted to explore how Carla perceived the major separations in her life, such as leaving home and going to college, and asked, "Did you move away from home to go to college, and if so, how did it feel to move away from home?"

"Home was really confusing for me," Carla said. She added that her college years, spent out of state, were the highlight for her because "I had a life there." She described having friends, her own apartment, and academic interests at school. The leader asked, "What was it about these experiences that made this time stand out to you?" Carla responded, "I guess maybe feeling like I was starting to find myself, I'm not sure. I just know that when I returned home, that was all lost." This answer was significant to the leader because it signaled that Carla appeared to lose herself when she returned home. Something about being with her mother at home left her feeling that there was no space for her to exist as a separate person. What was even more curious was Carla's decision to move back home. When asked about moving back home, Carla said she had no choice. This appeared to be expected in her Latina culture to care for her mother and also possibly influenced by her attachment to her mother.

Carla said that she had no current close friends and kept in sporadic contact with friends from college who lived far away from her. When the group leader asked her about her lack of current friends, she said that it was too hard to make good friends living at home. She also said that she felt ashamed of her career and reluctant to date because "there's nothing really attractive about my life . . . and besides I've never really trusted men."

Carla had seen multiple psychotherapists and psychiatrists over the past 15 years, with presenting concerns of depression and anxiety. She estimated that during that time, she had been prescribed as many as 20 psychotropic medications but that none of the diagnoses or medications had made a positive impact. Carla said that she found talking about her problems to be unhelpful, and she felt that the providers never really cared about her. The leader probed for specific examples of Carla's experiences with her past mental health care providers. Carla revealed that she felt that her psychiatrists frequently prescribed medications to her against her will, and she believed that they did not listen to her needs. Again, those in the role of a caregiver were mistrusted and disappointing. He asked Carla if she told the therapists when she was disappointed, and Carla said no, she did not. Carla said she just ended the treatment and never returned. He then asked about any positive experiences, and Carla could cite only one, which was with a psychiatrist who was flexible with regard to her medications. She said that his willingness to allow her more control in the treatment decision making helped her trust him. Notable to the group leader was the fact that this was the only positive experience she had shared about all of her therapy. When he asked Carla why she was ready for group now and why she felt that group would be different from her previous disappointing individual therapy experiences, Carla did not have an answer. She smiled and said that her former psychiatrist recommended group probably because "he didn't know what to do with me."

On the basis of these responses, the leader wanted to test how well Carla would respond to feedback she might receive in the group. He said, "Carla, I want to give you some feedback, similar to how you might get feedback in the group therapy. Would you be open to that? Would that be OK for you?" Carla nodded but looked anxious. The leader said, "Carla, I have appreciated your openness today. You seem to really want to join the group and try very hard to put on a happy face for me. On the other hand, I am also aware that you have been very disappointed by therapists in the past. This makes me wonder if I will not do or say something that may eventually disappoint you as well. I worry that you would decide to leave and not come back, and the group would not know why." Carla looked surprised and then rolled her eyes.

Her cheeriness disappeared, and the leader noticed that Carla was struggling with the feedback. When the leader asked her about the feelings that were coming up for her, she answered, "Frustrated, I don't know." Carla shut down. The leader decided to step back from Carla's immediate response of anger and tried to provide more information that might help her understand the goals of an interpersonal process group. He explained that the group is like a microcosm of outside relationships, and people get to learn how they come across to others and what things may be getting in the way of them feeling close to others. He spent some time discussing how an interpersonal process group operates and what it is like to be a group member in this type of group. Having described how process operates, the leader then asked Carla, "I noticed you rolled your eyes when I gave you feedback about you dropping out of group. What is it like to hear me wonder about this?" Carla said she wasn't sure. The leader said he noticed that Carla became silent. She pulled away and looked annoyed. He noted that in her avoidance of examining her role in their process, she seemed to be preemptively shutting down as a protective measure. The interview clearly indicated that Carla would struggle in the interpersonal process group, but before making a definitive decision, the leader wanted to include additional assessment tools.

The leader had asked Carla to complete the GTQ at the start of the interview, and he reviewed Carla's responses, which were consistent with her behaviors during the interview. Her responses were detailed for certain questions, incomplete or extremely vague for others. For example, on the family questions, Carla answered items asking how her parents showed caring to her ("My mother showed that she cared by telling me she loved me and never letting me leave her side"; "My dad was an alcoholic and didn't show me that he cared; work was more important than I was") or anger to her ("My dad gave me the silent treatment; my mom yelled all the time"). Although she did not respond to the question about her own role in her family, she described "having difficulty trusting others" and "anxiety about everything."

More important, Carla answered "I don't know" in response to the questions about the role that she played in the relationships that contributed to the difficulties she experienced. These responses indicated a withdrawal when it came to reflecting on herself and a lack of ability to tolerate threatening feedback. When Carla was asked to draw her family, she drew a small circle around herself situated within a larger circle of her mother. Far away, in the opposite corner were the words "everyone else" with no circles around them. This supported her description of herself as insignificant and engulfed by her mother, whom she often idealized and hated. On the interpersonal problems checklist, she indicated, "feeling too dependent on others," "losing my temper frequently," "avoiding social activities," "feeling isolated and lonely," "loneliness," "difficulty socializing," "difficulty trusting others," "feeling abandoned," "lacking of personal identity," "unable to make decisions without reassurance from others," and "feeling devastated when close relationships end."

For the group-specific questions, she put a question mark next to the item "I look forward to beginning group therapy." Interestingly, although she did not list any specific goals for group, she did list two things that might prevent her from reaching her goals, "myself" and "everyone else." In essence, she was aware that she could prevent herself from getting what she wanted in the group, and if she did not, everyone else in the group would. This response suggested a "me versus them" perspective.

The interview and GTQ responses offer moderate support for the conclusion that Carla has an insecure attachment style, most likely a fearful-avoidant attachment style given her high anxiety and avoidance. She displays a wish for closeness with others, experiences high anxiety in relationships, is quick to distance herself from others to prevent rejection, and engages in avoidant behaviors when threatened. We see shifts between hyperactivating strategies and deactivating strategies when Carla senses a potential threat. These dimensions of high anxiety and high avoidance are clearly supported by the interpersonal items checked on the GTQ. Furthermore, Carla's relationship patterns present a mix of dependency seeking and fear of abandonment. On the one hand, she feels angry and fearful about being rejected, and she expects others to abandon her, so she pushes people away. On the other hand, she is passive and dependent in her relationships, encouraging others to control her and fearful of being alone.

Although the group leader would often welcome members into the group with avoidant attachment styles (both fearful-avoidant and dismissing-avoidant), people with fearful-avoidant styles often struggle the most in interpersonal process therapy groups. The more fearful-avoidant individual tends to have more poorly regulated affect that is presented in combination with greater detachment. This combination can lead the fearful-avoidant individual to be scapegoated, and it can interfere with group cohesion. At this point in the intake, the leader was concerned that Carla's defensiveness and lack of self-reflection (e.g., quick responses of "I don't know" with little hesitation), high expressed negative emotion, and strong anxious fear of abandonment would jeopardize her ability to form an alliance within an interpersonal process group with more sophisticated members. For these reasons, he decided that Carla would not be an appropriate match for an interpersonal process group at that time.

When proposing alternate treatment options, the leader used the framework proposed by MacNair and Corazzini (1994), which is to offer individual therapy or group skills training (e.g., DBT) before admitting a patient to an interpersonal process group. Wanting to be sensitive to her presented issues of abandonment and control, the leader decided to present both options and give her a choice. The leader was aware that Carla would likely feel rejected and that he would need to process her reaction to the group intake. He explained to Carla that some people find individual treatment to be helpful in developing a sense of direction and momentum before joining a process group. He added that this might be useful in helping her develop her goals before starting group treatment. Alternatively, he argued that a DBT group was also a referral option. He explained to her that DBT groups are structured with built-in skills modules focusing on some of the areas that were relevant to her, such as her struggle to regulate her emotions, her anger and frustration in relationships, and her desire to receive direct feedback.

Having been presented with these treatment options, Carla seemed to become immediately agitated and stated that she had tried individual therapy and hadn't found it helpful at all. With anger in her voice, she stated, "What I need is for things to change." It was clear that the automatic cycle of rage and defensiveness was triggered the minute the leader suggested other treatment options. Years of feeling rejected and abandoned rose to the surface. The leader recognized this, listened to Carla, and empathized with her anger and frustration. After processing her feelings, Carla's anger lessened, and she rejected the individual therapy option and agreed to follow up on the referral to the DBT group.

Although the interview follow-up did not lead to accepting Carla into the process group, it is a useful teaching example for a number of reasons. First, we see that through the interview technique and assessment process, the leader was able to form a working hypothesis regarding the potential group member's attachment style and interpersonal functioning. Second, when considering her attachment style in conjunction with the patient's relationship history, defense mechanisms, and capacity to regulate affect, it was possible to make an estimation of group fit. Finally, in presenting several alternative treatment options and providing the patient with a choice, the leader was able to take the patient's functioning into consideration and address potential rejection issues that might arise from not being offered a place in the group.

ATTACHMENT AND GROUP COMPOSITION

In the preceding sections, we examined the role that attachment plays in the screening and placement of group members. Although patients may be suitable for group therapy, decisions about what type of group to place them in are often influenced by the existing or intended composition of the group. *Composition* is a term that refers to the combination of members, and associated individual characteristics, within a group (Piper, Ogrodniczuk, Joyce, Weideman, & Rosie, 2007; Piper, Ogrodniczuk, Joyce, & Weideman, 2011). Composing a group requires a balance of intrapersonal (e.g., individual qualities) and intragroup (e.g., type of group) considerations. Although there are exceptions, which are discussed in this section, a group leader's goal in composing a group is usually to assemble a mix of group members who will both support and challenge one another in the establishment and maintenance of a cohesive group environment (Bernard et al., 2008). Interestingly, there is no specific evidence that composition is the critical element in meeting this goal. The selection and preparation of group members may be more important in facilitating cohesion (Bernard et al., 2008). In addition, although many therapists believe in the importance of composition in determining outcome, there is a lack of empirical research examining this subject (Piper et al., 2007).

The most common approach to composing a group is the homogeneity–heterogeneity approach, which refers to assembling groups based on the similarity or dissimilarity of the group members (Kivlighan & Coleman, 1999; Lieberman, Wizlenberg, Golant, & DiMinno, 2005; Piper et al., 2011). Individuals in homogeneously composed groups all share a primary characteristic (e.g., an anxiety group in which all the members identify as being highly anxious persons). Heterogeneous groups are composed of individuals who differ with regard to a primary characteristic (Piper et al., 2007). Many therapists seem to prefer a homogeneous group (Lieberman et al., 2005; Perrone & Sedlacek, 2000). This preference may be based on cohesion theory (Yalom & Leszcz, 2005), which states that members who are more alike tend to find more in common, feel more comfortable, and establish a supportive atmosphere more quickly (Piper et al., 2011). On the other hand, there is little empirical research supporting the clinical preference for homogeneous groups (Piper et al., 2011). Furthermore, Piper and colleagues (2007), examining the characteristic of quality of object relations (QOR) in short-term therapy groups for complicated grief, found no difference between group type (homogeneous vs. heterogeneous) and outcome.

This study by Piper et al. (2007) examining the relationship between group composition and outcome is relevant to attachment theory for a number of reasons. First, there is a theoretical similarity between the constructs of attachment and QOR. Additionally, security of attachment and QOR have been found to be strongly related (Goldman & Anderson, 2007). QOR is defined as a person's tendency to establish certain types of relationships, on a continuum from primitive to mature (Piper et al., 2007). Persons with low QOR tend to engage in primitive relationships, and those with high QOR tend to engage in more mature relationships. Research has found that QOR is an important group composition variable because it predicts whether the group member will be able to remain in and benefit from the group over time (de Carufel & Piper, 1988; Piper et al., 1991). The more a person's relationships are mature and reciprocally rewarding, the more that person is able to tolerate the challenging aspects of interpretive therapy. There are obvious parallels here with dimensions of attachment security in that similar relationship patterns tend to exist across the two constructs.

Second, although Piper et al. (2007) did not find support for group composition type, they did find that placing a "critical mass" (p. 123) of high QOR group members in a group reinforces the mature functions of the group. In their study, they found that the higher the percentage of QOR for the patients in the group, the greater the improvement of members' anxiety symptoms. As long as this critical mass exists for the group, low QOR patients who are placed into a group of mostly high QOR group members will experience symptom improvements. The presence of too many members with low QOR will harm the cohesion of the group. A homogeneous group of low QOR group members will reinforce primitive interpersonal functions, such as low altruism, low self-disclosure, and lack of trust. In this type of negative group environment, a group member with high QOR would not improve because of the lack of group cohesion.

Other literature appears to support these findings. Marziali and Blum (1994) found high dropout rates for an interpersonal group that was homogeneous with regard to all of the members being diagnosed with BPD. They explained this finding by stating that many of the patients could not tolerate the regressed nature of the group and the lack of cohesion. Bernard and colleagues (2008) recommended heterogeneous groups with regard to the dimensions of affiliation and agency and observed that if a group was composed entirely of avoidant (low affiliation) or submissive group members (low agency), there would not be enough interpersonal tension in the group and, as a result, not enough opportunities for interpersonal learning among members.

In conclusion, when composing a group, the presence of group members with more developed relational capacities, more secure group members, or those with less attachment anxiety and avoidance benefits the rest of the group members, including those with less developed relational capacities (Bernard et al., 2008; Piper et al., 2007, 2011). Groups with members who are ready to engage, willing to take interpersonal risks, and able to display psychological mindedness in the here and now of group are more likely to have improved cohesion and growth (Bernard et al., 2008; Yalom & Leszcz, 2005). A group composed of enough more securely attached members helps ensure that the overall group can contain and tolerate the less mature relational dynamics of the members with more insecure attachment. Markin and Marmarosh (2010) recommended that group leaders fill groups with members who have secure functioning in either dyadic or group attachment. Although having at least some group members who are secure in both dyadic and group attachment is preferable, they acknowledged the difficulty in receiving referrals for these types of patients. For the reasons presented in this section, they recommended against filling a group with members who have both insecure dyadic and insecure group attachments.

ATTACHMENT AND GROUP PREPARATION

Pregroup preparation, usually in the form of orientation sessions, ranges in length from one or two individual sessions to multiple individual sessions with the group leaders. Often, these sessions occur after members are accepted into the group while the group therapist assembles the remaining members and before the group begins (Yalom & Leszcz, 2005). Multiple studies point to the importance of providing potential group members with an accurate depiction of what they will experience in the group during the preparation process (Bernard et al., 2008; MacNair & Corazzini, 1994; MacNair-Semands, 2002; Yalom & Leszcz, 2005). The group leader does this by helping each new group member anticipate what the group experience will be like, discussing the group rules and policies, and obtaining informed consent. Members' attachment styles can influence all of these preparation components in ways that are reviewed in the following sections.

Orientation Sessions

A broad consensus has been reached, through empirical study and clinical practice, that pregroup preparation benefits both the individual group members and the group as a whole (Bernard et al., 2008; Burlingame et al., 2001; Yalom & Leszcz, 2005). These orientation sessions are usually individual sessions designed to prepare the group member for group therapy and are different from any preparation that occurs in the group setting after the group has already begun (e.g., in the first few group sessions), a topic covered in one of the in-depth case studies in Chapter 12.

Yalom and Leszcz (2005) stated that it is important to meet at least periodically with the initial group candidates so as not to lose them during the time it takes to recruit the other group members. Orientation sessions featuring experiential and emotional preparation appear to be particularly beneficial because they provide more practice for what the group will elicit (Bernard et al., 2008; Burlingame et al., 2001; Yalom & Leszcz, 2005). Pregroup orientation sessions are also associated with increased group attendance rates (Bernard et al., 2008; MacNair-Semands, 2002; Piper & Perrault, 1989; Yalom & Leszcz, 2005).

There is additional consensus regarding the key objectives of the group preparation process. These objectives include forming a therapeutic alliance with the group member, assuaging any initial anxiety or misconceptions about beginning the group, offering clear information and education about group to facilitate appropriate informed consent, and developing consensus between the group leader and various group members about the group objectives (Bernard et al., 2008; Piper & Ogrodniczuk, 2004; Yalom & Leszcz, 2005).

Developing a healthy therapeutic alliance between the leaders and members is a key component of a successful group. Not only have reviews found a strong relationship between alliance and overall group outcome (Burlingame et al., 2006; Joyce, Piper, & Ogrodniczuk, 2007), they have also shown that pregroup preparation is critical in the initial development of alliance and the subsequent development of group cohesion (Burlingame et al., 2006; Joyce, Piper, & Ogrodniczuk, 2007). Yalom and Leszcz (2005) observed that the first component of creating strong alliances among group members is to have a shared mutual affiliation with the group leader. Burlingame and colleagues (2001) recommended the leader use the emerging alliance from the preparation session(s) to facilitate group cohesion when group therapy starts. When seen from an attachment perspective, the pregroup orientation sessions are important because attachment styles are likely to become activated during this preparation, helping familiarize the leader with the ways the new member negotiates interpersonal relationships. For example, a more preoccupied new member will likely engage in hyperactivating strategies during the preparation, and the leader can help the member understand how he or she is coping with the emotions that are triggered. This helps make it safer to explore what is becoming activated with the leader during the preparation phase, setting in motion the development of a secure base with the leader.

Although joining a group tends to be anxiety-inducing for most group members (Bernard et al., 2008; Yalom & Leszcz, 2005), this anxiety tends to manifest uniquely and differentially for individuals with insecure attachment styles. For example, those with higher levels of attachment anxiety tend to perceive positive increases in group therapy alliance over time, but they are also more likely to need increased group engagement across the sessions and through the process of rupture and repair (Kanninen, Salo, & Punamaki, 2000; Rom & Mikulincer, 2003; Tasca, Balfour, Ritchie, & Bissada, 2006; Tasca et al., 2007a, 2007b). In other words, it is important for these preoccupied individuals to feel that everyone in the group is getting closer over time. Fortunately, because unstructured groups (e.g., psychodynamic or interpersonal) provide numerous opportunities for here-and-now processing of the ruptures in the group, it is likely that these group members will ultimately perceive increasing group engagement deriving from this process (Tasca, Balfour, Ritchie, & Bissada, 2006; Tasca et al., 2007a, 2007b). Additionally, group conflict may be especially threatening to more preoccupied individuals who fear rejection. For this reason, it is important during the group preparation process to educate more preoccupied individuals about the types of interpersonal interactions that generally occur during the first few group sessions and the fluctuations in group engagement that are expected (Tasca, Balfour, et al., 2006; Tasca et al., 2007a, 2007b). Group leaders can also encourage and help more preoccupied individuals develop a self-reflective perspective to prepare them for the rupture and repair process of group therapy (Tasca et al., 2007a; Wallin, 2007).

On the other hand, individuals with greater attachment avoidance are more likely to disavow any anxiety that the new group may stimulate for them. More dismissing-avoidant individuals come to group perceiving other group members as less connected to one another and less dedicated to the therapy (Illing, Tasca, Balfour, & Bissada, 2011). In addition, their inclination to minimize group engagement in the initial stages of group therapy can also hamper the functioning of the group (Illing et al., 2011; Joyce, Piper, & Ogrodniczuk, 2007; Tasca et al., 2004). It is no surprise that those with greater attachment avoidance tend to experience a declining therapeutic alliance across the group sessions (Tasca et al., 2007a, 2007b) and are more likely to drop out of therapy (Tasca, Taylor, Bissada, Ritchie, & Balfour, 2004; Tasca et al., 2007a). Group therapists can best prepare more dismissing-avoidant group members for group therapy by spending additional time explaining the group norms and helping these members imagine how they would respond in interpersonally challenging group situations (Illing et al., 2011; Tasca et al., 2007a, 2007b; Yalom & Leszcz, 2005). Part of this work is increasing more dismissing-avoidant group members' motivation for group therapy (Tasca et al., 2007b). As a result, it is important to emphasize to these group members how the interpersonal exploration that occurs during group therapy interactions can be valuable to them (Tasca et al., 2007b), as well as address any concerns regarding emotional expression that they might have (Illing et al., 2011; Yalom & Leszcz, 2005).

Researchers have examined the misconceptions that many group members have about group therapy and how this hinders their ability to join the group (Nichols & Jenkinson, 2006). Nichols and Jenkinson (2006) argued that fears or negative myths group members had before starting the group led to them feeling overwhelmed or traumatized during initial sessions. They argued that addressing these negative myths before the group starts is critical. Marmarosh, Whipple, et al. (2009) studied the myths related to group therapy for those with more attachment anxiety and avoidance and found that more insecurely attached individuals revealed more fears about group therapy and endorsed more negative myths about group. These authors also recommended helping more insecurely attached group members address their anxieties and fears of group therapy during the orientation to group before the actual treatment begins.

Informed Consent and Group Rules: The Role of Mentalization

In general, informed consent is paramount in group therapy (Bernard et al., 2008). It can be obtained and given verbally or in written form. With regard to group therapy, it is important to do both, and usually this process occurs in the pregroup orientation session (or screening session, if it also serves as the orientation). A written informed consent form is usually some type of group contract that outlines how group operates and the expectations of each group member. This type of form also provides a useful opportunity to verbally anticipate and discuss the upcoming group experience in the orientation session, serving to prepare the new group member for group (Bernard et al., 2008). Yalom and Leszcz (2005) suggested that systematically preparing the patient for group is a "process of demystification" (p. 303) in which the patient is provided with a realistic understanding of group and any misconceptions are clarified.

According to Yalom and Leszcz (2005), preparation involves providing patients with an understanding of interpersonal therapy, describing how the therapy group will help with their interpersonal problems, offering suggestions about how to best utilize and participate in group, anticipating potential disappointments that might arise with group, developing an attendance contract and discussing the duration of the group, improving expectations about the potential success of group, and creating ground rules regarding subgrouping and confidentiality. They referred to this as a "cognitive approach" (p. 303) to group therapy preparation in that the group leader collaborates with the patient by using simple, straightforward language that he or she can understand for the purposes of clearly anticipating the expectations for group and making an informed choice about whether to join the therapy group.

When one considers Yalom and Leszcz's (2005) cognitive approach to preparation from an attachment perspective, their cognitive approach fosters group members' mentalization (Fonagy et al., 2002). As described in more detail in Chapters 1 and 5, mentalization involves the understanding of the internal mental states in oneself and others that underlie all behaviors and emotions. For this reason, verbally reviewing the written contract with group members, sometimes multiple times, is a useful way of helping them mentally reflect on their reactions to the group norms and expectations. For example, group contracts often describe a policy on outside contact. It could state:

> Making social plans to get together outside of the group is not permitted while individuals are active members of the therapy group. Relationships outside of group increase the chance of subgrouping inside the group and also tend to decrease emotional safety among the group members. In the event that there is a chance meeting or any other sustained interaction outside of the group, it is important to bring it back into the group so that it may be processed.

A more preoccupied group member with poor reflective capacities might read that section and immediately become upset that the leaders are controlling the group and inhibiting the possibility of making friends with any of the other group members. Or he or she might become convinced that subgrouping will happen in the group, that he or she will be excluded, and become upset anticipating joining group. Now the group member is upset, not thinking clearly, and anticipating an attachment injury. A more dismissing-avoidant group member might quickly read through the contract (if at all) and not consider any of the emotional and relational components. In the foregoing example, he or she might think, "Who cares about group members getting together? I don't want to talk with anyone outside of group anyway." Or "This contract is so stupid. Of course there will be subgrouping. Whatever." Although they may intellectually understand the information about the group process and rules, they may not be able to predict how they will react during a group session when attachment-based schemas are triggered. However, when the group leader keeps mentalization in mind and the contract is discussed collaboratively with the insecurely attached group member, an opportunity exists to explore reactions (or lack thereof) to the group norms and expectations during the preparation session(s).

As a result, it becomes important for the group leader to initiate the role of a secure base by addressing the group members' anxieties and fears that are activated during group preparation. Yalom and Leszcz (2005) described several cognitive domains of group preparation that facilitate member safety. The first domain is linking the members' symptoms and presenting concerns to interpersonal themes. By doing so, the group leader helps the group members understand how their interpersonal issues are related to their symptoms. Linking symptoms and interpersonal issues helps group members understand how group process will ameliorate their personal suffering and the symptoms that brought them into treatment. Without this link, members are uncertain how group will lessen their depression or anxiety.

Another domain of cognitive preparation is offering suggestions about how to best utilize and participate in group. The group leader works to explain to the members how their internal representations of self and others will be activated in the group and how they can influence the group interactions. For example, the leader may help an avoidant member understand how his withdrawal may come across in the group. The leader may even role-play a possible interaction with this member to see how receiving feedback would feel and to help the member prepare for the group process.

In addition to preparing for potential process, the leader may also discuss potential disappointments and the importance of respecting boundaries. As Marmarosh, Whipple, and colleagues (2009) observed, group leaders preparing more dismissing-avoidant individuals may want to focus on these patients' fears of being humiliated or exposed in groups, in addition to the efficacy of group therapy. By offering reassurance, addressing ways to cope with these fears, and expressing patience about the pace of these group members' self-disclosures and self-expression in group, the group leaders can help them prepare for potential frustrations while concurrently imagining constructive responses. This helps to create a proactive mental framework for members with a long history of interpersonal difficulties and also minimize the possibility of subsequent attendance disruptions that hinder the group process.

Yalom and Leszcz (2005) emphasized the need for repetition during preparation. Although they did not use attachment terminology, they noted that patient anxiety in pregroup orientation sessions can result in diminished or distorted memory recall. Members with high attachment avoidance tend to have vague and idealized recollections of attachment-related experiences (Main et al., 2003; Mikulincer & Shaver, 2007b; Tasca, Ritchie, et al., 2011). In addition, researchers have found that members with high attachment anxiety tend to have disconnected and rambling memory recall of attachment-related experiences (Main et al., 2003; Mikulincer & Shaver, 2007b; Tasca, Ritchie, et al., 2011). If the orientation sessions stimulate attachment-related memories—as they are likely to do—the information gathered during the orientation session may be poor or distorted. As a result, it can be useful to deliberately repeat important preparatory concepts in the first few group sessions, in addition to providing a weekly written summary of the previous session (Bernard et al., 2008; Burlingame et al., 2006; Yalom & Leszcz, 2005). These types of repetition also facilitate mentalization and a secure attachment to the group (Fonagy et al., 2002).

CONCLUSION

In this chapter, we examined the group screening, placement, and preparation processes from an attachment perspective. We described attachment phenomena (e.g., coherence of mind, reflective functioning) and their associated observable characteristics (e.g., affect, body posture, language, tone of voice) that can emerge during the screening interview and be useful in helping group leaders identify attachment anxiety and avoidance in group candidates. More important, we demonstrated how different groups may be more appropriate for group candidates with different levels of attachment anxiety and avoidance. Specifically, we provided the case example of Carla who was appropriate for a more structured group but not ready for an interpersonal process group. We believe that assessing candidates' attachment styles can help leaders determine who would be appropriate for their groups.

Screening is only the first step in successfully placing a group candidate into a group. Once an individual has been selected to join a therapy group, the preparation for the group is paramount. In the chapter, we discussed how the initial interview can help set the stage for the group process and help insecurely attached group members identify issues that they may struggle with during the group. It can be extremely helpful to review the group rules and begin to develop group cohesion via the interaction with the group leader during the preparation. We also addressed why the more insecurely attached group member, who may be more at risk of dropping out, can remain in group with preparation and placement into a group with an appropriate mix of secure and insecure group members.

5

PROCESSES THAT FOSTER SECURE ATTACHMENT IN GROUP PSYCHOTHERAPY

Attachment-based treatments aim to establish a secure base from which reparative experiences can occur and emotions can be regulated and understood (Beebe & Lachmann, 2002; Cozolino, 2002; Schore, 1994, 2003; Sroufe, 1996; D. Stern, 1985). For this to occur in group therapy, the leader is committed to creating a group climate in which individuals can explore their own attachment representations and the patterns of emotion regulation that are triggered during the group sessions (Clulow, 2001; Fosha, 2000; Hughes, 2007; Wallin, 2007). Regardless of the theoretical approach, the key therapeutic attachment-based processes in group treatment are empathic attunement, facilitating mentalization via group process and feedback, identification of transference and parataxic distortions, emotional and cognitive insight, corrective emotional experience, internalization, and group cohesion (see Table 5.1). The ways in which these processes influence cohesion are addressed throughout the chapter, and a specific section is devoted to how attachment styles influence group cohesion at the conclusion of the chapter.

http://dx.doi.org/10.1037/14186-006
Attachment in Group Psychotherapy, by C. L. Marmarosh, R. D. Markin, and E. B. Spiegel

TABLE 5.1
Attachment-Based Processes in Group Therapy

Attachment-based process	Goal
Empathic attunement and empathy of core affective experience	Facilitates trust, helps regulate painful emotions that are often avoided, reduces loneliness, and facilitates group cohesion; allows for corrective emotional experiences; facilitates changes in perceptions of self and others
Facilitation of mentalization	Facilitates self-understanding, emotion regulation, the ability to take perspective of others, and empathy; allows for intimacy
Identification of transference or parataxic distortions	Facilitates understanding of perceptions of others, ability to learn what is intolerable within the self, and obtain more accurate views of others; challenges current perceptions that are based on the past, not on current interactions; facilitates mentalization and empathy
Emotional/cognitive insight from interpersonal learning and feedback	Promotes deeper understanding of one's feelings and how they relate to what is happening in the group; links here-and-now reactions to the past; facilitates understanding of how one is responding to others; individuals learn to consider how they affect others and influence social relationships
Corrective emotional experiences with core affects	Challenges previous expectations of others and of the self; reinforces new ways of being through positive intimate exchanges; builds cohesion; fosters trust; increases intimacy
Internalization	Alters perceptions of self and others; group fosters the use of relationships when encountering difficult or painful situations outside of the group; fight–flight responses that are based on traumatic relationship experiences can be replaced with more secure relationship experiences
Group cohesion	Facilitates belongingness; contains emotions; motivates the navigation of ruptures; fosters internalization of group

EMPATHIC ATTUNEMENT: FACILITATING CHANGES IN MENTAL REPRESENTATIONS

The caregiver's empathy is essential in facilitating the child's ability to identify, tolerate, and effectively communicate emotions (Schore, 2003). The group leader, like the caregiver, facilitates the same thing in the therapy group. Yalom and Leszcz (2005) argued that "members are less likely to attack and blame one another if they can look beyond the surface behavior and become sensitive to one another's internal experiences and underlying intentions. Thus, empathy is a critical element in the successful group" (p. 42).

M. S. Corey and Corey (1997) added that leader empathy is what is "vitally related to trust" in group treatment (p. 143). White (2000) added that "empathy is crucial" (p. 10) for the cognitive behavioral group therapist to be able to know when to challenge and when not to challenge group members.

Empirical research suggests that without empathy in group therapy, the members are at risk of feeling misunderstood, and the group becomes more disengaged. Johnson, Burlingame, Olsen, Davies, and Gleave (2005) found that leader deficiencies in empathy are one component of the *negative relationship factor*, whereas leader empathy is a component of the *positive bonding relationship*, in group therapy. Kivlighan, Multon, and Brossart (1996) found that when leaders were more empathic, group members reported more relationship impacts in the group.

Unfortunately, being empathic is often confused with simply being nice, supportive, or accurately reflecting back what another group member says (Rowe & MacIsaac, 1991). Although these all require some level of active listening, empathy requires that the leader or fellow group member immerse himself or herself in the experience of another or the group based on how that unique other or group experiences the situation. It requires putting one's own perspective aside and stepping into the world of the other, while remaining separate, and seeing the world through the other's eyes.

It is important to note that being empathic does not imply that the leader does not share uncomfortable feedback, which may be perceived as confrontational, as long as the feedback is provided within an empathic stance. In group therapy, empathy can serve as a tool to facilitate trust and self-acceptance, deeper exploration of feelings, and an environment in which group members reveal more vulnerable parts of themselves and take risks (Greenberg & Elliott, 1997; Rowe & MacIsaac, 1991). During the group process, empathy is influenced by the security of the group members, the timing of the interventions, and the cohesion in the group. To empathize with members, the group leader must hold the group in mind. The following example demonstrates how the leader empathizes with the particular member and the group as a whole, eight sessions into the treatment. It illustrates how the leader pays attention to her own reactions over time and also immerses herself into the life of one specific member of the group. The goal of the group leader is to facilitate a secure base within the group so that the members can provide each other empathy and feedback and foster corrective emotional exchanges that challenge insecure working models of themselves and others.

Clinical Example: Therapist Empathy and Facilitating Mentalization

Eight weeks into the group, Sam, a more dismissing-avoidant member, was attending sessions regularly but avoiding intimacy in the group. Although he was committed, he avoided being open about himself and displayed the same detachment he described in outside relationships that led him to seek group therapy. He would focus on the other members' needs, supporting them, and avoided his own feelings, thoughts, or desires. Sometimes his detachment looked like disinterest, yet none of the members confronted him about his avoidant nature. Eventually, a fellow member, Tom, asked Sam what he was thinking. This question seemed to be inspired by Sam's silence and outward display of indifference after Tom revealed something personal in the session about his own childhood. Tom had been talking about his anger and how it got in the way of his relationships. Tom shared that his anger most likely originated from his emotionally abusive mother. When Tom challenges Sam about his thoughts in the group, Sam makes a joke.

Sam: I heard this thing about mothers in *The New York Times*. I think there is no such thing as a nonabusive mother. I think that is a requirement of motherhood. You know, it is a part of the definition of mother in the dictionary. [*Sam was moving away from his own emotions triggered by Tom's sharing, and he was deflecting feelings regarding a more serious conversation about maternal abuse by using humor.*]

Group: Laughs at Sam's joke [*The group members appear also to be uncomfortable with Tom's disclosure and what it has triggered. They share in the humor while Tom sits silently. The leader imagines the hurt and anger Tom is feeling and waits to see what will happen next.*]

Anne: [*a preoccupied member*] I have this problem I wanted to bring up into group today. It is this problem I seem to always run into, so you are all familiar with it. I know you have heard me talk about it before, but it is something I need to talk about again. I know I should share my feelings with my husband, as we have talked about in here, but he just does not seem to understand how frustrating it is. He just doesn't get it. [*Anne starts to go into details about her many complaints about her husband. The leader recognizes that the entire group is now struggling with the expression of conflict and how to express it in the session. All of the members have their own personal struggles with anger, conflict, and tolerating more vulnerable emotions. Instead of focusing on the process in the session, they are avoiding what is happening between them.*]

Joe: Anne, I think that you did the right thing by avoiding confronting him. Would it help to hear that all men are like that? They sometimes just don't get feelings. I'm not always good at that.

John: I hate when people label men as not being able to get feelings. I get feelings and last time I looked, I'm still a man. I think you just need to tell him at the right time. Do you rush in when he gets home at the end of the day? That never helps when you are tired to hear someone complain.

Anne: No, I wait. I always wait. I never rush in and try and approach him when he is tired. It just never seems to work. He never seems to care that much about what I'm feeling. No matter what I have tried, he can't hear me. *[Anne and the group members continue to share their reactions to Anne and her husband, a much safer topic for members. As the group members ask more questions about Anne and her husband, the group process becomes more boring and lifeless. Tom also remains silent.]*

Leader: I can't help but notice the increasing lack of energy in the group. It feels as if we can't solve this problem for Anne, and this gray fog is descending on us. I noticed that we all keep focusing on helping her deal with her anger at her husband without having to confront him. I wonder if we all struggle with the issue of avoidance of conflict in here and could help each other work on it in the group today, with one another. *[The leader empathizing with the group is able to imagine the underlying struggle to tolerate the discomfort that would come with moving toward more genuineness and vulnerability. The leader feels the time is right to facilitate an exploration about what is happening in the group, rather than continuing in a lifeless, de-energized manner.]*

Group: Silence *[The leader waits.]*

Leader: I noticed the silence and wonder what people are thinking or feeling?

Joe: I don't understand what you mean when you say a fog.

Anne: Yes, I think the group is helping me sort out my relationship with my husband, and sometimes it has been helpful.

Lynne: I get it. I felt like we changed the topic, and we are not really focusing on what is happening between us. I don't really know when we got derailed, so to speak.

Leader: I agree, Lynne. I could not help but go back in my mind to the beginning of the session. I felt there was a lot of energy early on, and I noticed that we moved away from that. Did anyone else notice that or recall when we got derailed? *[The leader is trying to help the members step back and think about the group process and what led them to move away from emotions in the group. This curiosity facilitates members' stepping back and mentalizing about the group experience.]*

Jason: I felt like things changed after Tom asked Sam what he was thinking. It felt like we moved away after that. *[The leader nods.]*

Leader:	Can you say more about what you noticed?
Jason:	Well, I don't want to put anyone on the spot, but I was wondering if Tom was upset at Sam. *[Other members look at Tom and Sam.]*
Anne:	I noticed that Tom stopped talking after that, and I was wondering if he was angry.
Tom:	Well, I think I just wanted to know why he was being quiet so I asked the question.
Leader:	Can you say more about that, Tom?
Tom:	*[Looking away from Sam.]* I don't remember. I just wanted to know what Sam was thinking. That is exactly what I asked him before he made it into a joke. *[It is clear Tom was uncomfortable and had feelings about the joking. There is another long silence.]*
Lynne:	I felt bad when that happened. I noticed the joke too and wondered if Sam did not want to go there. Telling a joke is one way to change the topic. I know I do that. *[Lynne is being empathic with Sam's discomfort but is not confronting him about the impact that his avoidance has on the group.]*
Tom:	I guess I felt like nothing seems to bother Sam. He is always so calm and together. Sometimes, he doesn't seem to care at all. He makes these jokes and people laugh, but I wonder what he struggles with in here. *[The leader motions for him to keep going. The leader also gestures to Tom to look at Sam as he gives this feedback. The leader feels it is important for the group to be more comfortable confronting Sam.]*
Leader:	Tom, can you help Sam understand how you came to see him as not feeling or caring about what you were saying in the group? *[The leader wants to help Tom focus more on the in-group behaviors so that Sam can see how he comes across in the here and now of the group process. Sam's dismissing-avoidant attachment style has led to deactivation of his emotions in the group. This is the issue he came to group to work on, and Tom is giving him important feedback.]*
Tom:	*[now looking at Sam.]* Look, I could be wrong, but I just shared all this personal stuff and it wasn't easy for me. I look over . . . and, well . . . you are either making a joke or looking disinterested. Last week I noticed you were playing with your cell phone. Sometimes I just don't think you can understand or that you care about this group. *[The group falls silent.]*

Although the leader was aware that Tom had good intentions and was hurt by Sam's withdrawal, she also knew well that Sam would have a hard time responding, given his pull to avoid emotions, specifically conflict. During the group intake, she learned that Sam endured years of physical abuse by a father who came home drunk and that he had few relational experiences of closeness that did not come with abuse. The leader was also aware that the group did not know about Sam's past. The leader, being empathic with Sam, believed that it was not that Sam could not understand what Tom was saying or that he did not care about Tom's painful experiences, but that Sam struggled to cope with similar feelings, and these feelings led him to withdraw, deactivate emotions, or use humor to lessen the intensity.

Tom had a more secure attachment style, and he was able to talk about his abuse and anger in the group. Sam, on the other hand, had a dismissing-avoidant attachment style and would deactivate when he felt threatened or overwhelmed with emotions. The leader imagined that Sam felt besieged during the session when Tom shared his childhood memories of abuse and later with the confrontation, but she also felt that Sam was able to tolerate this process in the group. Although she knew Sam would struggle with this confrontation, she also knew that Sam needed to begin to start looking at his automatic withdrawal in the sessions. The leader's empathy for Sam led her to determine that it was time for him, and other members with dismissing-avoidant attachment, to explore how their deactivation affects their relationships and maintains their isolation.

The leader was aware that Sam's reaction was important and that it was critical to find a way for him to express himself in the here and now of the session. Although the leader was focusing on Sam in the moment, she knew that all of the members could relate to the anxiety of here-and-now confrontations and fears of aggression; the leader also empathized with the group as a whole.

The leader was also hoping that by deepening the here-and-now interaction and facilitating members' genuine core emotional disclosures, the group would foster a corrective emotional experience for Sam if he was able to take the risk of revealing himself in the group.

Leader: [to Sam] I can see you are withdrawing now, and withdrawing may feel like the best thing to do right now—it is familiar for you . . . it can feel like the best option. But I believe you have much going on inside of you right now, much that the group does not know about, and this keeps you from feeling understood. The silence, the withdrawal, keeps you alone. Sam, this is a chance to do something different. [Sam makes eye contact with the leader for the first time in the session. Then he shakes his head in disagreement.]

Sam: Different? [He speaks softly and sarcastically.] I just do not choose to wear my heart on my sleeve. [He pauses.] You all think I do not get it. I get it, all right. You think I don't care.

[Sam stops himself. His face becomes red, and he is controlling what seems to be years of pent-up emotion.]

Leader: *[Not withdrawing, she encourages Sam with a soft yet forceful tone, matching Sam's intensity.]* Don't stop now, Sam. Tell us . . . tell Tom . . . keep going. *[Sam waits.]*

Sam: *[with a strained and pressured tone]* Why . . . why do I need to tell them . . . you . . . tell anyone anything?

Leader: *[pausing]* Because it matters, Sam. *[pausing again]* That is why. Because it happened. Because all of this rage and pain is eating you up inside. It is eating away at you and keeping you alone. *[The leader is helping Sam express his emotions in the session.]*

Sam: Tell them what? That my dad beat me to a pulp each night? Is that what I should tell everyone? *[He pauses.]* For what? For nothing. *[Again, he pauses.]* OK, Tom, I was quiet but I heard you. Your mom was horrible. I'm sorry I didn't look like I was listening to you. I did hear you. Maybe I am just sick of this. My dad beat me up almost every night. He would come home drunk off his ass. He would start with my mom and then he would pick on me. First, he would just yell insults, and that would make me feel like shit. Then, when that wasn't enough, he would take his fist and put it in my face. . . . I knew it would happen the minute he walked in the door. I just had to deal with it till I could leave home. I am so sick of this crap. You all think I don't understand or that I don't care? I know what it is like to feel alone. I have been on my own since I was 16. *[Sam's voice cracks.]* Why do you think I come to this group? It's because I can't have a successful relationship if my life depended on it. Because I am so messed up. *[Sam's anger suddenly lifts and as quickly as his rage emerged, so does his grief. He starts to tear up in the session. The leader notices the group is silent yet extremely present. She allows space for the group to empathize with Sam, who is starting to experience his core affects of rage and loss in the group. The leader feels the group will naturally reach out to Sam when he is bringing his true self to the session.]*

Tom: *[leaning toward Sam]* I am sorry, Sam. I had no idea. You're not any more messed up than the rest of us. I know what it's like to go through hell and the only way to get through it is to rely on yourself. It wasn't your fault. You think not caring will fix things, but you did nothing wrong. *[Tom's tone is extremely compassionate, and he is clearly empathic with Sam. Watching Tom express his sincere understanding to Sam was emotionally touching in the group. Sam struggles to stay connected with Tom and can only briefly look at him before quickly looking away.]*

Later in the session, the leader followed up on the importance of Tom's emotional response to Sam, and she asked Tom to say more about how he was feeling toward Sam after he was more vulnerable.

> Tom: Well, I feel like I understand Sam now. I was upset when I thought he wasn't listening. I had no idea what he was thinking or what was going on inside his head. Maybe it reminds me of my father who was also quiet and you couldn't tell if he cared. I am really surprised to hear we have so much in common. I guess I don't feel angry anymore. I am also really glad this happened. *[The group members share their experiences as well, and at the end of the session, Joe adds a bit of much-needed humor.]*

> Joe: I guess it is not just mothers that are in the dictionary under abusive. It must be an entire list of family members *[The group members burst into laughter. Sam laughs too and makes eye contact with Tom. Unlike before, when the group leader pursued Sam, this time, she feels that the group needs time to self-regulate before ending the session.]*

This example highlights how the leader's empathy allowed her to intuit Sam's readiness to tolerate the confrontation that would lead to the exploration of his withdrawal in the group. The leader was also aware that the members needed to step back from the emotional engagement at the end of the session. Empathy allows the leader to know when "going away" is a distraction versus when it enables the members to self-regulate. The leader's knowledge of the group members' attachment histories was also paramount because she was able to understand the roots of the deactivating and hyperactivating strategies within the group. Wallin (2007) stated, "Such knowledge can also strengthen our ability to imagine, understand, and empathically resonate with the subjective experience, as well as the childhood histories, of our patients" (p. 85). From an attachment perspective, group therapy is effective because it makes space for both the dissociated history and the possibility of new relational experiences.

After months of weekly group meetings, the group members truly began to trust one another by sharing more vulnerable feelings, revealing more private parts of themselves, and engaging in more mutual exchanges. These new exchanges facilitated corrective emotional experiences like Sam's. The group became more cohesive and a secure base for the members, who started taking risks and challenging automatic interpersonal patterns. Not only empathy can facilitate corrective emotional experiences; lapses in empathy can as well.

Empathic Failures: Opportunities to Foster Corrective Emotional Experience

Researchers have been focusing on the importance of therapeutic ruptures and their repairs in individual psychotherapy (Safran, Muran, Samstag,

& Stevens, 2002). Stone (1992) explained how repeated experiences of empathic failures within an empathic group environment foster the development of the self. From an attachment perspective, the leader's ability to identify these ruptures, process them, and own clinical errors is what fosters trust and deepens the sense of security group members experience within the group. Looking back on the session just described, Anne felt hurt when the leader ignored her and focused on Tom and Sam's relationship. In the next session, the leader noticed that Anne avoided making eye contact with her. She had no idea that Anne was hurt by what happened in the previous session, but she knew something was not right.

Leader: *[to Anne]* I noticed that you look away, and I was wondering if something was upsetting you. *[Anne looks extremely uncomfortable.]*

Anne: Everything is fine. *[Anne gives a half smile.]*

Leader: I hear what you're saying and want to respect that everything is fine. But I did notice you avoiding looking at me, and that is different. I worry that you wouldn't tell me if there was something bothering you, similar to what happens with your husband. If there was something bothering you, if I had done something that upset you, I wouldn't know and couldn't work it out with you. *[The leader wants to model a healthy confrontation and give Anne an opportunity to express her feelings in the group. The leader knows that this is something members struggle with and wants to model healthy acknowledgment of ruptures and repairs.]*

Anne looked at the leader for the first time that session and had tears in her eyes. When asked about the tears, she admitted to feeling hurt that the leader had cut her off during the previous session. The leader recalled her interruption and acknowledged how that hurt Anne.

The leader processed how it felt for Anne to be interrupted, and Anne said she felt alone and rejected, the way she had felt as a child. Anne grew up with a very ill mother who was in and out of hospitals. Because of her mother's health problems, she often missed how unhappy, angry, or alone Anne was feeling. The inconsistency in care left Anne focusing much of her childhood on her mother and her mother's well-being at the expense of her own exploration and development. Anne developed a more preoccupied attachment style that left her struggling to cope with her own feelings and extremely dissatisfied in relationships, including that with her husband, in which she often felt overwhelmed, forgotten, and needy.

When asked more about her tears in that moment, Anne said the tears actually represented her feeling touched by the group leader, who, unlike her mother and husband, noticed her reaction and seemed to be interested in how Anne felt. On the basis of the group processing her reaction, she later revealed experiencing hope that people could be different from how they had been in her past relationships. Again, we see the importance of the leader's empathy and ability to pick up on a rupture in the group session. Facilitating exploration of the rupture facilitated a repair that led to increased trust and hope. It also modeled healthy interpersonal relationships to members.

Triggering Pain and Hope

Experiencing another's empathy can be a "stunning experience" (Fosha, 2000, p. 226) for group members who finally feel they are not alone and exist in the heart and mind of another. According to Fosha (2000), empathy elicits positive affects such as love, gratitude, and hope. It is one of the main ingredients of a successful caregiving relationship and of a secure base. It is not uncommon to see a group member tear up after hearing fellow group members express true understanding of his or her feelings. When asked about this sudden display of emotion, the member frequently will say that he or she was surprised and moved by the other members' expressions of empathy. In the group session described earlier, Anne felt hope when the leader recognized her feelings of anger. Before that, Sam was touched when he noticed Tom tear up after he had revealed his own history of abuse. Sam later said it was something he thought about often because he had rarely experienced a male's compassion or sensitivity. He did not believe it could be possible or acceptable.

As much as empathy can instill hope, it can also provoke a profound sense of loss and pain for a group member who never experienced that level of attunement. It can reawaken longings, awareness of deprivation, and even rage (Fairbairn, 1952). Some people can become threatened or overwhelmed by that level of intimacy (Lachmann, 2008). Fosha argued that although empathy can awaken painful emotions and the desire to push those feelings away, it also facilitates the mourning of that loss. This is what happened for Sam. When the group revealed empathy for the pain of his childhood, he initially responded with a deepening of his grief. However, during the following group sessions, Sam often moved back to his familiar stance of self-sufficiency. The longings that were stirred in the earlier session felt exposing, and he needed to step back from the intensity of the experience. Although he was not in the same place he was we he began participating in the group, he continued to oscillate back to a position of safety until he could risk stepping back into a place of vulnerability. This process of exploration and retreat became one that was openly talked about within the group sessions.

Multiple Experiences of Empathy: Consensual Validation

Unlike individual therapy, in which the empathy comes mainly from the therapist, group therapy offers empathic attunement from multiple individuals and has the power to challenge powerful internal representations from the past. For Sam, the repeated experience of being understood, valued, and embraced by the group when he was vulnerable challenged his negative view of dependency and weakness. Over time, he learned that what felt safe in the past, being alone, was not as rewarding as being accepted for who he was with others. More important, he learned that others, especially men, were not always dangerous, rejecting, and abusive and that depending on others would not inevitably lead to disappointment. As Sam challenged his avoidance, other members were encouraged to challenge their attachment styles as well.

In group therapy, parataxic distortions and transference reactions are primarily modified through a process called *consensual validation* in which multiple leaders and members give the same feedback against which an individual group member can compare his or her own perceptions (Yalom & Leszcz, 2005). It is difficult for group members to deny or deflect their attachment distortions when multiple people offer the same feedback (Yalom & Leszcz, 2005). In essence, feedback from multiple others highlights and challenges insecure internal working model distortions of self and others, slowly altering automatic, engrained, and insecure attachment organizations.

Empathizing With Core Affects

Although empathy is considered one of the most important ingredients in group therapy, empathizing with defensive material or affect is not always helpful in treatment. As Wallin (2007) stated:

> Expressively empathizing with the patient's subjective experience can also be helpful, but only so long as our empathy is not confined to the patient's manifest feelings, but extends to emotions the patient may as yet be unable to feel or express. This caveat is especially significant when the feelings expressed (say anger or hostility) cover other feelings (of dependence or vulnerability, say) whose expression seems more problematic, but is potentially more adaptive. (p. 334)

The leader could have remained at the surface of Sam's experience, where he felt the desire to be "strong" and "not wear his heart on his sleeve." She could have stayed with the manifest content—the defensive affect, rage, or the defensive behavior, stoicism. Instead, she imagined herself into the mind of a young boy who is beaten repeatedly by a drunk and abusive father. She intuited that Sam blames himself at some level and that he disavows an incredible amount of grief and pain at losing a father and spending his entire life avoiding relationships. During the session, the leader empathized with what Fosha (2000) described as the core affects. In Fosha's (2000) model, core affects, no matter how painful or unbearable, help to heal and transform the patient. She argued that when an emotion is core, expressing it feels mutative and beneficial to the patient (Fosha, 2000). She defined *core emotional experience* as "all aspects of emotional life experienced directly and viscerally, in the absence of defenses" (p. 16). In contrast, defensive emotions engender the feeling of "going nowhere" (p. 17). Fosha (2000) argued that defensive emotions protect against underlying core affective experiences that are too overwhelming or frightening to experience. In essence, a defensive emotion facilitates the avoidance of more vulnerable and frightening core affects.

In the case material, we see Sam's defensive affect, anger, facilitating the avoidance of more vulnerable emotions of grief. When the leader empathizes with the core affects, Sam feels free to express more vulnerable feelings of loss, self-loathing, and loneliness. The group members are also touched by his revelation and move toward him rather than confronting him. The experience is mutative and facilitates cohesion within the group.

Although empathy is critical, it is not enough. Kohut (1984) was one of the first to describe the importance of alternating between empathy and explaining to facilitate cognitive insight and the linking of early experience and needs with what is happening in the here and now. Group researchers have found support for his theory in group therapy. Lieberman and Golant (2002) found that group leaders who provided empathy and helped members understand what was happening in the here and now of the group process reported more support and disclosure in the group, which then led to better group therapy outcomes. Even more convincing is evidence from a study by Gold, Patton, and Kivlighan (2009). They used a sophisticated statistical analysis to explore the influence of therapeutic factors and found only one change profile related to a decrease in group-member interpersonal problems. This profile was termed *experiencing and reflecting* and was described as sessions that alternated between focusing on affective factors and sessions that focused on behavioral and cognitive factors. We see evidence for the value of processing emotional experience and the importance of facilitating both emotional engagement and participants' ability to gain meaning from group interactions.

Group leaders facilitate insight in various ways: by making interpretations that link the past to the here and now, described later in this chapter, and by helping members reflect on their experiences in the moment and promoting their ability to observe what is happening within themselves, others, and the group. This reflective process is what Fonagy and his colleagues (2002) termed *mentalization*.

FACILITATING MENTALIZATION

Reflective capacity allows us to wonder what is in the mind of the other without it threatening our own sense of self. It is paramount to successful group therapy. For example, a securely attached group member is able to hear another member's experience of what happened in the group, even if it is different from his own experience of what happened. He is also able to be curious about the difference and reevaluate his own perceptions based on this conversation. There is an ability to hold on to different experiences and emotions simultaneously. "Mentalizing provides a buffer between feeling and action, which is necessary if impulses are to be caught before they become overwhelming, and if motivation of self and other are to be monitored and understood" (Fonagy & Target, 2008, p. 32). A lack of mentalization inhibits emotional closeness, the repair of ruptures, and intimacy. Reflective capacity develops alongside attachment and is correlated with secure attachment (Fonagy & Target, 2008; Gergely & Unoka, 2008).

More preoccupied individuals are likely to be overwhelmed by their own emotions, which inhibits their ability to reflect on what is happening in the group. They are also likely to be unaware that their past experiences are influencing their perceptions of the here and now. Their fears of rejection may be so powerful that they cannot listen to others and observe the group process. Rather than stepping back and exploring others' reactions in the group, they may believe others intentionally tried to attack them and may call forth activating strategies for getting attention that were developed in their relationships with attachment figures.

More dismissing-avoidant individuals, by contrast, may be so disconnected from personal vulnerability and their feelings that they cannot empathize with others or enter into their emotional world. Like Sam, they may simply withdraw into themselves to escape the inevitable rejection and lack of understanding they are certain will follow.

When we look back at the session with Sam, we see evidence of how the leader facilitates mentalization within the group session. The leader is aware that Sam is not responding to Tom because of inner emotions and conflicts that are being stirred up within him during the group process. He outwardly expresses withdrawal and indifference, but this does not mean he feels nothing or has no reactions under the surface. The group members, unaware of Sam's history, project onto him different emotions, reactions, thoughts based on their own personal histories. Tom perceives that Sam is not listening to him because he does not care. Through the group process, members start to question their assumptions based on their internal working models and appreciate how these models are based on their own personal history with their caregivers.

More important, the group leader is also able to move beyond the manifest content and observe the avoidance of conflict and anger that is holding the group hostage during the session. The leader waits to see what will unfold and then determines when it is time to help the group members confront their avoidance and explore what is happening in the group as a whole. The leader asks the participants to step back and reflect on the group process. She invites them to think about what is happening rather than just reacting. She asks them to focus on "when they felt energy" and "when things became less lively in the session." The leader encourages members to think about what they are feeling and what is happening between them; to share their perspectives with one another. Fonagy and colleagues (2002) supported the therapist inviting members into the process rather than always taking on the role of the expert who knows what is going on in others' minds. For example, the leader says, "I am feeling confused right now. We seem to be changing topics. I wonder what is going on in the group today?" Then she allows space for the group members to respond.

When the group members start to share their perspectives, they begin to observe that what they imagined to be true is not accurate. They are projections. Sam was not carefree during the session. Quite the opposite, he was overwhelmed and relying defensively on detachment. The members learn that what looks like disinterest on the outside may have deeper, more complicated roots on the inside. The members also learn to be curious about their immediate reactions and how they avoid conflict and intimacy. They come to realize that to know what is going on within another person's mind, they need to ask and then listen. They also learn that what is going on within them may be hidden from view and that what they see in others may be more indicative of their own personal feelings and interpersonal histories. Through the real relationships in the group and the reflective process, group members gain insight into who they are, why they feel and behave the way they do, and how previous experiences influence them.

IDENTIFYING TRANSFERENCE AND PARATAXIC DISTORTIONS

According to Wallin (2007), transference within an attachment-based treatment refers to the process of rigidly holding on to one perception of the other despite the fact that there are many plausible interpretations of his or her behavior. When group members struggle with insecure attachments, they often perceive others based on their previous experiences, and these perceptions are often inaccurate.

Yalom and Leszcz (2005) referred to these types of distortions as *parataxic distortions*, a term borrowed from Sullivan (1953) that refers to individuals' tendency to distort their perceptions of others. In group therapy, group members sometimes relate to one another not based on "realistic attributes" of the other but on the basis of a "personification existing chiefly in the former's own fantasy" (Yalom & Leszcz, 2005, p. 21). In attachment terms, group members experience the group, members, and leaders based on past internalized attachment relationships (Mallinckrodt & Chen, 2004; Wallin, 2007).

When using an attachment perspective to examine interpersonal behaviors among group members, the group leaders' overarching tasks are to (a) identify attachment-related behaviors, and (b) guide group members toward more secure organizations (Bowlby, 1988; Pistole, 1989, 1997). To get from point a to point b, group leaders help members identify how their internal working models distort their perception of themselves and others. For more preoccupied members, like Anne, these distortions usually involve perceiving the group as consistently unsupportive, unavailable, and rejecting (Bartholomew & Horowitz, 1991; Pistole, 1997) and themselves as helpless and not worthy of love and support (Bartholomew & Horowitz, 1991; Wallin, 2007). For more dismissing-avoidant members, like Sam, these distortions involve perceiving the group as demanding, engulfing, or irrelevant (Bartholomew & Horowitz, 1991; Pistole, 1997) and themselves as superior or self-sufficient (Mikulincer & Shaver, 2007b). Even more secure members, like Tom, rely on early interactions with significant others when interpreting people's behaviors and intentions.

Although an attachment perspective focuses on the identification of attachment-related behaviors and movement toward more secure internal representations of self and others, the level of intervention with regard to facilitating insight depends on the type of therapy group.

FACILITATING INSIGHT

Yalom and Leszcz (2005) described four levels of insight that are facilitated in groups. These levels range from Level 1, learning how others perceive oneself that may be different from what one expected (e.g., receiving interpersonal feedback about attachment-related behaviors), to Level 4, learning how earlier experiences in life led to the motivation to engage in specific interpersonal patterns within and outside the group (e.g., understanding that one's shame and fears of intimacy are based on early experiences of sexual abuse).

Yalom and Leszcz (2005) described the first type of insight as learning how one comes across to others based on the basic feedback one receives in the group. For example, Tom tells Sam how Sam's jokes make people laugh, but they keep members from getting to know him in the group. Tom is giving Sam interpersonal feedback that Sam is eventually able to use in the group to address how he affects others outside of the group. Yalom and Leszcz's second level of insight addresses more of the complexity in the interactions between oneself and others in the group. This insight is focused on how individuals learn about patterns in the way they relate with others. For example, with the help of Tom, who reveals facing similar struggles to those that challenge Sam, Sam learns that he too tends to avoid sharing his emotions with others in the group as a way of avoiding painful feelings. On the basis of his interactions in the group, Sam learns that he avoids depending on group members the same way he avoids depending on people in his life when he needs them. Sam is becoming aware of his deactivating strategies in the group. The third level of insight incorporates underlying motivation and members learning why they may do what they do interpersonally. For example, the group members explore why Sam avoids expressing his vulnerable emotions in the group. Over time, he acquires insight as to the origin of his avoidance, such as fears of being humiliated, disappointed, or shamed if he were to express his needs or feelings. The fourth level goes even deeper into this self-understanding to include the origins of Sam's underlying sense of shame. This includes linking Sam's physical abuse and emotional neglect with his fears of being humiliated or disappointed in relationships. In essence, a linkage is made between Sam's early experiences and his adult attachment style of avoidance. He learns in the group that his repeated painful interpersonal experiences with his caregivers early in life led him to wall off his neediness and cope with his vulnerability through self-sufficiency.

Attachment styles play a role in all these levels of insight regardless of whether they are the focus of a given session. For some groups, members may remain focused on the here and now (Levels 1 and 2) and mainly identify hyperactivating or deactivating strategies and how they influence relationships in the group. For other groups, members may go deeper into exploring the roots of this deactivation or hyperengagement to foster more empathy and understanding of interpersonal behaviors and reactions in the group.

Identifying Past Relational Patterns

Rutan and Stone (1993) argued that insight is an important component of group therapy and that group members need to have a new relational experience to gain insight. They stated:

> A sense of knowing one's own sensitivities and vulnerabilities helps one master everyday stresses. Insight enables the patient to spot a troublesome area of behavior pattern and, hopefully, avoid what would previously have become a problem situation. Certainly, it is not that all conflicts disappear, but many can be short-circuited through self-awareness. (pp. 140–141)

Sam was able to express his true emotions in the group and gain understanding that his feelings of anger and grief existed and were tolerable (i.e., emotional insight) and that his avoidance of his feelings kept him isolated (i.e., cognitive insight). In addition to this integrative insight (Gelso & Harbin, 2007), he was able to have an emotional experience with the group that facilitated his own sense of trust, belonging, and self-worth. These experiences led him to take more risks in the group and to practice being engaged with others. Because Sam had removed himself from relationships all his life, he was not skillful at empathizing with people, giving feedback, or even listening. He could engage in small talk, but he struggled with intimacy.

After 2 years of treatment, Sam achieved greater insight into how his detachment hurt others and left them feeling angry and alone. He learned that his way of expressing his own feelings was to withdraw, which creates feelings in others that are similar to his own disavowed feelings of anger, frustration, and disappointment. More important, he understood that he expressed his feelings indirectly, which was effective as a child because he had been repeatedly abused. Over time, he learned in group that he no longer needed to cope in the same way he did as a child and that sometimes the outcome he expects is not what will actually occur. He gained this insight after 2 years of therapy, but he is aware that he continues to struggle in relationships and continues to find it difficult to remain engaged when his instinct is to withdraw.

Striking When the Iron Is Hot or Cold

For some group members, it is helpful to make interpretations when the iron is hot and emotions are alive in the room; for other members, it is helpful to strike when the iron is cold, emotions are settled, and they can integrate feedback. Wallin (2007) described this as the "window of tolerance" (p. 297). This window is the amount of arousal an individual can experience without hindering his or her ability to process the experience. In essence, we are describing the optimal level of arousal that stimulates but does not overwhelm the group member. The optimal intervention will be different for a group member who denies the experience of painful emotions (dismissing-avoidant attachment pattern) compared with one who is flooded by the emotional world (anxious pattern).

For more preoccupied group members, who are more inclined to become overwhelmed with affect and struggle to think while feeling, interpretations that come too soon are likely to be rejected, perceived as attacking, or experienced as a rupture. In contrast, for dismissing-avoidant group members, those who are more inclined to become detached or withdraw, catching them in the emotion can help them link affective experiences before they are dissociated or disavowed.

The same is true for interpretations to the group as a whole. If the group is preoccupied and focused on issues of mistrust, paranoia, and fears of attack, it is likely that interpretations that stir up anxiety will not be helpful until later, when the group can tolerate them. If the group is detached and lifeless, an interpretation that infuses emotion can be enlivening and stimulating. Most important is that if the interpretation is met with resistance or is incorrect, the leader is able to facilitate a repair and own his or her misjudgment of the timing or content of the intervention.

One example of striking when the iron is hot occurs with Sam in our earlier example. Sam has a dismissing-avoidant attachment style and a tendency to "deal without feeling" (Fosha, 2000). The leader looks for opportunities to help Sam step into his emotional reactions in the group. This requires her to pay attention to both verbal and nonverbal expressions of emotion within the group. The leader encourages Sam to stay with his emotions, even though his gut instinct is to shut down and withdraw. She interprets his avoidance as being a self-protective reaction from his childhood, but one that is now toxic, serving only to maintain his isolation. Sam is then able to release intense rage and grief, which powerfully illuminates the history of loss and loneliness that has imprisoned him. This creates the opportunity for the group to react in a way that violates his expectations and pushes Sam to question his lifelong assumptions.

For Anne, the picture is quite different. Because of her preoccupied attachment style and tendency to hyperactivate emotions, striking when the iron is cold is a better approach. Sam's avoidant withdrawal continually activates her abandonment and sends her into painful cycles of underregulation within seconds. The leader has learned to catch moments of disruption and potential deregulation quickly and to process the experience before it escalates and becomes too hot. When Anne becomes deregulated, she is flooded with memories of abandonment and rejection, and the emotions are too powerful for her to think and feel at the same time.

During one session, Anne tries to engage Sam, but his face is blank. His lack of expression triggers Anne's unconscious memories of her own neglect and disregard. Her posture stiffens, her face grows tight, and eyebrows furrow. Within seconds, she is reacting in the context of a lifetime of being disregarded. The group leader observes the interaction and slows down this escalating cycle by helping Anne identify her feelings in the exact moment that her nonverbal behaviors surface. She says, "Anne, I noticed your face change just now, and I had this feeling something important happened." By slowing down the process, Anne's reaction is explored before it becomes too overwhelming, and she is able to understand the roots to her growing frustration. In essence, the leader facilitates Anne's ability to "feel and deal" at the same time (Fosha, 2000).

In addition to helping Anne understand what is happening to her, Sam is able to see how his silence and blank stare affects others. He is surprised to hear that Anne felt abandoned because his blankness is really a reflection of not knowing what to say to make her feel better. In addition, he reveals that he often feels paralyzed when Anne addresses him because he feels pressured to say "the right thing" or deal with her "punishing anger and disappointment." With the help of the leader's interpretations, Anne learns that her own automatic fears of being abandoned often leave others feeling anxious about letting her down, abandoning her. The group is able to recognize the cycle of Anne's hyperactivating behaviors, leading to deactivation in others, and the deactivation fueling more hyperactivation in response. This example is an excellent illustration of the benefits that can accrue to all group members by examining the complex reactions surrounding one member's response.

FACILITATING CORRECTIVE EMOTIONAL EXPERIENCES WITH CORE AFFECT

From an attachment perspective, the corrective emotional experience (Alexander & French, 1946) involves members experiencing core emotions in the group, having a different interpersonal experience, and internalizing the positive experience so it will replace traumatic past attachment experiences. These experiences are particularly powerful in a group because they occur with multiple people present, not just a therapist. In essence, the new relationships they experience in group have the power to revise insecure internal representations of self and other. When we go back to the clinical example in this chapter, it is not the leader who has the most powerful impact on Sam in the session. It is Tom's genuine and authentic confrontation and emotional support that foster the corrective emotional experience for Sam. Sam had never encountered a man who could be angry at him while being simultaneously vulnerable and compassionate. Although it was extremely uncomfortable for Sam to feel vulnerable and cared for and he initially retreated from it, he later revealed that he retreated because it felt "too intense." When he was asked to further describe this feeling, he said he felt a physical tightening and then the sensation of being unable to swallow. He said it was hard to speak. The leader noted that it sounded like he was describing the experience of feeling choked up. He felt something for the first time but could not put it into words. This encounter paved the way for Sam to express more emotions and move toward greater intimacy over time.

FACILITATING INTERNALIZATION

It is important to remember that just as we carry significant others with us as internal working models of self and others from childhood, we can also internalize new representations of self and others through our relationship with the therapy group. Group members can learn to carry the group with them (Marmarosh & Corazzini, 1997). How do leaders help members internalize the group experiences so that they can become more secure working models of self and others? Fosha (2000) argued that it is important for clinicians to process significant intimate moments—the corrective moments in therapy—and that this is where enormous opportunity lives to help clients experience something different. Furthermore,

> these are extraordinarily powerful and intimate interventions. They place intimacy front and center and gently announce that this is no ordinary discourse, but rather one whose goal for both the therapist and patient is risk taking against the backdrop of safety. (p. 239)

This is important in individual therapy, but it is critical in group therapy. Yalom and Leszcz (2005) emphasized the importance of helping group members recognize critical moments in the group and described how some group leaders invite members to observe the leaders' postgroup processing of the sessions each week.

Therapists can review important moments in depth with members immediately after they occur, asking, "What does it feel like in the group right now after we shared so much together?" or "I feel privileged to have witnessed such genuineness and courage in the group today, I wonder what it is like for you all to have experienced that in here?" According to Fosha (2000), reprocessing intimate moments in therapy facilitates the gradual taking in of these life-altering experiences and facilitates internalization. According to Rutan and Stone (1993), "internalization is the most advanced and durable mechanism of change" (p. 63).

From an attachment perspective, group treatment is the revision of internal representations of self and others. Rather than seeing the self as weak and flawed and others as strong and powerful, the more preoccupied group member is able to see the self as capable and equal to the others, as a valuable group member, not an outsider. With regard to the more dismissing-avoidant group member, rather than seeing the self as superior and self-sufficient and others being needy, he or she is able to see the self as both self-sufficient and dependent.

For example, Sam was later able to express that he felt himself withdrawing in the group. In the past, Sam would simply react, but now he was now able to step back, share what was happening within him, include others in this process, and link his experience to the group. Anne was able to stop herself in session and say that she felt herself becoming angry in the group and that she was aware this occurs when she feels hurt. Although she was not always clear about what threatened her during the session, she did not immediately feel that she was "bad," was able to identify a familiar pattern, and avoided projecting her anger onto someone else in the group.

FACILITATING GROUP COHESION

One of the most written about curative factors in group therapy is the relationship members develop with the group. According to Mikulincer and Shaver (2007b), group cohesion reflects the degree to which members experience the group as a secure base, similar to an early caregiver, a resource to turn to during times of distress. Despite the much-debated definition of group cohesion (Dion, 2000), it generally describes members' feelings of belonging to the group and their sense of kinship toward other members (Joyce, Piper, & Ogrodniczuk, 2007). According to Yalom and Leszcz (2005), this feeling of "we'ness" is not only a necessary condition for meaningful group work, it is also a prerequisite for change. It sets the foundation for more challenging aspects of group work that require risk taking and tolerance of conflict. G. Corey (2008) agreed and stated that "without a sense of 'groupness' the group remains fragmented, the members become frozen behind their defenses, and their work is of necessity superficial" (p. 111).

Empirical studies have supported the importance of cohesion and have shown that group members who experience more cohesion in their groups are more inclined to weather the ups and downs of the group process (Budman, Soldz, Demby, Davis, & Merry, 1993; Kottler, 1994), effectively expose more vulnerable parts of themselves in the group (Tschuschke & Dies, 1994), and have significantly more change in group therapy regardless of the type of treatment (Joyce et al., 2007; van Andel, Erdman, Karsdorp, Appels, & Trijsburg, 2003). Researchers have also found that group cohesion is related to process variables that include group members' attendance (Connelly, Piper, DeCarufel, & Debanne, 1986), decision to drop out (Hand, Lamontagne, & Marks, 1974), participation in group (Budman et al., 1993), ability to tolerate conflict (MacKenzie, 1994), and satisfaction with the group (Perrone & Sedlacek, 2000). Although many studies support the importance of group cohesion, few have provided empirical support linking attachment styles to the development of group therapy cohesion.

Chen and Mallinckrodt (2002) and Mallinckrodt and Chen (2004) were the first to study the influence of attachment in short-term artificial counseling groups and found that avoidant members of groups were less attracted to the group and less accurate at appraising other members' interpersonal traits. Specifically, Chen and Mallinckrodt studied graduate students participating in an interpersonal group as part of a course requirement. They found that members high in attachment anxiety displayed problematic interpersonal behaviors in the group, such as nonassertiveness, vindictiveness, and intrusiveness. They also found that attachment avoidance was negatively correlated with group attraction, a measure similar to group cohesion. In addition, they found that attachment anxiety and avoidance were both associated with inaccurate perceptions of themselves and others in the group. Anxiously attached members perceived excessive friendliness in others, whereas avoidant group members overestimated hostility in others. These findings support how internal working models influence how group members perceive other group members' behaviors and intentions in the group. These perceptions are likely to influence how one feels about the group members, its leaders, and the group as a whole as well as the development of cohesion. What can the leader do to facilitate cohesion for insecurely attached group members?

Leader Factors That Encourage Cohesion

Burlingame, Fuhriman, and Johnson (2001) emphasized group leader behaviors that engender cohesive groups, captured in six empirically based principles focusing on group leader factors that foster group cohesion. These principles describe how the leader can engender group cohesion through initial group planning, verbal interactions in the group, and the facilitation of emotional intimacy in the group (all of which parallel the curative processes we have focused on throughout this chapter). The principles emphasize the leader being empathic to group members from the moment he or she meets the members during the screening process to the facilitation of deeper emotional experiences later in treatment.

The authors argued that the leader should model here-and-now feedback, guide effective interpersonal exchanges, and foster an environment in which members feel safe. Although they did not address how group members' attachment styles may influence this recommendation, we believe the leader may benefit from being aware of the role attachment styles may play in this process. For example, it may be helpful to consider that insecurely attached group members may be less experienced in giving feedback and more challenged when it comes to receiving feedback. More preoccupied members may avoid giving feedback for fear of being rejected or causing conflict, and they may be more sensitive when receiving feedback as well. More dismissing-avoidant members, like Sam, may withdraw and not fully appreciate the purpose behind interpersonal processes. They may struggle to identify feelings and dismiss the importance of sharing feedback. As we see in the case example, the group leader needed to interrupt the process to provide more assistance to these group members and model helpful ways of interacting effectively. The leader also needed to empathize with members who were negatively affected by insensitive behaviors, like Sam's avoidance or Anne's complaining about outside relationships, and provide more assistance to members as they processed ruptures when they occur to facilitate cohesion. By allowing Sam to express his true feelings in the group rather than detaching brought the group closer and facilitated the cohesion necessary for future risk taking.

Two principles emphasize the importance of the leader being sensitive to the timing of interventions and modeling emotional engagement and presence in the session (Burlingame et al., 2001). We already addressed the importance of the leader considering how best to facilitate insight. In the case examples, we see how the leader intervened differently depending on the group members' ability to process hear-and-now interactions that often stir emotions. The leader also modeled presence when she expressed awareness of the group moving away from enlivening interactions between members both when she spoke to Sam's underlying pain and pushed him to express himself and when she asked Anne what was happening in the relationship that caused Anne to avoid eye contact. All of these interventions facilitated members' becoming more vulnerable and trusting the group, which added to the group cohesion.

Positive Effect of Cohesion

One of the basic notions of Bowlby's (1988) theory is that a secure base facilitates security of attachment, and therefore, a cohesive group should facilitate security of attachment. Rom and Mikulincer (2003) found that cohesion improved the functioning of soldiers who were anxiously attached. A cohesive group bolstered these soldiers, who were seeking a sense of approval and felt security. In essence, the military group functioned as a secure base and reduced the negative impact of the anxiety and distress the anxious soldiers experienced. The group, facilitating a sense of belonging, improved the soldiers' abilities to perform the group tasks.

Although cohesion facilitated the functioning of anxious members, it failed to improve the functioning of avoidant members, who tended to emphasize self-reliance. As a matter of fact, soldiers with avoidant attachments felt worse in cohesive groups because it challenged their internal desire for independence and their negative attitudes toward dependency. This is significant information for group therapists who may assume that all members enjoy the benefits of cohesive groups. In reality, some members are challenged as the group becomes more cohesive, and they may be more at risk of dropping out. If they resist the impulse to leave, however, these members may reap the benefits over time. Dinger and Schauenburg (2010) found that increasing cohesion was especially important to positive changes in more avoidant members where the central problem was related to difficulties with connection. In essence, if these more avoidant members remain in group treatment and face their struggles with intimacy, they increase their sense of belonging in the group, and symptoms are reduced.

CONCLUSION

The movement from an insecure stance predominated by withdrawal or emotional flooding to a more secure stance predominated by engagement and emotional regulation is the main goal of group therapy from an attachment perspective. The leader attempts to help individual members identify attachment-based representations that are quickly enacted within the group, facilitate corrective emotional experiences, and revise anxious and avoidant internal mental models of self and others. The leader's goal is to help the group become a secure base that provides members with a sense of felt security so that they can explore parts of themselves in the process and emotional intimacy within the group can develop.

Riva, Wachtel, and Lasky (2004) argued that "an essential leader behavior is to foster a group climate that is safe, positive, and supportive, yet strong enough to, at times, withstand highly charged emotions, challenges, and interactions between members" (p. 41). The leader's ability to consider the experience of the group and the members at any given time facilitates safety and risk taking.

Through the leader's empathy, the process for exploration becomes possible. Emotional sensitivity in the group fosters regulation and the space to explore the link between emotional responses and thoughts and experiences that are often uncomfortable or out of awareness. Once members feel safe enough to explore their reactions and reflect on their experiences, they gain a sense of self-observation and the capacity to think about their own and others' personal reactions in the group; they gain the ability to mentalize. More important, members repeatedly practice these skills during the group process and begin to develop more sophisticated ways of identifying, expressing, and tolerating emotions in themselves and others. Members learn to become more vulnerable and to explore what inhibits closeness in relationships. Yalom and Leszcz (2005) argued that group members' empathic capacity

> facilitates the transfer of learning from the therapy group to the client's larger world. Without a sense of the internal world of others, relationships are confusing, frustrating, and repetitive as we mindlessly enlist others as players with predetermined roles in our own stories, without regard to their actual motivations and aspirations. (p. 179)

Insights gained through these interpersonal interactions lead to corrective emotional experiences that, over time, become internalized. These new internalized representations of self and other replace previous representations of insecure attachments, and they allow for intimacy and the pursuit of secure adult relationships outside the group. Feeling less alone, being more trusting of others, and experiencing the self as worthwhile not only facilitate the reduction of symptoms but also increase life satisfaction.

6

TREATING THE PREOCCUPIED GROUP MEMBER

Therapy groups that focus on how past attachment experiences are relived within the here and now of group member relationships may be particularly effective for group members with a more preoccupied attachment. We want to remind the reader that although the term *preoccupied* often denotes an attachment category, we define preoccupied members as members who report high levels of attachment anxiety but low attachment avoidance. These individuals often come to group with presenting problems that reflect past attachment traumas and difficulty meeting current attachment needs in interpersonal relationships (Tasca, Illing, Lybanon-Daigle, Bissada, & Balfour, 2003; Tasca, Ritchie, et al., 2006).

This chapter is divided into three parts. First, we discuss the dynamics that are likely to unfold between group members with a more preoccupied attachment and the group as a whole and between more preoccupied members and other members of similar and different attachments. Second, we outline

http://dx.doi.org/10.1037/14186-007
Attachment in Group Psychotherapy, by C. L. Marmarosh, R. D. Markin, and E. B. Spiegel
Copyright © 2013 by the American Psychological Association. All rights reserved.

group therapy goals for more preoccupied members and offer suggestions on how group therapy can facilitate the achievement of these goals. Last, a case example is used to illustrate attachment-related problems for more preoccupied group members as well as possible group leader interventions.

PREOCCUPIED MEMBERS AND THE GROUP

Patients with more preoccupied attachments are often experts in reading what other people want from them, and they are skilled at charming others, at least initially (Wallin, 2007). These individuals have developed expertise in pleasing others because in childhood they had to read the mood and state of mind of their caregivers carefully to have their attachment needs met (Connors, 2011; Dozier, Stovall, & Albus, 1999). For this reason, more preoccupied members are initially well liked by the group because they are perhaps overattuned to the wishes and needs of others. Part of the preoccupied member's initial charm is that he or she often comes across as vulnerable and needing to be cared for in relationships. In response, the group can be pulled to "rescue" the preoccupied group member, treating him or her as helpless and emotionally fragile (Wallin, 2007). Consistent with this, Mikulincer (1998) found that when individuals who reported higher attachment anxiety were under stress, they magnified their perceived deficiencies and attempted to engage others to gain their compassion and support. The following example illustrates this dynamic.

Challenges to Cohesion

In one therapy group, the members develop a norm for calling each other out, fueled by some underlying hostility and competitiveness. One particular group member, however, is spared from this dynamic and always seems to get a pass from the group. When the group leader points out how this group member is treated differently and somehow seems untouchable, the other members reply that although they are personally "strong enough to take it," they feel that she is so "sensitive," "sweet," and "emotional" that they have to take care of her and protect her. In return for taking care of and protecting this "helpless" group member, the others feel needed, stronger, more competent, and special. Because the more preoccupied member is adept at mirroring members and making them feel special and validated, to challenge her would risk their place on the pedestal on which she has placed them. However, by protecting this group member, they unintentionally reinforce her image of herself as fragile and helpless.

The initial charm of group members with a more preoccupied attachment belies a host of attachment insecurities. As these attachment insecurities play out within member-to-member relationships, the group is likely to move from feeling protective of and close to the preoccupied member to becoming frustrated with and even resentful of him or her. More preoccupied individuals tend to seek unqualified closeness in romantic relationships, are preoccupied and jealous, and tend to idealize their partners and rely excessively on them (Feeney & Noller, 1990). Typically, these traits eventually make others feel suffocated, frustrated, and resentful of the individual's constant need for reassurance and closeness, both within the therapy group and in other relationships outside the group (Bartholomew & Horowitz, 1991). In group, other members eventually withdraw from the more preoccupied member's intensity and neediness, as do significant others outside of the group. Sadly, this dramatic shift from initially feeling close to and cared for by the group to feeling rejected by and distant from it recapitulates early familial dynamics in which the more preoccupied member's attachment needs were attended to inconsistently by a caregiver.

The group's conflicting feelings toward the preoccupied group member parallel the preoccupied member's mixed feelings toward the group. Because preoccupied group members have a tendency to idealize others and crave connections, they are likely initially to perceive the group in a positive light and to quickly develop intense feelings of connectedness and belonging to the group (Bartholomew & Horowitz, 1991; Rom & Mikulincer, 2003). Accordingly, preoccupied group members have been found to form personal goals around maintaining closeness to the group (Rom & Mikulincer, 2003). However, over time, these members often become angry over perceived slights from others and feel rejected and disappointed by individual group members or leaders and/or the group itself (Bartholomew & Horowitz, 1991; Smith, Murphy, & Coats, 1999). The tendency for preoccupied group members to hold positive and negative feelings about the group is supported by research showing that more preoccupied individuals hold positive and negative views of their romantic partner on conscious and implicit levels and feel ambivalent about their motivation for closeness because of past traumatic attachment experiences (Mikulincer, Shaver, Bar-On, & Ein-Dor, 2010).

Interactions With Other Group Members

How individual group members respond to more preoccupied members may depend, in part, on the other group members' attachments. Specifically, group members with a more dismissing-avoidant style may feel frustrated or even disgusted with more preoccupied members' intense need for closeness.

More dismissing-avoidant members are ashamed of and disown their attachment needs. Thus, to see these needs amplified in another person may feel threatening to a more dismissing-avoidant group member. In contrast, more preoccupied members may feel a sense of affiliation with one another and join together in an implicit agreement to soothe one another's attachment anxiety, which could be "good" in the sense that their attachment needs are met or "bad" in the sense that these attachment insecurities are amplified rather than challenged. Interestingly, in several groups the authors have led, multiple preoccupied members in the same group have been helpful to each other in that each individual mirrored back to the other how he or she came across in relationships. For example, Susan and Shannon became fast friends in the group, constantly affirming and validating one another and making grand gestures of caring and support for the other. However, as group progressed, little by little, Shannon grew frustrated with Susan's constant need for reassurance from her. Eventually, when the group leader asked if there was some underlying tension in their relationship, Shannon replied, "I now know what it's like to be in a relationship with me, and I would leave myself too!" Seeing a reflection of herself in Susan gave Shannon insight into how she came across in relationships, motivating her to try different interpersonal behaviors.

Interpersonal Strengths

It is important to appreciate the strengths that preoccupied group members bring to the group and not just the interpersonal struggles with which they often enter group therapy. Although every individual has his or her own unique strengths, some generalizations may apply across members with a more preoccupied attachment. More preoccupied members are often the most dedicated group members, never missing a session and always checking in with others and showing concern (Pistole, 1997). Tasca, Taylor, Bissada, Ritchie, and Balfour (2004) found evidence to suggest that more anxious members are less likely to drop out of group therapy because of their fear of losing the treatment relationship. Harel, Shechtman, and Cutrona (2011) found that more anxious group members in supportive-expressive–type therapy groups were more likely both to receive support from the group and to provide support to other members. This study speaks to the notion that although more anxious patients often come across as needy, constantly eliciting positive support from others (Brennan, Clark, & Shaver, 1998), their tendency to also give support to others is an interpersonal strength and a positive ingroup behavior. For members with a more preoccupied attachment, their greatest interpersonal struggle—that is, the ability and desire to care and connect with personal others and groups—is also their greatest interpersonal strength.

GROUP THERAPY GOALS FOR THE MORE PREOCCUPIED GROUP MEMBERS

Increasing Mentalization

Because of their early attachment experiences with a preoccupied and inconsistent attachment figure, more preoccupied group members have a difficult time regulating and making meaning out of their intense emotional experiences or appreciating the thoughts and feelings of others (Fonagy, Gergely, Jurist, & Target, 2002; Fosha, 2000; Main, Goldwyn, & Hesse, 2003; Tasca, Foot, et al., 2011). Difficulty recognizing and describing both one's own thoughts and feelings and those of others limits the ability of more preoccupied group members to form intimate relationships, both inside and outside of the group, and to make use of group therapy (Tasca, Foot, et al., 2011). We suggest that the group leader can help facilitate mentalization in more preoccupied members by verbalizing feelings, facilitating group member insight into the feelings that underlie behaviors, and encouraging interpersonal feedback within the here and now of the group. These three processes help interrupt more preoccupied members' concern about self-criticism and anger toward others over perceived slights, which typically interfere with reflective functioning (Tasca, Foot, et al., 2011).

Verbalizing Feelings: Putting Emotional Experiences Into Words

More preoccupied patients have a difficult time using language to verbalize their emotional experiences (Tasca, Foot, et al., 2011; Wallin, 2007). As a result, they have difficulty gaining enough distance from their feelings to cognitively reflect on them and may become overwhelmed by their emotions (Mikulincer & Florian, 1998; Mikulincer, Shaver, Sapir-Lavid, & Avihou-Kanza, 2009). Other group members, as well as the leaders, can model how to verbalize and reflect on one's feelings. In fact, Yalom and Leszcz (2005) noted that imitating behavior is a major therapeutic factor in group therapy. By asking questions, offering interpretations, sharing personal experiences, and giving suggestions and guidance, the group can also help more preoccupied members explore and identify their feelings. The following vignette demonstrates the difficulty more preoccupied members have verbalizing and reflecting on their emotional experiences and suggests how the group can help these members build their reflective functioning abilities by putting their emotional experiences into words.

Case Example: Developing Mentalization in Group

Alice, a more preoccupied group member, became instantly self-critical when John expressed disappointment in the group and immediately blamed herself for his discontent. Her automatic reaction was to try to alleviate his anger and disappointment to preserve her own sense of safety in the relationship. In the group, however, a third group member, Tom, challenged John about his disappointment and asked if it was possible that John had not gotten anything from the group because he had yet to "put himself out there." This direct confrontation allowed Alice to consider an alternative to her knee-jerk reaction of self-blame.

The group leader took this opportunity to ask Alice directly if even a small part of her felt angry toward John. In general, Alice was disconnected from her feelings of anger because she feared that expressing anger would lead to others abandoning her. Instead of expressing anger in a healthy way, she would internalize her anger and become plagued by self-condemnation. However, seeing another group member model healthy confrontation, coupled with prompting by the group leader, helped Alice to reflect more deeply on her emotional reactions in the moment and put them into words.

Facilitating Insight Into Underlying Feelings

When individuals have a difficult time reflecting on and understanding their feelings, thoughts, and behaviors, they often engage in self-destructive behaviors impulsively, without knowing why they did so. It is essential for the group, with the group leader's guidance, to be curious and offer interpretations that help the more preoccupied members reflect on their experience, so that they ultimately achieve some insight into the feelings that underlie their behaviors.

Case Example: Achieving Insight in Group

Casey, a more preoccupied group member, could not understand why she overdosed on medication after last week's group session. Instead, in the group session, she cycled through self-criticism and anger over what she perceived to be her roommate's lack of caring. She did not directly address her anger at the other group members for her perception of their lack of caring. Instead, she focused on her anger at herself and her roommate. The group leader attempted to interrupt Casey's self-criticism and anger by asking her, "I wonder why you overdosed after last week's group? Could it have something to do with your feelings about the group last week?" Essentially, the group leader, with the help of the group, facilitated Casey's ability to step back and reflect on the underlying feelings and motivations and gain insight into her self-destructive or maladaptive behaviors.

Encouraging Interpersonal Feedback

Interpersonal feedback, delivered within the here and now, can facilitate reflective functioning by helping the group member receiving the feedback to empathize with other members' states of mind. In group therapy, more preoccupied patients have the opportunity to check their perception of another member's thoughts and feelings. This process is key for those who have a difficult time describing the thoughts and feelings of others and how these are experienced in the minds of others (Fonagy et al., 2002). Feedback from other group members about how they experience the more preoccupied member can help build reflective functioning.

Case Example: Building Mentalization Through
Group Member Interpersonal Feedback

Alice was hypersensitive to rejection from other members. She was particularly fearful of being rejected by Ben, who had a family history of feeling like a disappointment to others. Some of the other group members were encouraging Ben to express his feelings of anger directly rather than feeling disappointed in himself. Ben turned to Alice and said, "I feel like you are always watching me, just waiting for me to do something to hurt you. It feels like a test, which makes me want to keep my distance from you." The group leader went on to help Alice develop her reflective functioning abilities by asking her how she thought Ben felt about her in that moment and then asked Ben if Alice's perception was accurate. This process allowed Alice to check her perception of another person's feelings and intentions against interpersonal feedback from that other person, helping her to comprehend another person's state of mind more accurately. In response to the group leader's inquiry, Alice hyperfocused in on Ben's negative feedback and imagined that Ben hated her. However, Ben clarified that he really wanted to please Alice and felt inadequate when he could not seem to find the right words to comfort her. Because Ben's interpersonal feedback challenged Alice's negative view of herself and her perception of others' feelings and motivations, his feedback helped Alice to better recognize and depict the thoughts and feelings others and to begin to challenge her negative view of herself.

Helping Preoccupied Group Members Regulate Affect

To paraphrase Diana Fosha (2003), more preoccupied group members *feel* (and *reel*) but they do not *deal*. Consistent with this, patients with a preoccupied attachment have been found to exhibit out-of-control emotions and poor self-regulatory skills and to exaggerate negative affect (Mikulincer &

Florian, 1998; Mikulincer et al., 2009). These patients may exaggerate negative affect because they readily and repeatedly reaccess painful attachment-related memories, which maintains their constant agitated state (Mikulincer, 1995). In group therapy, more preoccupied members may thus overwhelm themselves and the group with the intensity of their emotions and their dependency needs. Tasca, Foot, et al. (2011) suggested that the intense emotions experienced by preoccupied group members need to be "downregulated." However, we propose that although preoccupied group members need to learn to experience certain emotions less, they actually need to learn to experience other kinds of emotions more.

As described in Chapter 5 of this volume, Fosha (2000) distinguished between *core affects* that when experienced are mutative and healing for the patient, and *defensive emotions*, which mask or guard against these underlying core affective experiences. She defined core *affective experience* as "all aspects of emotional life experienced directly and viscerally, in the absence of defenses and anxiety-including, but not necessarily limited to, categorical emotions and self and relational affective experiences" (Fosha, 2000, p. 16). In contrast, defensive affects occur when "the individual leads with one affect so as not to feel another, feared to be more painful" (p. 115). Fosha (2000) also described *red signal affects*, such as anxiety, fear, and shame, that are experienced intensely enough to "signal psychic threat" (p. 114). We propose that more preoccupied group members need help "downregulating" defensive emotions and red signal affects and "upregulating" core affective experiences.

How can group leaders distinguish between emotions that are defensive and need to be lessened and emotions that are core and need to be intensified for group members with more attachment anxiety? Wallin (2007) argued that more anxious patients have learned to exclude rage and loss from conscious awareness because these emotions were not empathically responded to in early attachment relationships, a process Bowlby (1988) called *defensive exclusion*. Patients with more preoccupied attachments may escalate feelings of anger toward the self, as self-criticism, to defend against these core emotions of rage, authentic loss, and sadness, which felt unsafe to experience in early attachment relationships. Maintaining a constant state of anger and disappointment in others and in oneself is by no means pleasant, but that patient may consider these emotions more bearable than the underlying feelings of rage and loss. Essentially, the more preoccupied group member leads with anger and self-criticism to keep from feeling the more unbearable feelings associated with past attachment traumas. Similarly, the more preoccupied group member's overwhelming anxiety over rejection may be conceptualized as a red signal affect that alerts him or her to real or imagined threats of loss and abandonment. Although this anxiety serves the purpose of protecting more preoccupied members from further loss and rejection, red signal anxiety is problematic for these patients because it leaves them feeling constantly threatened and needing to defend themselves against possible losses (Mikulincer & Shaver, 2003).

Self-criticism, anger, and fear of rejection often interfere with more preoccupied group members' ability to reflect on their emotional experiences (Tasca, Foot, et al., 2011). This may be viewed as a process in which more preoccupied members' defensive and red signal affects interfere with their ability to experience and process core affects. In Fosha's (2000) model, when expressed and processed to completion, core affects lead to an experientially different place. In contrast, defensive emotions and red signal affects linger, and the experience of these emotions is often described by group leaders and members as "going around in circles," "not going anywhere," and "being stuck" (Fosha, 2000, p. 17). In this sense, more preoccupied group members may appear to "reel in" their emotions (or, more specifically, their feelings of helplessness, anger, self-loathing, and anxiety) and exhibit poor reflective functioning abilities, frustrating the group because they cannot move past these defensive affects to the underlying core affective experiences. How can group leaders help members with a preoccupied attachment dial down defensive emotions so that core emotions can be experienced and processed within the safety of the group? The group leader may choose to interpret the defensive function of defensive or red signal affects (Fosha, 2000).

Case Example: Interpreting Defensive Affect to Help Regulate Group Member Affect

Jane, a more preoccupied group member, pressed the group for specific advice and support on what she should do about a conflict with her boss. The rest of the group grew frustrated with her passive role in solving this problem and her continued pressure on them to offer advice. The group leader noticed this dynamic and chose to interpret the defensive function of Jane's feeling of helplessness. She asked,

> Jane, I wonder if it is difficult for you to look within yourself for answers to this very personal problem because there is this fear inside of you that worries that if you do, we won't be around to help you anymore if you should need us?

This interpretation allowed Jane to get in touch with her deep-rooted fear of abandonment, and the group leader helped Jane explore her fears as they played out in the group. Moving past her stance of helplessness and emotionality to explore her fears and insecurities openly allowed the group to feel empathy for Jane and support her more effectively.

Alternatively, a group leader might attempt to bypass the defensive emotions all together (Fosha, 2000). For example, when the group tried to help Jane explore her feelings about her boss, Jane became preoccupied with the fear that the group was annoyed with her, just like her boss. Jane's anxiety over the group's rejection kept her from reflecting on the feelings about her relationship with her boss. The group leader attempted to bypass Jane's anxiety altogether and asked,

> Jane, it seems like when we try to help you reflect on your feelings about something, this anxiety over rejection gets stronger and keeps us from understanding what's going on for you. Are you willing to put this anxiety aside for just a few minutes so we can all try to better understand what is happening for you?

With preoccupied group members, who fear rejection, it is important for the group leader to empathize with their attempts to explore and expand on their feelings (Prenn, 2011). As the group leader, it is critical to keep in mind that preoccupied group members typically defend against experiencing their full range of emotions. Intense and authentic sadness, rage, and loss often lie underneath these patients' carefully crafted defenses. It is essential that the group leader help the group to act as a secure attachment figure for the preoccupied member, empathizing with, validating, and containing his or her core affects as they arise in the group.

Reducing Fear of Loss and Abandonment: Group Cohesion and the Wish to Belong

Experiencing a sense of safety and belonging within a cohesive therapy group may attenuate anxious members' fear of loss and abandonment and their neediness in interpersonal relationships (Tasca, Foot, et al., 2011). From an attachment perspective, group cohesion reflects the degree to which the participants perceive the group as a potential secure base or safe haven that provides a sense of safety, belonging, and intimacy (Mikulincer & Shaver, 2007a). Although group members with an anxious attachment are likely to project onto the group their mental representation of others as rejecting and disappointing, Mikulincer and Shaver (2007a) suggested that a highly cohesive group may moderate these projections, leading anxious members to develop a more secure attachment to the group despite their generally insecure internal working models. Consistent with this, Rom and Mikulincer (2003) found that group cohesion improved the socioemotional and instrumental functioning of group members and reduced the detrimental effects of attachment anxiety on instrumental functioning during group tasks. One interpretation of these findings is that the experience of cohesion signaled support, closeness, and consensus to the more preoccupied group members, giving them the freedom to concentrate less on their fears of rejection and loss and more on the tasks of the group. Similarly, group cohesion may provide more preoccupied members with the necessary sense of safety and belonging to engage in the therapeutic tasks of group therapy. To facilitate a preoccupied member's experience of group cohesion, a group leader may ask,

> Tim, I hear the group saying that they really missed you last week when you didn't come to group because you are a vital part of this group. What is it like for you to be a part of something and to hear this feedback?

Essentially, group cohesion may free more preoccupied members to explore alternative ways of perceiving, feeling, and interacting with the group that challenges their insecure internal working model (Mikulincer & Shaver, 2007a; Rom & Mikulincer, 2003). Group cohesion may facilitate more secure internal working models for more preoccupied members because it provides them with the sense of belonging and acceptance that they did not experience in childhood. Feeling like a part of a larger group may challenge more preoccupied members' belief that they are fundamentally unlovable and that others will reject or abandon them, while shaping a more positive view of the self as someone worthy of group membership.

Case Example: A Preoccupied Group Member

Krista was a 22-year-old woman diagnosed with generalized anxiety disorder and described by both her individual and subsequent group therapist as possessing a "histrionic-like personality," characterized by excessive emotionality and attention-seeking behaviors (American Psychiatric Association, 2000). She had a history of excessive alcohol use and self-cutting. She also had a history of bingeing and purging, although these symptoms were not active during her time in the group. At the prescreen interview, Krista told the group leader that she wanted to join the therapy group because she often felt overwhelmed by anxiety, did not like or know herself, and felt cut off from herself. Despite her presenting problems, Krista was an exceptional doctoral student in physics with a competitive research grant. She worked in the research laboratory of a professor in her PhD program, whom she said she looked up to as a father figure. On first impression, Krista presented as likable, cooperative, motivated for treatment, and easy to get along with. However, underneath the compliant exterior were deep attachment insecurities.

Krista described her father as available and loving but only when she expressed an interest in his pursuits. According to Krista, her father was a "huge narcissist" who would disappear for weeks at a time with no explanation. Upon his return from these prolonged absences, he would shower her with presents and attention, calling Krista his "best girl." It was when discussing her mother that Krista became the most emotionally charged and overwhelmed. She told the group that her mother has been depressed "on and off" for as long as she could remember. Krista described her relationship with her mother as incredibly close and more "like friends than your typical mother–daughter relationship." However, Krista often became preoccupied with feelings of anger toward her mother, saying she did not allow Krista to be herself or "grow up." In the past, Krista's attempts to express her independence and autonomy were met with feelings of rage from her mother, which caused Krista to feel guilty and anxious. Similarly, in the therapy group, as soon as Krista started to feel angry, she immediately experienced guilt and anxiety before she had the chance to fully experience her anger.

Not surprisingly, Krista's romantic relationship history was fraught with complications. She reported a series of intense but short-lived romantic relationships in which she changed herself to please her boyfriend. She reported having sexual relations early in relationships to foster commitment, but she typically ended up feeling rejected by men despite her efforts to please them. She tended to be attracted to men who were more detached and in control of their emotions, something she admired in them.

In the first few sessions of group therapy, Krista self-disclosed her feelings, made connections between group members, supported other members, expressed her desire for intimacy in the group, and even made a few helpful process comments about members' interactions. At first, the leader was delighted to have her in the group. However, as group progressed, Krista's attachment dynamics were triggered and re-created within the social microcosm of the group (Yalom & Leszcz, 2005). Krista became increasingly frustrated that group members failed to reveal more or make more gestures toward establishing intimacy, and her frustration was expressed passive aggressively. When the group participants commented on their perception that she seemed frustrated, Krista ardently denied this, profusely apologized, and expressed an overwhelming fear of offending the group. In general, Krista was preoccupied with the fear of offending group members and with being rejected by them.

Krista often projected her fear that others hated her onto the group, which was actually indicative of her own self-hatred. When Krista was by herself, she felt lonely and anxious; she drank or cut herself to cope with her emotions. Underneath her anxiety and panic over being alone was her negative view of herself and her fear that others would reject her. Her feelings of loneliness were not helped by the fact that she tended to seek out individuals who cannot meet her attachment needs for some reason. At the same time, she often failed to notice instances in which her attachment needs were being met, such as when other group members showed her support and caring. Krista's tendency to magnify instances of rejection and minimize instances of support and caring made sense in light of her early attachment experiences, in which her attachment objects were preoccupied, inconsistent, and unempathic. In what follows, we use the case of Krista to illustrate attachment-related problems for group members with a more preoccupied attachment and offer possible group leader interventions.

Reflective Functioning and Mentalizing

Because Krista's primary attachment figures did not accurately empathize with or emotionally regulate her as a child, she never learned to reflect on her feelings, desires, and intentions as separate from those of others. Experiencing her rage toward her parents was too threatening for Krista, so she internalized this rage and blamed herself (Fonagy et al., 2002). As one might expect, in the therapy group, rather than engaging in self-reflection, Krista would become self-critical, which effectively put a stop to deeper exploration. The group leader's goal was to help Krista gain some distance from her overwhelming emotions by interrupting her self-criticism and examining the feelings and reasons behind her behaviors (Tasca, Foot, et al., 2011). In the following vignette, the group leader uses group member feedback to help Krista reflect on and cognitively understand the feelings and intentions of others as well as her own.

Lucy: I can tell that Krista cut herself, and it really scares me.

Leader: Krista, how does it feel to hear that you cutting yourself makes Lucy scared? [*The group leader encourages Krista to reflect on her emotional reactions in relation to the feelings of another person.*]

Krista: I feel really bad. Like I'm a drain on the group and I'm afraid that you are all going to hate me now for putting you through this. [*Krista cannot differentiate between her own self-hatred and the feelings and intentions of others in the group. She also avoids Lucy's concern for her.*]

Leader: Krista, you mentioned the group hating you, but what do you feel about what Lucy just said? You said you feel bad. Can you say more?

Krista: I feel bad, but I guess I am not really sure why she is scared.

Leader: Lucy, can you say more to Krista about what scares you?

Lucy: Well, I worry that Krista will hurt herself by accident. I also imagine that she is in a lot of pain. She does not really talk about that, but I can imagine it when I see her scars. [*Lucy is modeling reflective functioning by seeing below the surface and identifying the painful emotions motivating the self-destructive behaviors.*]

Krista: That makes me feel awful. I do not want to worry you. I am sure you wish I would leave the group so you would not have to deal with me.

Leader: Krista, it occurs to me that your self-criticism gets in the way of you taking in the more positive feelings associated with Lucy's feedback—that is, that she is genuinely concerned. What do you think makes it difficult to hear this? [Here Krista's self-criticism gets in the way of her appreciating the mental state—feelings, intentions—of Lucy because she projects her self-hatred onto Lucy. The group leader encourages Krista to reflect on this process.]

Krista: You're right. I just can't believe you care. It is easier to think you wish I was gone. I just automatically imagine you think I am awful to be with [looking at Lucy].

Lucy: I do not think you're awful at all. I really worry that you will eventually hurt yourself. I know that sometimes it's hard for me to take in the good things that people say about me because I have my father's critical voice in my head, maybe that's the way it is for you, Krista? [Lucy, a more secure member, models reflective functioning and challenges Krista's negative internal working model of others that anticipates rejection, interfering with Lucy's ability to accurately appreciate the feelings and intentions of others.]

Leader: I appreciate you sharing that, Lucy. Krista, I know it's hard, but I'm going to ask you to put your self-criticism aside for just a few moments and take in Lucy's feedback that she is worried about you. With self-criticism aside, how did you feel the moment after Lucy said she worries about you? [The group leader asks Krista to put self-criticism aside to reflect upon and identify her feelings.]

Krista is touched that Lucy genuinely cares about her, and the group leader helps Krista process this new and corrective experience of feeling less lonely, supported, and cared for. In the process, Krista is better able to reflect on her own feelings that arose in this interaction with Lucy and depict the feelings and intentions of Lucy.

Poor Self-Regulation of Emotion

For patients like Krista, with a preoccupied attachment, negative emotions are identified but become escalated and maximized to the point where the patient feels out of control (Mikulincer et al., 2009; Mikulincer & Florian, 1998). Without the ability to make sense of or reflect on their emotions, anxious patients are often overwhelmed by them, sometimes leading to destructive, yet momentarily self-soothing, behaviors. Krista relied on drinking, cutting, sexual acting out, and, in the past, bingeing and purging to regulate her emotions. This is consistent with a study by Tasca et al. (2009) that found evidence to suggest that patients with an eating disorder and attachment anxiety experience hyperactivation of emotions that may result in symptoms of bingeing and purging perhaps as a way to cope.

Consistent with Fosha's (2000) theory on different types of emotional experiences elaborated on in the previous section, Krista was stuck in a defensive place emotionally and was blocked off from her core affect, cycling around and around between helplessness, self-loathing, and anxiety over being rejected. Here the group leader's goal was to help diminish Krista's defensive emotions and red signal anxiety so that core affective experiences could emerge and could be worked through and processed to completion, interrupting the overwhelming and endless cycle of anger, disappointment, and self-loathing.

Leader: Krista, it seems like when we get to this place of trying to understand your feelings and behaviors in the group, anger, toward yourself and your mom, comes in the room and distracts us. I know it's hard, but if you weren't feeling angry with yourself or with your mom, how would you feel right now? [*The group leader points out defensive emotions and asks the patient to put them aside so core affects can surface.*]

Krista: I don't know. I'm confused. What does this have to do with my professor? [*The patient's defenses are activated upon the leader's request to put defensive emotions aside.*]

Leader: Confusion . . . self-criticism . . . anger. . . . I wonder if these are all ways of protecting yourself from some painful feelings. Just for a moment, let's try and put them aside and understand what's going on for you now. Is it OK if we try that together? [*The group leader interprets defensive affect and tries again to bypass defensive emotions with the patient's permission.*]

Krista: [*pause*] I just feel empty and lonely and like really in need (*starts to cry*). [*The patient's core affects start to surface, which are then elaborated on and validated within the group.*]

Leader: Who in here do you feel least lonely with? [*The group leader hopes to facilitate a corrective emotional experience in which Krista experiences a secure attachment relationship and feels safe to express core affect.*]

Krista: I guess Kim.

Leader: Can you tell Kim how you are feeling right now?

Krista: [*looking at Kim.*] Sometimes I just feel so empty. I hate being by myself, it's like being with a stranger. I know it sounds pathetic but sometimes I just want a hug.

Leader:	Kim, what is your reaction to Krista right now?
Kim:	I feel sad for her. I want to give her a hug.
Leader:	How does that make you feel, Krista?
Krista:	I feel anxious. I can feel my whole body tense. I don't want to be a burden to you, Kim. I'm afraid you might abandon me if I become too much for you. [red signal anxiety]
Leader:	If you weren't feeling anxious, what would it feel like to know Kim wanted to hug you? [The group leader asks Krista to put red signal anxiety aside.]
Krista:	Amazing . . . less lonely [getting in touch with core affect].

The group continues to help Krista to more deeply experience and process her core emotions as they arise. With anxiety and self-criticism aside, Krista is able to get in touch with core emotions related to feeling accepted and cared for by Kim but also her deep loss over not having this type of attachment relationship in the past.

Fear of One's Own Autonomy and Individuation

As a child, Krista quickly learned that dependency was reinforced with attention and affection, whereas separation was punished with abandonment, rage, or rejection. With both her mother and father, dependency and merger were reinforced, and Krista's autonomy and individual sense of self were defensively excluded. Krista's anxiety over challenging the group and expressing her opinions and needs is likely a result of these early attachment experiences in which autonomous expressions were punished by caregivers. In the vignette that follows, the group leader's goal was to help the group use conflict to enhance intimacy and group cohesion so that preoccupied members like Krista have experiences in which separateness and assertiveness do not lead to abandonment as feared but rather to enhanced closeness.

During the storming stage of the group, a conflict arose between members who wanted to continue the group and thought it was helpful and members who wanted to terminate the group and believed the therapy to be ineffective. Krista blamed herself for those members who wanted to leave. Although most members denied negative feelings toward her, a more dismissing-avoidant group member, Chris, told Krista that he found her neediness excessive and would probably not be friends with her if they met outside of the group. In response to this, Krista looked Chris directly in his eyes and asked, "Why do you hate me so much?" She immediately ran out of the group room crying. The group leader left the room and tried to encourage Krista to come back into the group; however, the group session ended, and the interaction would need to be processed next week. As seen in the vignette that follows, at the beginning of the next group session, Krista quickly and fervently began berating herself for what transpired with Chris, blaming herself for the entire interaction and the conflict that ensued.

Krista: I just want to apologize again to the group for my comments last week.

Chris: I don't understand. You said that you felt that we were being superficial and now you are saying that you didn't mean that?

Krista: I'm so sorry! Sometimes stupid things come out of my mouth.

Alice: Well, I did kind of feel like we were talking about surface stuff last week.

Chris: Well, I didn't feel that way!

Krista: Please stop arguing about this! I shouldn't have said anything.

Chris: I feel like you are lying, Krista. Just tell us how you really feel!

Krista: I am not lying. I can't believe you would even say that. *[tearing up]*

Leader: Krista, I know you are hurt, but I think it's important to think more about what Chris is expressing in here. Chris, you sound very angry at Krista. Something about Krista saying the group was being superficial last week and now apologizing is making you very upset.

Chris: Well, I feel as though she is just apologizing to avoid making people angry. It does not feel genuine.

Alice: I feel that way, too. I want to talk more about the group and the way that Krista felt about it last week. Krista, I was glad you said what you did, and I want to talk more about it.

Leader: It sounds like all of you are expressing the desire to say what you feel and to be honest in here. Even if it is uncomfortable and causes conflict. Krista, it seems like when you expressed a different opinion from others in the group, that you felt pretty anxious and quickly took it back. As a result, we don't always get to see the stronger, more assertive side of you. What do you think feels scary about showing those parts of yourself to the group?

Krista: I don't know. I have a hard time trusting people. I hear that the group wants me to say what I really think or feel. I just worry that I will end up being punished if I do. I worry that everyone is angry with each other now because of me and somehow I'll get in trouble for it.

Alice: I was not really angry at Chris today, I just didn't agree with him. I'm definitely not angry with you for expressing your opinion. I admired you for saying what you did last week. To be honest, I felt disappointed when you took it back this week.

Krista: [tearing up] I have never heard that before. That you admired me. I left here last week worrying that you would hate me.

Hyperactivating Strategies

Patients like Krista, with a preoccupied attachment, attempt to minimize emotional distance to regulate their anxiety over loss and rejection (Bartholomew & Horowitz, 1991). Preoccupied patients tend to overemphasize the risks associated with interpersonal relationships (Boon & Griffin, 1996). Thus, they maintain their attachment system in an activated state, characterized by heightened vigilance regarding actual and potential attachment threats and physical and psychological proximity-seeking strategies (Mikulincer & Shaver, 2003). Krista's motto when it came to relationships was, "The best offense is a good defense!" She brushed over the other members' and leaders' behaviors with a fine-tooth comb for possible signs of rejection. Sadly, these hyperactivating strategies had the unintended consequence of pushing others in the group away, the very result that Krista feared. Here, the group leader's goal is to facilitate experiences within the group that reduce the more preoccupied member's fear of rejection and loss, rendering hyperactivating strategies in interpersonal relationships no longer necessary.

Processing group member feedback in the here and now challenged Krista's insecure internal working models. Several group members gave Krista feedback, noting that they felt frustrated with her continually pressing them for reassurance, they felt closer to her when she was not seeking reassurance, and they felt their concern for her went unrecognized. Although this feedback was initially hurtful to Krista, the group leader helped her to see that, from this feedback, she did not need to work so hard to be accepted by the group, unlike her experiences with her parents where she had to be continually vigilant to get her attachment needs met.

Surprisingly, the most powerful corrective emotional experience for Krista arose from feedback from Chris, a more dismissing-avoidant group member, who once looked down on Krista's desire for intimacy and need for reassurance. Chris made great strides in group therapy, and these gains allowed him to see Krista and his reactions to her from a different perspective. Upon terminating from the group, Chris revealed to Krista,

> I think it was scary for me to see you so eager to be close to others in the group. I was afraid of getting suffocated, but there was also a small part of me that was envious of how easily you felt close to people because it has always been so hard for me.

Hearing this feedback from Chris brought tears to Krista's eyes. Unlike Krista's parents, Chris was able to own how his attachment insecurities prevented him from meeting Krista's attachment needs, challenging Krista's self-critical belief that it was her fault that others have failed to meet these precious needs. Furthermore, Chris's feedback that he actually admired Krista's comfort with closeness greatly challenged her view of others as disapproving and rejecting and, unlike previous attachment experiences, made her feel valued and cared for.

CONCLUSION

This chapter sought to capture and describe the plight of the more preoccupied group member, who often feels as if she might fall apart if left alone, rejected, or abandoned. Her sense of self is so dependent on the approval of others that to be alone brings up feelings of desperate need and palpable anxiety. Group therapy has the unique power to alleviate these patients' attachment anxieties by providing them with a sense of belonging and acceptance not previously experienced. Group therapy also provides these patients with interpersonal feedback that calls into question their insecure internal working models while facilitating more secure internal working models, characterized by trust in others' and in their own strengths and intrinsic value. In the case of Krista, we see an individual plagued with self-doubt and a fear of abandonment who is so overwhelmed by her emotions that she resorts to acting-out behaviors to cope with her inner world. However, we also see how the group in many ways serves as a secure attachment object for Krista, helping her to regulate her emotions and form healthy attachments based on a more flexible model of others as available and the self as competent and worthy.

7

TREATING THE DISMISSING-AVOIDANT GROUP MEMBER

This chapter focuses on more dismissing-avoidant group members—those members with high attachment avoidance and low attachment anxiety. We focus on how these members relate to others in the group and how group therapy can facilitate changes for them by enacting past working models of self and other in the group. The chapter is divided into three parts. First, we discuss dynamics that are likely to unfold between group members with a more dismissing-avoidant attachment and the group. Second, we describe how the leader's attachment influences the work with more dismissive group members. Finally, we outline group therapy goals for more dismissing-avoidant members and offer suggestions on how group therapy can facilitate the achievement of these goals. A case example is used to illustrate attachment-related problems for more dismissing-avoidant group members as well as possible group leader interventions.

http://dx.doi.org/10.1037/14186-008
Attachment in Group Psychotherapy, by C. L. Marmarosh, R. D. Markin, and E. B. Spiegel

THE MORE DISMISSIVE MEMBERS AND THE GROUP

According to Wallin (2007), more dismissing-avoidant patients often avoid emotions that stir up feelings of vulnerability, and they have a particularly difficult time coping with these emotions when they are stirred up in treatment. Rather than expressing their internal experiences verbally, they often rely on subtle cues to express their underlying emotions (Guerrero, 1996; Wallin, 2007). These patients are more inclined to say everything is fine while clenching their fists, averting eye contact, or smiling during emotionally painful interactions. Dismissive adults prefer more physical distance from others (Kaitz, Bar-Him, Lehrer, & Grossman, 2004) and demonstrate less facial gazing, vocal and physical supportiveness, and listening to their partners in videos interacting with a romantic partner (Guerrero, 1996).

In addition, these more dismissing-avoidant individuals often engage in defensive self-enhancement, which means they suppress negative aspects of themselves and instead focus on their strengths (Mikulincer & Shaver, 2007b). The simultaneous suppression of negative emotions and expression of grandiosity further mask any aspect of a true self. The avoidance of emotions and self-inflation are examples of the deactivation that characterizes these individuals. They have learned to dismiss their needs for others, including group members, leaders, and the group as a whole. Researchers have shown that more dismissing-avoidant individuals tend to dismiss the benefits of the group, focus on their personal goals versus group goals, and have negative attitudes toward the groups that they belong to (Rom & Mikulincer, 2003).

For example, Amy would minimize the importance of the leaders by interrupting them while they were talking, devalue the members by rejecting their feedback, and minimize the importance of the group by comparing the group with other groups that were more desirable. Over time, other members started to confront Amy about her inability to value them. One member, Frank, revealed that he believed Amy thought she was "too good for the group." Amy agreed and did not seem to mind the feedback. She often perceived the group's confronting her as evidence that they were envious of her. Group members eventually rejected Amy. When the leader explored her reactions to being left out, she shared that this was not new for her. She was often rejected as a child, although she did not reflect on this with any emotion. It became evident that she had learned to reject others as a way of bolstering her own self-esteem and protecting herself from inevitable rejection. Despite this revelation, group therapy continued to be a challenging process for Amy, and she eventually dropped out of the group.

Challenges to Cohesion

Group therapy is challenging for more dismissive-avoidant individuals because the act of seeking help challenges their internal working model of themselves as strong and of others being weak. Needing the group or acknowledging their vulnerability in the group has the potential to rouse early painful losses that originally led to deactivation (Beebe & Lachmann, 2002; Schore, 1994). Rom and Mikulincer (2003) actually found that individuals with more dismissing-avoidant attachments had greater group-specific anxiety because the stress of joining a group inhibited their ability to deny anxiety. Unfortunately, continuing to defend against this vulnerability with self-sufficiency and superiority leaves them lonely and rejected (Fosha, 2000). Mikulincer and Shaver (2007b) stated that even though avoidant individuals experience loneliness, they continue to deactivate and remove themselves from social relationships. Not surprisingly, Kirkpatrick and Hazan (1994) found that greater avoidance was correlated with an increased likelihood of being single and alone.

The difficulties these members struggle with not only leads them to be more inclined to struggle in the group process but can often lead to premature termination from group treatment. Tasca and colleagues (2004) found that women with more attachment avoidance were more likely to drop out of group therapy. Because these group members are challenging in group and at risk of premature termination, it is helpful for group leaders to keep their avoidance of painful pasts in mind. Although they can often appear arrogant or independent on the surface, they have turned off proximity-seeking behaviors and are often seeking relationships but without the ability to accept intimacy (Mikulincer & Shaver, 2007b).

Interactions With Other Group Members

Because dismissing-avoidant group members avoid the direct expression of their true feelings or internal states or are completely unaware of them (Fraley & Shaver, 2000), it is sometimes difficult to identify their underlying emotions or presenting problems (Cassidy, 1994; Main & Weston, 1982; Wallin, 2007). One way to understand how these individuals truly experience themselves in the group is through the feelings and experiences they induce in others they interact with via projective identification (Wallin, 2007).

Bion (1961) was the first to apply the concept of projective identification to groups and defined projective identification as the process of a member disowning unacceptable aspects of himself or herself and projecting them onto the group as a whole, its leaders, or specific members. Yalom and Leszcz

(2005) defined projective identification in group as the "process of projecting some of one's own (but disavowed) internal attributes into another, toward whom one subsequently feels an uncanny attraction–repulsion" (pp. 365–366). Rutan and Stone (1993) clarified that projective identification is a two-party system because it requires one who projects the unwanted parts and another or multiple others who accept the projections in the group. By exploring projective identification, we can learn what is going on inside of the dismissive group member who may not have awareness of his or her underlying feelings or needs, and we can see what is being activated in the group. A wonderful example of projective identification in a group with a more dismissing-avoidant member is depicted in Yalom's (Yalom & Gadban, 1990) video demonstrations of group therapy, described next.

Case Example: Interactions With a More Dismissive Group Member

Dan, a more dismissing-avoidant group member, comes late to group consistently and avoids participating fully in the sessions. Yalom is the first to confront Dan about not participating in the group. At first, the members express their desire to have Dan participate in the group, but his vacant reactions lead them to question why he is even coming to group in the first place. During the session, he blames his work for his lateness and his wife for his problems, and he minimizes the members' request to have him participate. Gradually, during the session, the members become more and more frustrated, and eventually, they become aggressive in their attempts to get a reaction from him. Yalom recruits all the female group members to "tell Dan what it would be like to be with him 24/7 . . . to be married to him." Dan continues to look calm, cool, and collected while each female member tells him how challenging it would be to be his wife. Not surprisingly, he becomes more defensive and appears to withdraw even more.

At some point in the session, a female member reveals that Dan had told her in private that he was frustrated with the group and often felt that it was a waste of his time. We also learn that as a child, Dan struggled with his parent's alcoholism and his own feelings of inadequacy and rejection. We can imagine that Dan's bids for emotional connection were often unmet, and he learned to disavow his own needs, feelings of anger, or his experience of disappointment in relationships. These disregarded parts of him appear to be induced in the others through his passive-aggressive behaviors, which also happens in his marriage. He denies having any needs or feeling angry while those around him feel completely needy and enraged.

This example highlights how the more dismissing-avoidant member, Dan, is not forthcoming about his true feelings of resentment and anger, and he does not appear to be aware of how his own needs are easily dismissed.

He withdraws into his work and continues to struggle with relationship issues. The group becomes a microcosm of his outside world (Yalom & Leszcz, 2005), with Dan re-creating a similar dynamic in the group to his relationships with his coworkers and wife. Those who interact with Dan find themselves angry and alone. Projective identification is one significant way more dismissing-avoidant individuals can express their underlying emotions in the group without having to be weak or needy (Cassidy, 1994). If the group leader can process this enactment in the session, the leader has a powerful tool to explore what is happening in the group and within individual members.

Group members, like Dan, who have dismissing-avoidant attachments (high avoidance and low anxiety), often engender complex feelings in other members. Alice, a more preoccupied group member, starts to blame herself during the session and worries that something she said in group angered Dan and made him come late. She swallows her own feelings of anger and instead appears concerned that Dan is angry with her. It is not uncommon for more preoccupied members to be activated by more dismissing-avoidant members because the dismissing-avoidant member's rejection and neglect activate the more preoccupied person's worst fears. More preoccupied individuals often doubt themselves and personalize reactions in the group. When they are activated, they tend also to increase pursuit of the more dismissing-avoidant individual and can be intrusive in their attempt to increase intimacy (Lavy, 2006). This pursuit often leads more dismissing-avoidant individuals to withdraw even more (Bartholomew & Allison, 2006).

Secure members are critical to the group process because, like secure individuals in a couple, they tend to buffer the effects of members with a more dismissing-avoidant attachment (Ben-Ari & Lavee, 2005; Feeney, 2005). Secure partners are more forgiving (Mikulincer, Shaver, & Slav, 2006), can express vulnerable feelings (Feeney, 1995), can self-soothe (Mikulincer & Shaver, 2007c), are more compassionate (Mikulincer & Shaver, 2007c), and can model how to address conflict (Paley, Cox, Burchinal, & Payne, 1999). Likewise, the leader's attachment style is also critical to facilitating a secure base in the group.

THE GROUP LEADER'S ATTACHMENT STYLE AND THE DISMISSIVE GROUP MEMBER

Wallin (2007) argued that how a therapist responds to the patient's projection and the enactments is influenced by his or her own attachment orientation. A more dismissing-avoidant therapist may engage in deactivation, avoiding the patient, whereas a more preoccupied therapist may engage in hyperactivation, becoming overly obsequious or intrusive and pursuing.

The secure group leader is able to regulate his or her emotions, facilitate curiosity about his or her experience in the group, and help group members observe their reactions in the here and now. Yalom and Leszcz (2005) described this as the leader "retaining or regaining our objectivity" (p. 45). In the video, Yalom does this by stepping back from the enactment to reflect on the process that is evolving in the group. He wonders aloud what is happening when Dan withdraws and the group becomes "louder and more shrill" as they attempt to get Dan to speak more authentically. In attachment terms, Yalom is exploring the deactivating behavior in one group member and how it is pulling for hyperactivating behaviors in the others. At the same time, Yalom is facilitating group members' mentalization by having them step back and reflect on the emotionally charged group process so that they can make sense of what is happening within themselves and in the group.

GROUP THERAPY GOALS FOR MORE DISMISSIVE GROUP MEMBERS

The major task of group therapy is to help a more dismissive member move from an avoidant orientation to one that is more relational and secure. This requires that the individual rework internal models of others as weak and inferior and of the self as superior and self-sufficient. This is no easy task and involves challenging these implicit patterns of relating as they occur in the here and now of the group. Because dismissive members have learned to disavow painful emotions such as shame and aloneness, they are excellent at intellectualizing, but they often lack the capacity to access emotions and experience them relationally (Fosha, 2000; Holmes, 1996; Main & Weston, 1982; Wallin, 2007). Here we discuss how empathy, insight, mentalization, and emotional regulation are key treatment ingredients to helping a dismissive group member move toward more attachment security.

Using Empathy to Experience Core Affect: Walking the Tightrope

One of the reasons dismissive individuals do not have access to certain painful emotions is because of their defensive exclusion of attachment-based memories and thoughts (Fraley & Shaver, 1997, 2000; Schore, 1994). When it comes to more dismissing-avoidant group members, it is helpful to keep in mind their struggle with vulnerability and experience of shame. Early in their development, they were most likely met with indifference, disdain, or even disgust when revealing vulnerable affective experiences (Main & Weston, 1982; Schore, 1994). The group leader must balance the need to confront the member's avoidance while also remaining sensitive to his or her underlying humiliation.

In the early phases of group therapy, when the group is forming, more dismissing-avoidant individuals tend to be more sensitive to the pressures of belonging and struggling to determine how group can help them while also maintaining their distance. This struggle is often typified by coming late, missing sessions, giving advice, remaining silent, telling jokes, or talking about outside events that are safe to talk about. It is important to keep in mind that these individuals may not be able to identify how they are really feeling, let alone be able to share what they are feeling with others.

An empathic leader holds back from challenging, too soon, the natural defenses that these individuals have relied on over the course of their lifetimes. It is helpful for the leaders to acknowledge these members' self-sufficiency and their independence in the group, which is at odds with opening up and joining the group. These members struggle with a challenging dilemma: *If I want to stay strong and rely on myself, I will be alone; if I open up and depend on the group, I will be weak and needy.* In the face of this dilemma, the group leader can admire the group member's independence, which has gotten him this far, but the leader can also comment on how this self-sufficiency has left the member alone and feeling disconnected to people, the issue that most likely brought him to group treatment in the first place. To change means they will have to start feeling.

In addition, researchers (Mikulincer, Birnbaum, Woddis, & Nachmias, 2000) have shown that more avoidant individuals easily suppress attachment-based concerns if they are not under stress, but they lose this ability in certain situations. Group therapy, with its many ongoing processes, can function as a stressful environment for these members and allow for more underlying attachment-based processes to surface. The following case example demonstrates how the group process activated Raj and facilitated his exploration of his attachments in the group.

Case Example: Using Empathy to Elicit Core Affect

Raj was a 45-year-old, single, engineering professor with an obsessive type personality. He was a workaholic who valued his career and academic success. Although he was doing well in his professional life, his relationships failed miserably. He was single and wanted to be married, but he was detached and judgmental. He was also triggered by people's demands on him and often distanced himself from needing anything or anyone. One way he avoided depending on others was focusing on his work and obsessing about the details of his research. He often would fall silent in the group when others were vulnerable, and he would give logical advice that always felt a bit patronizing. It was as if he did not know how to connect or have social skills. Although group members repeatedly gave him feedback, he never seemed to be able to change the way he engaged with the group. Raj intellectually understood that he avoided his needs and feelings, but he could not help it or access more vulnerable parts of himself. He would often say with a sense of annoyance, "I just don't understand what you want from me."

During one session, Raj reacted to Nancy, a group member who was describing her dependence on her boyfriend.

Raj: Why do you care so much what your boyfriend thinks? You should be more independent. I was independent since the age of 5. *[The group is again frustrated by Raj's arrogance, superiority, or lack of empathy, but this time, Raj leaves a clue that the leader immediately follows. The leader knows the group could go down the same "frustrated feedback track."]*

Leader: You have been independent for so long, since you were 5 years old. What was going on at that time, Raj? *[The leader imagines that Raj is not trying to be difficult but is just unable to tolerate any expression of neediness. She speaks in an open tone and thinks he would feel safer if the leader acknowledges his strength and independence. She hopes that this empathy will lessen his defensiveness and allow him to explore what part of his childhood is related to his self-sufficiency.]*

Raj: *[struggling at first]* Nothing. I was just an independent child. That's all.

Leader: Raj, this is important. Let's think about it. What might have been going on that made you feel you were strong and independent since, as you said, the age of 5.

Raj: *[without emotion]* Well. One thing was being the one in my family chosen to be sent to boarding school. I think when I was 5. Why is this important, anyway? Why are you asking me about this?

Leader: That's a good question. It is my experience that we all bring our past experiences into our current relationships and that what happened when you were 5 might help us understand how you feel in the group, why independence is so important to you, and why you respond the way you do to members, like Nancy, when they reveal their needs. Does that make sense? *[This intervention is aimed not only at clarifying things for Raj but also at helping the other group members empathize and mentalize as to the deeper roots to Raj's behaviors in the group.]*

Raj: *[seeming to appreciate how the information could be useful]* I guess it sounds logical. Although I don't think that anything that happened to me at 5 is impacting me in here.

Leader: I know. Maybe this may not be relevant, but let's see where it goes. I know others in here may benefit from getting to know you better.

Raj: Well. You know I was born in India and moved here later in life to go to college. It is very common in India to send children to boarding school to learn English to get an education. I was honored to be the one selected in my family. I did very well and graduated at the top of my class. *[Raj focuses on educating the members and defensively showing off his success.]*

Leader: You adapted so well and were extremely successful at such a young age. You said that is when you became independent. Can you say more about that—about the experience going to boarding school. *[The leader empathizes with Raj. She does not immediately challenge his defenses at this time and instead explores his success to help him open up more about his experience.]*

Raj: *[spoken without emotion]* Well, I was told I would be going to school and that this was a good thing for the family. Then we packed that night, and we left in the morning. I saw them a year later.

Julie: WHAT?! You did not see them for a year?

Raj: Well, I didn't know that it would be a year *[said with slight annoyance]*.

Mary: Still. That's horrible. You were only 5 years old. You were so young. I am a schoolteacher, and I think that is a young age to be away from your family for a year.

Raj: *[looking disgusted]* You don't seem to understand. It wasn't horrible. It made me who I am, and I owe my family so much for that opportunity. *[Raj feels misunderstood and leans back in his chair. The leader, sensing the increasing defensiveness and wanting to respect Raj's cultural background, empathizes with his experience of not being understood.]*

Leader: Raj, I wonder if the group is not as familiar with Indian culture, and it is very important for us to appreciate the value of education and being selected to attend school. You have something important to share with us. Could you tell us what it was like for you? *[The leader attempts to empathize with Raj and repair the rupture to continue to make space for him to express himself.]*

Mary: I'm sorry, I jumped in. I would like to know more. I have strong reactions when it comes to children. *[Mary is more secure than some of the other members and is able to acknowledge her own anxiety. She expresses interest in bringing Raj into the group despite his hurtful responses in the past.]*

Nancy was silent during the interaction, and the leader was keeping her in mind because Raj had judged Nancy earlier in the session. The group leader was also trying to facilitate Raj's openness in the group. She felt her way into his experience and empathized with his strength while facilitating some curiosity about his experience of being independent at such a young age. The leader was aware that exploring Raj's memories of being 5 years old would likely expose his more vulnerable emotions and possibly move toward his affect. This would also be more challenging for Raj, whose attachment needs were consistently denied.

Facilitating Emotional Insight Into Underlying Feelings and Defenses

Fosha (2000) described how more dismissing-avoidant individuals have learned to deal without feeling, and the price they pay for not feeling is "isolation, alienation, emotional impoverishment, and at the best, a brittle consolidation of self" (p. 43). The group leaders must facilitate a secure base within the therapy group for dismissive individuals to feel there is any value at all to exploring their emotions within a relational context. Group member–leader interactions are likely to trigger these unwanted emotions immediately and offer multiple opportunities to understand their instinctive avoidance. For example, Raj was triggered in the group by a fellow group member's openness about her dependency on her boyfriend, and that is when he proudly announced that he was independent since he was 5.

Researchers (Mikulincer, Shaver, Gillath, & Nitzberg, 2005) have found that more dismissing-avoidant individuals are motivated by egoistic outcomes, and the group leader may need to start with helping the dismissing-avoidant member identify a selfish motive to open up in the group. The leader focuses on Raj's strength and independence, and she maintains Raj's specialness in the group by addressing his ethnic background and the lack of the group members' knowledge of his diversity. He is the expert who can explain something to the group. The leader also addressed the cultural diversity in the group to facilitate safety for other members in the group who come from a different background to promote an openness and respect to differences (DeLucia-Waack, 2011).

Clinicians (Fosha, 2000) and researchers (Main & Weston, 1982) have described how dismissive group members, like Raj, are more likely to rely on repression and avoidance when core affects surface because these core affects were not welcomed in their earlier attachment relationships. In the following example, we see how the group leader took note of Raj's nonverbal reactions and continued to explore his childhood in the group to increase his disclosure of personal information that could lead to emotional expression.

The leader sensed Raj's need to defend his cultural background and was also aware that he might feel unique in being the only Indian American in the group. Raj seemed to appreciate the acknowledgment that he was different and that he could educate the group about his ethnic group identity.

> Raj: Well, I came from a large family in India. I am the oldest. I have two younger brothers and two younger sisters.

> Steve: Were you all close?

> Raj: I guess that depends on how you define closeness. I was closest to my grandparents, I suppose. Due to the limited space in the house, I slept with my grandparents at night and spent the days with my brothers and sisters. It was a busy house. [At this point, Raj folds his arms around himself as if to contain himself.]

> Leader: That must have been so different to suddenly go from sleeping with your grandparents every night and having all of your family around you to being on your own at school. [The leader considers that for Raj, this may be an important memory of his grandparents and has triggering feelings within him; however, at this point, she focuses only on how different this experience was for him.]

> Raj: [His expression has changed, and he avoids eye contact.] I never really thought about it that way. It was very different from living at home. I have a big family [pauses]. But I knew I was the lucky one to have this opportunity. [Raj's struggle to suppress his attachment needs is profound. The group members have had a glimpse into his experience of loss, and the leader continues to track his reactions within the group, knowing that his experiences will lead to more vulnerability.]

Increasing Mentalization

In addition to empathizing with underlying emotions, it is critical for the group leader to help more dismissing-avoidant group members, like Raj, find ways of reflecting on these emotions in the group. We suggest that the group leader can help facilitate mentalization in dismissive members by verbalizing feelings slowly, facilitating group member insight into the feelings that underlie behaviors, and encouraging interpersonal feedback within the here and now of the group. These three processes help to interrupt dismissive members' avoidance of affect, which typically interferes with reflective functioning (Tasca, Foot, et al., 2011).

Emotional Regulation: Verbalizing and Tolerating Feelings

One way the group leader can help more dismissing-avoidant individuals put emotional experience into words is to reflect back the emotions that are nonverbally being expressed in a slow manner that is not experienced as intrusive. The group members and leaders can also explore a memory that comes to mind in the group that triggers more emotions. In the case of Raj, the group leader felt that it would be important to help him identify some feelings in the group given his resistance to the group's interpersonal feedback and was isolating himself more and more from the group process.

Raj: Come to think of it, I never knew I would not see them for a year. I thought I would see them.

Mary: Was that customary in India? Not to see your parents or family for that long a time in boarding school? [This question reflects more curiosity and openness to Raj's cultural background and exposes what is cultural vs. what is specific to Raj's family.]

Raj: [paused] No. Other parents did come to visit, but my family lived too far away. They could not come each week. It makes sense, and it would not be practical. They had to work and did not have the money to visit. [Although Raj is still minimizing the experience, it is clear this question has touched on his emotions.]

Steve: So they lived too far away to visit you. Wow. It must have been hard to hear that they would not come to see you for a year. [Again, a group member is curious about Raj's experience and genuinely interested. This is different from past group interactions.]

Raj: Well, they did not really tell me that. I figured it out over time.

Steve: How did you figure that out?

Raj: I guess I realized it when they didn't come. I would go to the front hall where all of us would go to see our families on the weekend. I would go each weekend to wait, and they never came. Eventually, I realized they were not coming, and I stopped going. [Although Raj still speaks with the same matter-of-fact tone, his feelings are palpable in the room. The group is silent.]

Nancy: [in a compassionate tone, reaching out] Wow. You waited and they never came. You really must have been a strong kid to deal with that and to do so well in school on your own.

Raj: [said in a slower tone] I know it sounds worse than it was. I mean it was hard on me, but it was not so bad. [Raj again tries to protect himself from the feelings that are starting to come to the surface.]

Leader: Raj, it may not have been so bad, but you said it was hard. I imagine that 5-year-old must have been very disappointed and had many feelings before he decided to give up. Am I correct? Do your recall what that 5-year-old may have felt each week while waiting? You know, before he decided it would best to move on.

Raj: *[speaking even more slowly]* I never thought about this. I have never thought about what he was feeling each week. I don't know. He . . . well I mean I . . . I just waited. It was hard to wait there. I am not sure this is that important. *[Raj continues to hold back, but he is more open than he has ever been in the group.]*

Leader: It feels to me like this is an important time in your life, Raj. This is when you learned to become so independent. Can you recall one specific time when you were waiting to help us really understand what it was like for you? What made it so hard? *[The leader honors Raj's independence and then tries to help him explore a memory that helps him identify his feelings as a child, which may be more tolerable than his feelings as an adult.]*

Raj: I don't know. It was a long time ago. I guess there was this one time.

With the help of the group members, who became intrigued by his past and continued asking him questions, Raj eventually recounted one specific day. He described going to the front room early to get a seat right across from the front door, and he eagerly waited for his family to visit. Each time the door opened, he imagined it would be his mother walking through. Each time, it would be someone else's family, and he would watch them reunite. It was never his family, and it would happen more than a dozen times.

Raj: Eventually, I just stopped waiting for them to come. On the weekends, I would stay in my room and focus on my schoolwork. This ended up to be a good thing since I did so well. *[Although Raj is positive about the outcome of the experience, his face becomes red, and he appears uncomfortable with the feelings that are coming up. He looks sad. The group is present and engaged.]*

Leader: Raj, for a moment I saw something in your eyes, and it looked like you felt sad just now. Is that how you felt?

Raj: I never really thought about this time in my life as sad. I was sad. I have not really gone back there in a long time. *[Pauses]* I just don't want to focus on sadness now. I don't see the point. It doesn't change anything.

Steve: I can really relate to that. I also ask myself, "What is the point?" sometimes. "Why do I need to focus on feeling angry or sad?"

Leader: So what do you tell yourself, Steve, when you ask yourself that?

Steve: It has taken me a long time to realize that shutting off my feelings from when I was growing up made sense when I was a kid, but now it has pushed others away and kept me alone. It is hard to believe that these feelings can have a purpose. I remember the first time in this group when I shared my experience of my father's alcoholism and how that triggered all of this anger I had pent up for years. At the time, I could not see how that anger was influencing all of my relationships especially with my own kids. *[Steve is a member who is also high in avoidance but less so than Raj. He is able to empathize with Raj's deactivation of emotions, but he is also able to offer a different perspective on how disavowal of painful feelings can have a negative impact on current relationships.]*

This clinical example highlights how group members can help each other process and explore emotional reactions. Although Raj quickly moves away from his sadness, he is able to acknowledge the sadness he felt as a child for the first time in group. He also raises his experience as a child who is sitting with painful emotions without a caregiver to comfort or soothe him. Raj indicated that he learned to focus on schoolwork to avoid being overwhelmed with his intense feelings of longing, disappointment, and anger. This was adaptive as a 5-year-old struggling to survive repeated disappointments. This detachment and withdrawal from emotions is not adaptive in his current life, however. Steve, another more dismissing-avoidant group member, is able to empathize with Raj and express his own struggles with identifying and tolerating emotions and how this influences current relationships. More important, during this session, Raj has moved from being judgmental toward Nancy for expressing emotional vulnerability and neediness to focusing on the root of his own disavowal of needs. He also offers the group an opportunity to connect with him and his struggles to avoid his feelings.

Encouraging Interpersonal Feedback

When working with dismissive group members, it is helpful to encourage the group not only to challenge their avoidance but to recognize their risk taking. As Raj revealed more in the session, group members seemed to be more engaged with him. They appeared interested and thoughtful as he was describing his experience. Raj's disclosures had an important impact on the members, who then started to share their painful experiences to connect with him. The group members, like Steve, shared their own past that related to Raj to demonstrate their understanding of the use of avoidance to manage more painful emotions. Although members were able to relate, the experience of increasing intimacy caused Raj to withdraw again. He felt the support group members offered was not always helpful, and he was ambivalent about being similar to the other group members. The compassion he was receiving felt uncomfortable to him, and he did not want to be weak and needy. The leader aimed to help Raj use the group feedback to foster some insight into how his avoidance was perceived by other people and how this may have an impact on him outside the group.

Leader: Raj, I wonder what your experience of the group has been like today?

Raj: I don't know. It is very different from what I expected. People seem to like it when I talk about this side of me from the past, but I'm not sure I see the point in the long run. If I were you, I would want to hear how I can help address your problems, not how I was feeling sad when I was young.

Nancy: To be honest, this is the first time I have ever felt like I knew you. I think this is the only time that you have shared anything about yourself. You always give advice, like a professor, and you do it as though you have it all figured out. You have the answers.

Leader: Nancy, how does that make you feel?

Nancy: It makes me feel worse. I feel like you think you're better, and it makes me feel angry. I'd much rather hear about your struggles, too. Hearing about your experience has made me feel like we're not so different after all.

Steve: Exactly. I really appreciated you sharing what you did even if you don't think it was helpful. I think I understand why you focus on your work so much. I used to think you just didn't care, but I think you focus on solving problems because you learned as a kid that feelings are not helpful. I also struggle with that, so I get it.

Raj: So you want me to talk more about my childhood?

Nancy: No, I guess what I am saying is I want you to talk more about yourself and give less advice. Just be you in here.

Leader: Nancy, can you share more with Raj about your experience with him earlier in the session versus now?

Nancy: Sure. I guess I was annoyed when he said I should not be so dependent on my boyfriend. [The leader motions for Nancy to talk directly to Raj.] I should be more like you, independent. Like you have been since you were 5 [talking to Raj]. I felt like you were being critical of me. But now that I have gotten to know more about you, I see that there is a reason why you don't want to depend on people. You don't want to be disappointed. I relate to that, and I don't want to be disappointed either.

Leader: Raj, what do you hear Nancy saying?

Raj: I didn't know I came across as perfect. I don't think I'm perfect. [It is hard for Raj to take in the positive feedback.]

Mary: I don't think you realize that when you give only advice, you come across as having all the answers. It feels like you're perfect or better than us.

Raj: Do others think that way? [*Several group members nod their heads in agreement.*]

The intervention described was the first time Raj acknowledged any feelings, described anything personal in the group, and was able to hear group members' feedback. This was a major and important step for Raj, who continued to courageously struggle to take in the group's feedback over time.

We can see the importance of using the past to enhance our understanding of the here-and-now interactions in the room with a more dismissing-avoidant group member (Bowlby, 1988). Before this session, the leaders and members continually provided feedback to Raj, but the feedback was not penetrating his defensiveness. He was not able to access his feelings with ease, and every bone in his body was rejecting vulnerability. The group's confrontations never seemed to affect Raj, and this only served to frustrate the group members. To foster a new pattern of interpersonal interaction and emotion regulation, the leader engaged with Raj with more curiosity to foster a new experience.

The leader invited him to explore the roots of his deactivation and take a closer look at his reaction and eventually his underlying feelings. Once the details of his childhood became more apparent to the leader and the other members, the group became more accepting of him and could understand his behaviors in the group. Eventually, the members' reactions began to become a more salient factor in the process as they expressed empathy for Raj and also feedback as to how his vulnerability was more attractive to them compared with his superiority. Not surprisingly, Raj did not trust the positive feedback he received from group members. This is consistent with work by Brennan and Morris (1997), who described how more dismissing-avoidant individuals tend to reject other's feedback in general, especially positive feedback that activates their dependency needs. Future group sessions focused on helping Raj continue to gain insight into his ambivalence to emotional closeness in the group and the way he came across to others. Although the interaction did not alter Raj's attachment behaviors immediately, it initiated a process in which Raj could begin to develop a more cohesive narrative of himself, learn to slowly tolerate emotions, and gain insight into how and why he pushed others away.

CONCLUSION

Group therapy has the unique power to facilitate incredible growth for members who come to the group with a long history of interpersonal avoidance and emotional detachment. Group therapy provides these patients with interpersonal feedback that calls into question their devaluation of others and idealization of themselves. The group members have the power to confront these dismissing-avoidant interpersonal strategies if the leader helps them explore the underlying motivation behind emotional detachment. For some group members high in avoidance and low in anxiety, interpersonal feedback with regard to their defensiveness can engender insight, but for some group members within this avoidant dimension, receiving challenging interpersonal feedback will only provoke more defensiveness. The group leader's task is to know when to allow the group to challenge the more dismissing-avoidant group members and when to try a different strategy. These members are at risk of being a scapegoat if the interpersonal feedback does not penetrate the defensiveness. The leader must facilitate empathy and mentalization to foster insight within the group. To do this, it is important for the leader to facilitate a different interpersonal experience by slowly making space for these individuals to reveal the underlying motivation for their self-sufficiency. Providing this window into the more dismissing-avoidant group member's feelings facilitates empathy in the group and connects this member with others, facilitating cohesion.

As we look back on the case of Raj, we see how he was slowly able to gain insight into the impact of his actions on others in the group when he was seen in a different light. Raj was able to expose a different part of himself in the group, and other members were able to see how he needed to protect himself from the feelings he had as a child. Only after the others really saw him were they able to provide helpful feedback that could be digested by and meaningful to Raj.

8

TREATING THE FEARFUL-AVOIDANT GROUP MEMBER

The more fearful-avoidant group member, one who is high on both attachment anxiety and avoidance, engages in both deactivating and hyperactivating strategies and can benefit from group therapy. However, these individuals also need to be carefully screened for the appropriate group. This chapter is divided into three parts. First, we discuss how more fearful-avoidant attachment relates to what has been described in the literature as disorganized attachment and how high attachment anxiety and avoidance influence group work. Second, we describe how the leader's attachment influences the work with more fearful-avoidant group members. Last, we outline group therapy goals for these members and offer suggestions on how it can facilitate achievement of these goals. A case example is used to illustrate attachment-related problems for more fearful-avoidant group members as well as possible group leader interventions.

http://dx.doi.org/10.1037/14186-009
Attachment in Group Psychotherapy, by C. L. Marmarosh, R. D. Markin, and E. B. Spiegel
Copyright © 2013 by the American Psychological Association. All rights reserved.

FEARFUL ATTACHMENT AND THE DISORGANIZED
ATTACHMENT STYLE

Mikulincer and Shaver (2007b) argued that the fearful-avoidant attachment style resembles the disorganized infant attachment style because fearful individuals oscillate between high anxiety and high avoidance and have been unable to adapt one strategy that facilitates security. They noted the parallel between the back-and-forth attachment behaviors in adults and the reactions disorganized children have to the Strange Situation. In their research, they found simultaneous activation of security and fear that led to unusual behaviors in children such as freezing, dropping to the floor, or gazing blankly at the caregiver who returns (Main & Hesse, 1992). Main and Hesse (1990, 1992) described the confused and chaotic reactions children have when they are reunited with a caregiver who represents both security and terror. The child remains "caught between contradictory impulses to approach and avoid" the frightening parent (Wallin, 2007, p. 22). In many ways, these disoriented behaviors may be adaptive because the child is caught in a painful experience in which the one who provides comfort is also the one who causes the intense pain and fear. Theoretically, the disorganized attachment is linked with a history of trauma and abuse, and this is what leads to the individual being conflicted between the caregiver who sometimes provides safety and the same caregiver who threatens his or her existence. Empirical studies have linked disorganized attachment to a history of abuse and fearful avoidance to inhibition, severe mourning reactions, trauma symptoms, and alcohol use (Mikulincer & Shaver, 2007b).

MORE FEARFUL-AVOIDANT ATTACHMENT
AND THE QUIET BORDERLINE

Given the strong link between early trauma in childhood and disorganized attachment in later life (Sroufe, Egeland, Carlson, & Collins, 2005), researchers have also linked more fearful-avoidant attachment and borderline personality disorder (BPD; Dozier, Stovall, & Albus, 1999; Fonagy, Gergely, Jurist, & Target, 2002; Schore, 2002). BPD is characterized by affective instability, relationship difficulties, experiences of rage, self-destructive thoughts and behaviors, increased rates of posttraumatic stress disorder, and an inner sense of emptiness (Clarkin, Levy, Lenzenweger, & Kernberg, 2004; Gunderson & Sabo, 1993). Traditionally, BPD has been linked with the more preoccupied attachment style (Fonagy et al., 2002). Sroufe et al. (2005) compared different infant attachments assessed at 12 and 18 months of life and found that disorganized attachment in infancy was more related of BPD in adulthood. It appears that the dimension of attachment anxiety overlaps in both more preoccupied and more fearful-avoidant individuals, and BPD may have different expressions of symptoms. The literature on BPD has differentiated two relational styles of BPD, the quiet borderline and the raging borderline. The quiet borderline does not engage in the traditional acting-out, hyperactivating behavior that we see most commonly in BPD. Instead, the quiet borderline pulls inward, withdraws, and rages internally with the silent treatment (Sherwood & Cohen, 1994).

According to Sherwood and Cohen (1994), quiet borderline patients are adept at sensing what roles others might want them to play, and they are even more masterful at becoming what others want them to be. They have an unstable underlying identity, and their true self is experienced as deficient. In therapy, these "as-if" patients try to sense what the therapist expects of them. In group therapy, these patients tend to hide in the group rather than engage in hyperactivating strategies. It appears that "acting-out" individuals with BPD tend to be higher on the anxiety dimension (those who demonstrate more hyperactivating strategies), whereas "acting-in" individuals with BPD are more fearful-avoidant adults (those who are sensitive to abandonment but also disengage or withdraw in relationships). Similarly, Mikulincer and Shaver (2007b) described the link between fearful-avoidant attachment and covert narcissism. Unlike the overt narcissist, or phallic narcissist, who expresses grandiosity and superiority, the covert narcissist, also called the depleted narcissist, is sensitive to rejection, has idealized expectations of the self, and is prone to entitlement.

THE MORE FEARFUL-AVOIDANT MEMBER AND THE GROUP

More fearful-avoidant group members (high in attachment anxiety and avoidance) can both facilitate and inhibit group process. Because these members are easily activated in the group and engage in both avoidance and care-seeking behaviors, they tend to slowly activate other members in the group as well. Their deactivation and disavowal of emotions often leads them to act in ways that engender intense feelings in others, similar to the more dismissing-avoidant group member (see Chapter 7, this volume). Unlike the more dismissing-avoidant member, however, they are able to seek out reassurance from the group and display longings for closeness. At times, these alternating cycles of clinging and then withdrawing can frustrate other group members, who are left confused and uncertain how to maintain a relationship with them. Because of this challenge, group leaders need to be even more perceptive and pay careful attention to the group member's subtle nonverbal behaviors.

During the group process, more fearful-avoidant members can also become more disorganized as the cohesion in an interpersonal process group increases because the attachment-related issues become more salient. The felt pressure to be vulnerable along with the intense desire to protect oneself from being retraumatized creates ambivalence to the treatment. Just as they appear to be more connected to the group, they may start to withdraw and consider leaving treatment because of the intense emotions that are triggered.

Because members with both elevated anxiety and avoidance often have a history of trauma (Fonagy et al., 2002; Mikulincer & Shaver, 2007b), their ability to make sense of their increasingly intense emotions is compromised, and they find some way to self-soothe, such as missing sessions, using drugs or medications, overeating, or drinking alcohol. Hughes (2007) described the use of dissociation to avoid the risk of retraumatization in attachment-based family therapy. He discussed the importance of the *therapeutic window,* a term used by Briere and Scott (2006). The window refers to the exploration of traumatic experiences when the awareness of the trauma is not too emotionally intense or overwhelming but also not when the trauma is being repressed or denied.

Interactions With Other Group Members

It is not uncommon for more fearful-avoidant group members to look for a group member with whom they can align who meets their needs for emotional regulation. More fearful-avoidant members tend to be drawn to secure members who are able to regulate emotions. Interestingly, more fearful-avoidant members are also attracted to more dismissing-avoidant members because the latter do not press the former for emotional closeness and allow them the safety of distance. Unfortunately, these members who are more dismissing may also activate traumatic memories of abuse or neglect in the more fearful members. It is not uncommon for early caregivers of more fearful-avoidant members to be cold, rejecting, and emotionally detached (Sroufe et al., 2005). Although insecure group members can activate the earlier traumatic memories of more fearfully attached group members, this process can be therapeutic if the more fearful member is able to tolerate the group process and challenge the more dismissing members in the group.

In addition, more fearful-avoidant members can benefit from other insecurely attached members in the group who may understand their internal experience. For example, more dismissing-avoidant members share the propensity to withdraw in relationships, and they have the potential to confront more fearful-avoidant members about their withdrawal and detachment. More preoccupied members are excellent at detecting emotional reactions in other people although they are not always good at providing support

(Simpson, Ickes, & Grich, 1999). Their attunement may be useful in detecting more fearful-avoidant members' subtle reactions in the group.

More secure group members also have the potential to facilitate the group process (Ben-Ari & Lavee, 2005). Specifically, secure members can help more fearful-avoidant members express positive emotions such as gratitude and joy after positive interpersonal interactions, express guilt after making a mistake, and express anger and forgiveness when others make mistakes (Mikulincer & Shaver, 2007b). More secure members can also approach others in need and help them through an emotional crisis because they are not as activated by neediness or overwhelmed with emotions. In addition, more secure group members can model the use of supportive interactions with others (Mikulincer & Florian, 1997). In essence, more secure group members can facilitate the overall safety in the group for more fearful-avoidant group members.

The Group Leader's Attachment Style and the More Fearful-Avoidant Member

Group leaders who have more insecure attachments are more likely to get pulled into the push and pull dynamics of more fearful-avoidant group members. The leader who is higher on anxiety is often concerned with being liked and accepted in the group and is more easily emotionally activated (Rom & Mikulincer, 2003). In addition, this leader is more inclined to detect the subtle nonverbal expressions of emotion and become overwhelmed with the more fearful-avoidant member's trauma or withdrawal in the group. Because more preoccupied leaders are not always able to reflect on their experience when emotionally triggered, they may be more inclined to pursue these members, try and rescue them, or experience hopelessness when they are unable to help them. They may also fear the withdrawal and anger of more fearful group members, which inhibits these members' growth (Mikulincer & Shaver, 2007b). Although these are possibilities, group researchers have found that anxious military leaders tend to have a positive impact on group cohesion because they emphasize disclosure, emotions, and interdependence (Davidovitz, Mikulincer, Shaver, Ijzak, & Popper, 2007), but this may be similar to a more anxious individual therapist who initially facilitates the alliance but does not necessarily facilitate change over time (Sauer, Lopez, & Gormley, 2003).

More dismissing-avoidant leaders, in contrast, who are avoidant of emotions and less empathic may inhibit the emotional growth of more fearful-avoidant group members. One can assume that a more dismissing-avoidant leader with preoccupied and fearful-avoidant group members who are seeking emotional regulation would be at a disadvantage. Psychotherapy researchers have found that therapist avoidance has a negative impact on session depth

(Romano, Fitzpatrick, & Janzen, 2008) and treatment outcome with more anxious clients in individual treatment (Marmarosh, Bieri, Fauchi-Schutt, Barrone, & Choi, 2011). Davidovitz et al. (2007) found that avoidance in the leader of a military group had the worst impact on more avoidant soldiers in the unit, but they also found that it had a detrimental impact on all soldiers' mental health over time, even the secure soldiers who were initially buffered. This is extremely important in group therapy, in which a more avoidant leader, who is either more fearful or dismissing, could cause more distress in group members.

Perhaps with no other population is having a secure group leader more important than with the more fearful-avoidant group members. The history of trauma, the combination of withdrawal and insecurity, and the difficulties with emotion regulation make a more secure leader one of the most important components of the treatment. More secure leaders are better at tolerating stress, mentalizing, and moving toward and away from intimacy to meet the needs of insecure group members (Mikulincer & Shaver, 2007b). Because of this, it is important for group leaders to reflect on their own earlier relational experiences and how their own attachments are affecting their groups.

GROUP THERAPY GOALS FOR MORE FEARFUL-AVOIDANT GROUP MEMBERS

The major task of group therapy is helping a more fearful-avoidant member move from an avoidant orientation to one that is more relational and secure. Because more fearful-avoidant members often have a history of trauma and engage in both hyperactivating and deactivating strategies, they often struggle with the capacity to access and tolerate emotions and experience them relationally (Fosha, 2000; Holmes, 1996; Wallin, 2007). It is not surprising that empirically supported treatments for BPD prioritize emotion regulation (Linehan, 1993; Linehan et al., 2002) and insight into maladaptive internal representations of self and others (Bateman & Fonagy, 2003, 2006; Clarkin, Yeomans, & Kernberg, 2006). In what follows, we use a case description to demonstrate how automatic fear responses are activated during interactions in the group, how the secure base of the group can facilitate corrective emotional experiences, and how insight into the origins of internal models of self and others can help more fearful-avoidant members move toward more security.

Using Empathy to Facilitate Emotion Regulation

Group therapy offers the opportunity to have multiple relationship experiences that can trigger implicit representations of self and others, and it provides a larger context to explore and make sense of these automatic relationship patterns and how emotions are regulated (Hopper, 2001; Stone & Gustafson, 1982; Wilberg & Karterud, 2001). According to Wallin (2007), patients who come to treatment with disorganized attachments, or what we refer to as fearful-avoidant attachment, need to regulate painful emotions and be able to integrate their contradictory impulses to merge and withdraw. He argued that to do this, the therapist (in this case, the group) must act as a secure base for the patient so he or she can learn to "tolerate, modulate, and communicate feelings that were previously unbearable" (p. 103). The secure base of the group therapy is derived from the group's ability to foster mentalization and emotion regulation.

Fostering Mentalization

One of the most precious things lost when one experiences ongoing abuse is the ability to feel safe enough to wonder what is going on in another's mind (Fonagy et al., 2002). The ability to reflect on another's internal experience is critical to the maintenance of healthy intimate relationships; however, those who have been abused or traumatized early in life have learned to avoid considering the minds of others to avoid comprehending the hatred and aggression that was directed toward them (Fonagy & Target, 2008; Fonagy, Target, Gergely, Jurist, & Bateman, 2003). Fonagy et al. (2002) argued that a "mentalizing stance is also unlikely to develop in a child who generally feels treated as an uncared for physical object" (p. 353). More fearful-avoidant individuals learn to rely on their own perceptions when interpreting other people's intentions and motivations. They do not have the same freedom to wonder about interpersonal experiences. They exist in a world where "ideas are too terrifying to think about and feelings too intense to experience" (Fonagy et al., 2002, p. 373). They are frightened and instinctively engage in a fight–flight response. According to Bateman and Fonagy (2003),

> If children see the hatred and denigration in the mind of the caregiver, they are forced to experience themselves as unlovable and hateful; if they expose themselves by letting the caregiver know what they experience, they will be humiliated, and what they felt proud about becomes shameful; if they show vulnerability, it will be exploited or ridiculed. (p. 191)

This experience is the origin of insecure attachments.

Although mentalization can be turned off to cope with trauma, it can also be the key to resilience when coping with a traumatic past. Mothers who were deprived as children and were able to accurately reflect on the history of their trauma tended to have secure children, whereas the mothers who were traumatized and lacked reflective capacity had children with insecure attachments. The mother's ability to reflect on the root of her childhood deprivation and trauma reduced the mother's self-blame and fostered her ability to cope with the loss. Mothers who did not have this reflective capacity were unable to make sense of their childhood trauma and unfortunately were more likely to pass it onto their own children (Fonagy et al., 2002).

It is no wonder that helping more fearful-avoidant individuals consider the minds of others, engage with more openness and curiosity, and feel safe enough to trust others is often the focus of their treatments (Bateman & Fonagy, 2003, 2006). The following case example describes how the group process stimulates a fearful-avoidant group member's trauma and how the group facilitates the member's ability to access his feelings of anger and tease apart what are realistic perceptions of others and what issues are based on his past experiences.

Case Example: A More Fearful-Avoidant Group Member

John never dated and led a lonely life. Although he was extremely intelligent and did well in graduate school, he was extremely insecure and timid. He was referred to individual therapy by his graduate advisor, who noticed that he would drift off in class and appeared disconnected from his classmates. After a year in individual therapy, his therapist referred him to group therapy to address his diagnosis and social anxiety and to explore his continued pattern of avoidance in group settings. With the exception of a few comments, John was a silent group member for 2 months.

When John joined the group, he was reserved and offered little to the group process. On the surface, he was extremely agreeable, but the leaders often wondered what he was really thinking or feeling. Although he was diagnosed with social anxiety, his withdrawal seemed more profound, and his lack of intimate relationships since childhood indicated a more complex issue. The signed release of information to the individual therapist was invaluable. When the group leaders consulted with his therapist, she revealed that John was frustrated in group and complained about the leader's intrusiveness during their individual sessions. Specifically, she revealed that John was extremely angry toward the male leader, but he could not fully explain why and did not feel safe enough to share it in the group. The group leaders appreciated the feedback and agreed to allow the individual therapist time to work with John around his reaction to the leaders and his feelings about the group process. Having a release of information was critical to preventing a split between the good individual therapist and the traumatizing group.

After several weeks, the therapist, with John's permission, revealed to the group leaders that John had recently revealed a history of sexual trauma at age 5 and was struggling with memories of abuse that were being triggered in the group by the male leader. The individual therapist had not been aware of the early abuse and only learned of it when they were exploring John's reactions to the leader. John had never spoken about the abuse to anyone, denied a history of trauma during the intake, and said he did not think this event was relevant. After the therapist learned of the abuse, she hypothesized that the abuse was the root to John's more profound avoidance of relationships and especially his avoidance of sexual intimacy. The leaders felt this information was invaluable, and they agreed not to bring it into the group at this time. The group leaders discussed ways of addressing the here-and-now interactions in the group and how the trauma could be addressed without exposing John who was just beginning to talk about this in his individual treatment.

Verbalizing Feelings: Putting Emotional Experiences Into Words

One of the most challenging aspects of working with more fearful-avoidant group members is the difficulty helping them find words to express their emotional reactions in the group. These group members often struggle to express their feelings, and some dissociate to cope with unbearable emotions and memories (Briere & Scott, 2006; Wallin, 2007). Traumatic memories can be triggered within seconds, and this makes these individuals especially vulnerable in group therapy. The following example demonstrates how the group process activates John's automatic fear response and how the leader tries to follow up on his emotional reaction multiple times to help John put his feelings into words.

Male Leader:	I wonder why the group is being so generous and polite when people come late to or miss a session.
Janice:	I don't want people to feel badly. If they can't make it, they should be able to miss the session if they have to *[avoiding conflict]*.
Sean:	I agree. I really hate it when people get upset when you really can't make it here on time. The traffic is really awful. It is a waste of time to get upset over that *[more avoidance]*.
Female Leader:	What about others? Does anyone else share a similar or different opinion? *[opening up the process to others who may feel differently]*
Alex:	Well, I guess it makes it harder on us when people come late and we need to start over or review what we have talked about. I know why it is important to be here, and I am not sure what else you want us to do *[looks to male group leader and is first to acknowledge the importance of*

members being at the group and the challenge when people are late].

Michelle: I just don't think we should focus on lateness. There are more important issues to address in the group. I want to hear more about what happened to Susan from last week. *[moves back to avoidance of conflict.]*

Male Leader: What about what Alex said? I think the group is not addressing what he said about it being hard when people are not here. Let me put it another way, what does it mean if we don't care if people show up or are not here? *[The group falls silent, and the male leader pushes a little more than he has had in the past to facilitate the conflict in the group.]*

John: It means nothing. The group is fine *[said with a tightness and agitation in his voice].*

Susan: That doesn't sound fine to me *[using humor to lessen the tension].*

Sean: I wanted to talk about something different. Is it OK if I change the topic? *[More avoidance of the conflict emerging in the here and now of the group.]*

Female Leader: Sean, do you mind if we continue with this a bit longer and get to what you want to raise in a moment? *[Sean nods yes.]* John, you said we were fine, and it felt like you had feelings about what is happening in the group now. Is that correct? *[slowly moving toward John's feelings]*

John: No, not at all. I didn't mean anything by that. *[John smiles and quickly retreats back to a safe place, and his frustration appears to evaporate.]*

Female Leader: John, I feel torn. On one hand, I want to accept that this did not mean anything, but on the other hand, I noticed you seemed to have feelings that quickly faded away. I could easily accept that you do not have those feelings anymore, but those feelings seem to be way too important to just ignore. I wonder if you struggle with whether to share them with us and what would happen if you did. I wonder if the entire group is avoiding these feelings as well.

John: I guess I am not sure it is worth wasting the group's time with this *[looking uncomfortable].*

Sean: You are not wasting our time. You never take up group time *[supporting John but also maintaining his own avoidance of his own reactions].*

Janice: I agree. You are so quiet. I think it is fine to take up the time here.

Male Leader: I know this feels risky, but what would it look like if you didn't filter what you were feeling John and just said it like it is, without worrying what anyone thought [*trying to facilitate John's expression of his reactions in the group*].

John: That's it [*points angrily at the leader*]. What you are doing right now. You keep trying to "make" problems . . . make us feel things we don't feel. I think you basically want to intentionally stir up things in the group. You get off on it. [*John is extremely angry and finally being more honest about his perceptions of the male leader as being aggressive and sadistic.*]

Female Leader: [*to John*] It makes you angry. You feel he is intentionally trying to stir up things in the group that don't exist and he enjoys manipulating everyone? Is that correct? [*empathizing with John's anger and clarifying his underlying internal representation that is being activated*]

John: He sits back calmly and wants us to start fighting with one another. He doesn't listen and never backs off. Look, when we say it is fine when people come late, it's fine. Stop making it something that it's not. [*John is being more honest and revealing more of his anger. He is also standing up for himself and the group members.*]

Although the male leader wore the attributes of an overly aggressive leader to help John explore his experience in the group and identify his internal representation of earlier abusive or neglectful caregivers (Lichtenberg, Lachmann, & Fossage, 2011), the leader also expressed his true self, which was open, engaged, and authentic. The leader did not get defensive or quickly apologize, which would have prevented John from freely expressing his anger. Toward the end of the session, the male leader acknowledged that it took courage for John to confront him in the group, the first member to do so, and stand up for others in the group as well.

Identifying Transference and Parataxic Distortions

One of the helpful benefits of group therapy is having multiple perspectives on the group process. More fearful-avoidant members often project intense malevolent intentions onto others on the basis of their previous traumatic attachment experiences (Wallin, 2007). Unlike individual therapy in which the patient can only compare his or her view of reality with the therapist's perceptions, group therapy allows members to hear multiple perspectives and compare their views of the group process. The space to hear and explore different perspectives can help the more fearful-avoidant member tease apart what aspect of their perceptions is based on reality and what is based on the past.

> *Female Leader:* So what do others think about what John is saying? *[The coleader knew it would be important to have other group members share their experience of the male coleader.]*

> *Susan:* I can understand the part about Mike pushing us. I do think he is pushing us to confront each other more, and we all seem to want to avoid that. It frustrates me too because I don't really like conflict. I just don't want to get angry with anyone in here. *[Susan expresses insight into her own avoidance of anger but also a different subjectivity with regard to the intentionality in Mike. This facilitates mentalization by exploring different perceptions and linking the avoidance of feelings with intentions.]*

> *Alex:* I felt annoyed today too, if you want the truth. I feel like Mike wants us to be more open with one another about being late. I don't really like it when people come late, and I didn't want to share that because I didn't want Sarah to feel bad *[the member who often comes late]*. I also really appreciate Mike and his being honest. Sometimes we are just too nice, and we never say what we really think. I never saw Mike as overly aggressive or intentionally mean. I am sorry John, I know that is how you perceive him, but I just don't see that.

> *Susan:* Oh, me too. I think Mike was trying to help us, even though I also don't like it. I was surprised to hear that John felt it was intentionally nasty. I don't think you get off on it *[said to Mike and indicating her desire to take care of him]*.

Group members became curious about John's belief that the leader was deliberately hurtful, and almost all expressed their experience of the leader as being a caring and compassionate person. Some of the more secure group members, such as Alex, attributed the leader's confrontation of the missed sessions to his caring about the group, not as him being abusive or sadistic.

The female coleader was able to help the group members explore their different impressions of the leader and help them wonder about why they may be different. The group consensus that the leader was frustrating them but not acting abusively in the group helped John become less defensive and more curious about his reactions. He was able to wonder with the group about his automatic perception of the leader and how this was triggered in the session.

Encouraging Interpersonal Feedback

Different group members, with different attachment histories, expressed different reactions in the session. The more secure members like Alex revealed fears of expressing anger directly to one another and worries about offending each other. More preoccupied members, like Susan, revealed fears of being rejected by the group if they were to express anger or confront members directly and engaged in caretaking of the leader when she feared his possible retaliation. Their fears of being rejected were their main concerns. More dismissive members, on the other hand, like Michelle, acknowledged disagreeing with the need to attend sessions but denied any feelings about it. She said she was not angry at all and was not sure why attendance in the group was relevant.

After group members shared their reactions, the leaders invited them to talk more specifically about how they felt about hearing from specific members who did express anger in the group today, especially anger at the leader. Unlike members' different concerns and fears, all the group members praised John for initiating the conversation and asserting himself with the leaders. Even though the members did not share the same perception of the male leader as being abusive, they appreciated his raising this difficult topic in the group. Unlike his past experience of being victimized and then silenced, John took a risk and stood up to authority by directly expressing his anger.

Facilitating Insight Into Core Affect and Impact of Trauma

With the help of the group and his individual therapist, John was able to slowly sort out his experience of feeling violated in the group. He was able to identify his automatic perceptions of the leader having hostile motives and begin to tease apart what triggered this perception in the session. It appeared that the male leader's continued pursuit of the group activated something in John.

John said he felt trapped and suffocated. When the group members asked him more about being trapped, he said he felt "it is important for group members to be able to come and go in the group as they need to without feeling pressured or attacked." The male leader empathized with John's need to feel in control and desire to protect himself but also asked more about his perception of group members being attacked. The leader's goal was to help John make meaning out of his automatic reaction in the group. Although the leader empathized with John's need to alleviate his sense of pressure and admired his courage to confront the leader, he also raised the possibility that John seemed to view all conflict or pressure as attacking and sadistic. The leader raised the possibility that sometimes conflict could be useful and could even lead to more trust in the group, such as John expressing his frustration and standing up for himself in the session.

Months later, the individual therapist told the leaders that this event in the group was significant for John because he said it helped them talk more openly about his automatic reactions in relationships and anger. The group experience activated his implicit perceptions of himself as a victim and of others as abusers and helped John realize how his sexual abuse as a child continued to have an impact on him as an adult. Liotti (2004) found that people with past trauma had internalized three self-experiences: self as victim, self as abuser, and self as rescuer. He argues that these three roles are constructed because of the emotional trauma with the caregivers. The group was helping John identify these different parts of himself as he interacted within the group. Sometimes he felt like a victim who was a child, and at other times he felt abusive. He also noticed that he felt this desire to rush in and protect the other group members when conflict or intimacy made him feel uncomfortable. The group process was extremely helpful to John and his individual therapist, who were able to work together to sort out what was being activated in the group.

The individual therapist noted that the male leader was still perceived as threatening despite the leader's ongoing empathy and support of John in the sessions. During the individual therapy, John revealed being even more mistrustful of the male leader's supportive reaction to him, and this led to a deeper exploration of his sexual abuse and the horrible manipulation he endured. The therapist noted that although John did not trust the male leader, he was moved by the group members' praise of him during the session. Again, it was the group members' support of his anger, their perceptions of the group process, interpersonal feedback, and praise that facilitated John's risk taking and the corrective emotional experience that followed. Over time and with repeated experiences of the threat response in the group, John was able to move slowly toward a more secure attachment to the group.

GROUP WITH INDIVIDUAL TREATMENT FOR THE MORE FEARFUL-AVOIDANT GROUP MEMBER

Silvers (1998) described how combined individual and group therapy facilitate changes for individuals with interpersonal difficulties that stem from a history of trauma. He argues that trauma causes the individual to withdraw during threatening interpersonal experiences, and group provides a rich environment to address these issues. Unlike individual treatment, the group has the potential to activate complex reactions in multiple people. The traumatized individual has the opportunity to gain insight and flexibility when dealing with intense emotional reactions and painful memories of abuse. Although group treatment is central, individual treatment is also critical because it can provide a place where overwhelming emotions and past traumas can be explored and understood. The security of individual therapy helps the group member explore what is being activated in a safe and contained environment, and the individual is later able to bring it to the group when he or she is able to.

In our example, John's history of sexual trauma is stirred in group therapy by the male leader. This trauma had not been addressed after a year in individual treatment. This is a clear example of how group can activate aspects of the self that are not always accessible in individual therapy. Although individual therapy does not provoke the trauma, it is essential in helping John explore his traumatic reactions and continue to engage in the group process. The secure base of individual therapy helped John develop a secure attachment to the group and develop more secure attachments to diverse members within the group. Empirical evidence supports this type of combined group–individual therapy for patients with long-standing interpersonal difficulties, such as John (Bateman & Fonagy, 2001; de Zulueta & Mark, 2000; Hopper, 2001; Linehan, Tutek, Heard, & Armstrong, 1994). Individuals with fearful-avoidant attachments and histories of trauma tend to need more support and benefit from having multiple secure attachments.

PREMATURE DROPOUT OF GROUP AND THE MORE FEARFUL-AVOIDANT ATTACHMENT

Because group therapy is challenging for members with more fearful-avoidance, it is helpful to understand what may be risk factors of dropping out of treatment for these individuals (Stiwne, 1994; Wilberg et al., 2003). Hummelen, Wilberg, and Karterud (2007) asked eight female borderline patients who dropped out of outpatient group treatment how they experienced the group and what led them to end treatment prematurely. As expected, group members who dropped out said they had difficulty coping with the strong emotions that were generated in the treatment. Specifically, individuals described difficulties with rage, hate, powerlessness, shame, and intense anxiety. They also spoke about intense feelings of aggression toward the leaders, whom they perceived were unable to recognize the challenges the group members were experiencing in the groups.

This patient felt a strong rage and contempt toward the therapists, related to her perception of their being unwilling to deal with her suffering or admit their own shortcomings. She felt that the therapists were just like her father who was described as a cynical and cold-hearted man. Furthermore, she had a strong sense of falseness and self-contempt; she often felt extremely shameful and terrified, experiencing an overwhelming fear of being "disguised" and rejected. (p. 78)

This example clearly shows how the patient had a negative view of others (as coldhearted) and negative view of herself (with self-contempt). Unfortunately, this more fearful-avoidant member hid her feelings and dropped out of the group to cope with the emotions that were triggered in the group.

These group members were unable to express themselves in the group and had difficulty linking their relationship difficulties outside of the group to the challenges they were having in the group process. They even "conceived of the group as the causative factor of their symptoms and interpersonal difficulties" (Hummelen et al., 2007, p. 82). This study sheds light on what is likely happening to more fearful-avoidant group members who often struggle in the group. They have difficulty coping with their feelings, are unable to see how the group can help them, and tend to blame the group for the distress they experience in group. Group leaders can best help these members if they can keep in mind their sensitivity to rejection and intense emotions, be aware that they may externalize responsibility for their feelings and be sympathetic to their desire to leave the group to maintain their sense of safety, control, and self-cohesion (Stone & Gustafson, 1982).

CONCLUSION

Group therapy can facilitate the activation and working through of traumatic relationships for members who come to the group with a long-history of elevated attachment anxiety and avoidance. Group therapy provides these patients with interpersonal feedback that calls into question their mistrust of others and devaluation of themselves. In addition, the group has the power to confront these disorganized interpersonal strategies if the leader helps group members explore the underlying emotional dysregulation and cycles of hyperactivation and deactivation.

It is important for group leaders to be aware that these members are at risk of dropping out of treatment if they cannot find a way to regulate the emotions that are intensely triggered in the group sessions. The leader must facilitate empathy, mentalization, insight, and a sense of safety so that the member can start to reveal more honest and frightening projections of malevolence onto others. Having two leaders can often facilitate this process because one can help the member process reactions if the other is activating a flight–fight response. This can also be done by working with an individual therapist who also works with the group member. Although more fearful-avoidant members like John may come to the group inhibited, they can benefit the group. John facilitated the expression of conflict and helped members express their avoidance of conflict in the sessions. Group therapy offers these individuals emotional support, alternative perspectives on the group process, interpersonal feedback, and the capacity to make sense of their automatic reactions.

9

ATTACHMENT AND SPECIAL GROUP POPULATIONS: EATING DISORDERS, SUBSTANCE ABUSE, AND TRAUMA

This chapter examines the role that attachment plays in group therapy with special populations in the areas of eating disorders, substance abuse, and trauma. For each of these three populations, we explore the theoretical and empirical connections to attachment theory, highlight important research findings on attachment in group therapy, and propose attachment-based interventions for group therapists when working with group members with a history of an eating disorder, substance abuse, or trauma.

ATTACHMENT AND EATING DISORDERS

Theoretical and Empirical Links

Individuals with an insecure attachment may be particularly vulnerable to developing eating disorder symptoms because women diagnosed with an eating disorder have been found to possess higher levels of attachment insecurity

http://dx.doi.org/10.1037/14186-010
Attachment in Group Psychotherapy, by C. L. Marmarosh, R. D. Markin, and E. B. Spiegel

(Barone & Guiducci, 2009; Fonagy et al., 1996; Illing, Tasca, Balfour, & Bissada, 2010; Tasca, Foot, et al., 2011). One reason for this may be that individuals with an insecure attachment have difficulty regulating their emotions (e.g., Wallin, 2007). As a result, they may develop eating disorder symptoms as a way of providing some sense of affect regulation (Tasca, Foot, et al., 2011). Tasca et al. (2009) found that, in their study, eating disorder patients with attachment anxiety demonstrated more emotional hyperactivation (e.g., reactivity), which was related to bingeing and purging. In contrast, eating disorder patients with attachment avoidance demonstrated more emotional deactivation (e.g., restricting emotions), which was related to food restriction. In both cases, the specific eating disorder symptom (bingeing and purging vs. food restriction) mirrored the patient's attachment strategy for regulating affect, either restricting food as one restricts emotions or bingeing and purging as a way to cope with overwhelming affect. In addition to difficulty regulating affect, patients with eating disorders have been found to have significantly lower coherence of mind than people in the general population (Barone & Guiducci, 2009; Fonagy et al., 1996). Tasca, Foot, et al. (2011) suggested that eating disorder symptoms interrupt narrative coherence and keep the patient from processing important yet painful attachment-related memories. Taken together, these studies provide some tentative evidence that attachment insecurities may lead to eating disorder symptoms for some patients and that these symptoms serve the function of coping with painful attachment-related emotions and memories. In contrast, an alternative hypothesis is that patients with an eating disorder are more vulnerable to developing an insecure attachment. Future research should investigate further the direction and relationship between eating disorders and insecure attachment.

Group Therapy for Eating Disorders From an Attachment Perspective

Tasca and colleagues (Tasca, Balfour, Ritchie, & Bissada, 2006, 2007a) studied attachment as a predictor of outcome and as an outcome variable in and of itself for women with binge-eating disorder (BED) in either group psychodynamic-interpersonal psychotherapy (GPIP) or group cognitive behavioral therapy (GCBT). GPIP focuses on how members' maladaptive relationship patterns are re-created within the group and how group member interactions can be used to challenge these patterns inside and outside of the group (Tasca, Balfour, et al., 2006; Tasca et al., 2007a). In contrast, GCBT aims to reduce problematic behaviors such as dietary restriction, monitors eating behaviors and cognitions, and considers more adaptive coping strategies and reasonable expectations (Tasca, Balfour, et al., 2006; Tasca et al., 2007a). The results of these studies suggest that both group treatments were successful in helping members reduce their days binged (Tasca, Balfour, et al., 2006;

Tasca et al., 2007a) and depression (Tasca et al., 2007a). Furthermore, over the course of both treatment groups, positive changes in insecure attachment were demonstrated for group members (Tasca, Balfour, et al., 2006; Tasca et al., 2007a). Tasca et al. (2007a) suggested that common factors transpired across GPIP and GCBT to explain similar changes in attachment and symptoms. For example, the positive interpersonal context and group interactions that all were found in both treatments (Tasca et al., 2007a) may have facilitated changes in self-reported attachment. Thus, regardless of the particular treatment context, group members may internalize positive therapeutic interactions, helping them to modify maladaptive attachment-related schemas (Tasca et al., 2007a).

Interestingly, a group member's need for approval predicted improvement in depression in GPIP but not in GCBT (Tasca et al., 2007a). Tasca et al. (Tasca, Balfour, et al., 2006; Tasca et al., 2007b) posited that more anxious members, those elevated on the dimension of attachment anxiety, may benefit from GPIP because this therapy focuses on group member relationships and the interpersonal issues underlying the members' eating disorders. These members, who need to feel close to others and are sensitive to the affective tone of relationships, may be a particularly good fit for the interpersonal dynamic nature of GPIP. This is consistent with previous research (Tasca, Balfour, et al., 2006) that has found higher attachment anxiety scores to be associated with improvements in days binged for women with BED who received GPIP but not GCBT. In contrast, Tasca et al. (2007a) did not find a relationship between change in avoidance and improved symptoms in either treatment condition. Perhaps the interpersonal focus of GPIP is not as salient to more avoidant members, those elevated on the dimension of avoidance, who deny their need for closeness and are inherently self-critical (Tasca et al., 2007a). Furthermore, Tasca and colleagues (2007a) suggested that because GCBT is highly didactic and educational, changes in attachment may not be necessary for symptomatic improvements. This is consistent with findings from Tasca, Balfour, et al. (2006) suggesting that lower attachment anxiety scores are associated with improvement in days binged for women with BED in GCBT. Alternatively, among those receiving GCBT, the lack of a relationship between change in avoidance and symptom improvement may be attributed to the higher dropout rate associated with attachment avoidance in GCBT (Tasca et al., 2007a). Although Tasca et al. (Tasca, Balfour, et al., 2006a; Tasca et al., 2007a) provided some evidence to suggest that altering insecure attachment models leads to symptom improvement for more anxiously attached members in GPIP, the results for more avoidantly attached group members with an eating disorder are less clear, and more research is needed on the role that attachment plays in the process and outcome of group therapy for these members.

Suggestions for group leaders are as follows.

1. *Common factors may explain positive changes in attachment across group treatments.* Regardless of the particular group therapy modality, to facilitate secure attachments for group members, group leaders should promote a positive group climate and group therapy alliance (Tasca et al., 2007a).

2. *Attachment style may be matched with group treatment to facilitate a successful outcome.* The research suggests that for patients diagnosed with BED and have high attachment anxiety (Tasca, Balfour, et al., 2006; Tasca et al., 2007a) or a high need for approval (Tasca, Balfour, et al., 2006), group treatments, such as GPIP, that focus on the underlying interpersonal and affective issues behind the symptoms may be particularly helpful in facilitating a successful outcome. Although the findings are less clear when it comes to patients with BED and more avoidant attachment, groups that are more structured and skills based, such as GCBT, appear to be more effective for group members with more avoidance (Tasca, Balfour, et al., 2006), although other studies have not found a difference in outcome for eating disorder patients with more avoidant attachments (Tasca et al., 2007a).

3. *Group leaders can be mindful that although ruptures and repairs in the alliance occur throughout the life of GPIP groups, the underlying group climate should be positive, collaborative, and less conflictual for more preoccupied members.* Tasca, Ritchie, and colleagues (2006) found that although, overall, ruptures and repairs in the alliance transpired over the course of GPIP, group members with a more anxious attachment needed to experience the underlying group climate as increasingly engaged over the course of the therapy to have a positive outcome. The researchers suggest that these individuals need to experience more group cohesion to meet their attachment needs and to make full use of the therapy (Rom & Mikulincer, 2003; Tasca, Ritchie, et al., 2006).

4. *Interpersonal or psychodynamic group therapists may want to identify more avoidant members in a pregroup assessment and actively prepare them for the emotional stressors that may come with a relationship-focused treatment.* Research has found that patients with an eating disorder and higher attachment avoidance are less likely to perceive a positive therapy alliance (Tasca et al., 2007b), less likely to perceive an engaged group climate (Illing, Tasca, Balfour, & Bissada, 2011), and more likely to drop out of treat-

ment (Tasca et al., 2004). Preparation may include information about the benefits and stressors of interpersonal exploration in group therapy, as well as typical group norms regarding cohesion and self-disclosure (Illing et al., 2011; Tasca et al., 2007b).

ATTACHMENT AND SUBSTANCE ABUSE

Theoretical and Empirical Links

Theoretically, secure attachments help individuals self-regulate various internal experiences (e.g., affect, behavior, cognition, interpersonal relatedness, physiology, sense of self; Padykula & Conklin, 2010). However, when a person is insecurely attached, self-regulation is compromised and internal experiences become more imbalanced and extreme. For example, individuals with an insecure attachment are more likely to feel (physiologically and affectively) hyperaroused and overemotional, in the case of a more anxious attachment, or dissociated and alexithymic, in the case of a more avoidant attachment (Padykula & Conklin, 2010). Thus, for some, substances become a way of coping with and managing painful internal experiences (Padykula & Conklin, 2010). Specifically, more anxiously attached individuals tend to abuse substances to help them regulate their affective distress, which often feels too overwhelming to manage effectively. More avoidant individuals, in contrast, tend to abuse substances to detach from emotional awareness of their problems (see Mikulincer & Shaver, 2007b).

In other words, insecurely attached individuals may be more likely to turn to substances to regulate their emotions because they never had a secure attachment figure to serve this vital function. Similarly, individuals with an insecure attachment may initially turn to substances as a substitute for the missing relational intimacy that comes from not having a reliable attachment figure (Flores, 2001, 2004; Höfler & Kooyman, 1996). According to Höfler and Kooyman (1996), substances allow insecurely attached individuals to shift their attachment needs from an unreliable person(s) to an object that is seen as impersonal, secret, and secure. This pseudo-attachment relationship with a substance, although temporary and addictive, fills a relational void for some individuals.

Group Therapy for Substance Abuse From an Attachment Perspective

Most of the literature on group therapy for substance abuse from an attachment perspective is theoretical. Theoretically, group therapy is effective in treating substance abuse because the group serves as a secure base for the members, helping them to transition their attachment needs from substances onto the group itself (Flores, 2001, 2004). As group members immerse themselves into the group, they become a part of a larger, interconnected experience that is greater than their own isolated and relationally empty experiences (Flores, 2001). In this way, the group comes to serve the attachment functions (emotional regulation, a sense of belonging and connectedness) that substances once filled. In a rare study on attachment in groups for substance abuse, Polansky, Lauterbach, Litzke, Coulter, and Sommers (2006) studied the curative factors of an attachment-based parenting group for insecurely attached mothers suffering from addiction. The authors found increases in the mothers' reflective functioning and concluded that this occurred as a function of the safe, supportive, and nonjudgmental group environment. The group also increased the quantity and quality of the group members' communication with their children. The group members experienced what it feels like to be known and accepted, basic qualities of a secure attachment, perhaps leading to positive outcomes in reflective functioning and verbal communication (Polansky et al., 2006).

Suggestions for group leaders are as follows.

1. *Particularly in the initial stages of group, group leaders can be supportive and directive, focusing on creating a structured and secure group environment.* Early in recovery, individuals with addictions often have difficulty tolerating the neutral stance and lack of gratification from a more classically oriented psychodynamic group therapist (Flores, 2001). Flores (2001) theorized that this is because therapist neutrality heightens member transference and promotes regression, which is too much for these patients to handle at this vulnerable stage in recovery. By actively working to facilitate a safe, supportive, and structured group environment, the group leader helps group members come to rely on the group as a secure base. Group structure and support helps group members contain their anxiety, diminishing their temptation to use (Flores, 2001).

2. *Focus on balancing affect containment in the beginning stages of group with affect expression in the later stages.* The longer group members can maintain sobriety and emotional stability, the easier it is for them to look at their internal experiences more closely, ultimately increasing reflective functioning abilities. As reflective functioning increases, group members are increasingly able to tolerate more insight-oriented work (Flores, 2001).

ATTACHMENT AND TRAUMA

Theoretical and Empirical Links

Here we consider attachment and both posttraumatic stress disorder (PTSD) and complex trauma (C-PTSD). C-PTSD is a deep psychological injury resulting from extended interpersonal trauma (e.g., emotional, physical, sexual abuse).

Attachment and PTSD

Herman (1992) described two major and oscillating posttraumatic stress responses: intrusion (i.e., flashbacks, images, and emotions related to the event) and constriction (i.e., numbing, denial, and inhibition). Secure attachment acts "as a protective shield against PTSD" (Mikulincer & Shaver, 2007b, p. 388) by providing access to the feelings of safety and security that come with internalized positive mental representations of secure attachment figures. In contrast, more anxious attachment intensifies the intrusive reactions of posttraumatic stress because more anxiously attached individuals are already more likely to be hyperaroused. Alternatively, persons with more attachment avoidance who already deactivate their emotions are more likely to restrict or numb their posttraumatic stress reactions and have more severe posttraumatic avoidant responses (see Mikulincer & Shaver, 2007b, for a review).

Attachment and C-PTSD

An insecure attachment may develop as a reaction to complex trauma early in life (Pearlman & Courtois, 2005; Schore, 2003; van der Kolk et al., 2005). Consistent with this, an association between insecure attachment and PTSD symptom severity has been observed among adults who were sexually or physically abused as children (e.g., Muller, Sicoli & Lemieux, 2000; Twaite & Rodriguez-Srednicki, 2004). Although similar to PTSD, the primary differentiation of complex trauma from PTSD is in the significant developmental damage done to the victim's sense of self and associated psychological functions (Herman, 1992).

Group Therapy for Trauma From an Attachment Perspective

Although more research is needed, several studies have found that group members with more attachment avoidance appear to have poorer outcomes in trauma groups, whereas members with a more anxious attachment appear to have better outcomes in these groups (Muller & Rosenkranz, 2009; Saunders & Edelson, 1999). For instance, Muller and Rosenkranz (2009) studied attachment in an inpatient program for PTSD (of which relational group therapy was one of several components of treatment) and found that positive changes in attachment were associated with symptom reduction during treatment as well as maintenance after treatment. However, although both attachment anxiety and avoidance decreased during treatment, reductions in attachment anxiety were maintained 6 months after treatment, whereas attachment avoidance increased in the 6 months after treatment. They concluded that attachment avoidance may be more resistant than attachment anxiety to relationally based treatments. Similarly, in their case study of a long-term psychodynamic trauma group, Saunders and Edelson (1999) found that group members with a dismissing-avoidant style took significantly more time than other members to experience positive outcomes in group. Perhaps this is because although insight and bonding with other group members were possible for the dismissing-avoidant members in this study, they were quick to retreat to older, trauma-based, internal working models when their attachment systems were activated. The authors concluded that process groups, because of their relational nature, may be too threatening for dismissing-avoidant members with a history of trauma. In contrast, the authors concluded that because the more anxiously attached members in their trauma group were more open to emotional experiences and relational intimacy, they were able to make better use of the group.

Suggestions for group leaders are as follows.

1. *Engage in an active stance with an emphasis on here-and-now inter-actions.* Members in trauma groups have a high potential of experiencing flashbacks and reenactments in the group process, which can lead to affective flooding, dissociation, and/or decreased mentalization (de Zulueta & Mark, 2000; Saunders & Edelson, 1999). Keeping more preoccupied group members engaged in the here and now of group may minimize the overwhelming affect associated with the reexperiencing of the traumatic material (de Zulueta & Mark, 2000). For more dismissing-avoidant members, gently but directly encouraging identification and labeling of internal experiences in the here and now may help minimize possible deactivation or dissociation (Fonagy & Bateman, 2006; Karterud & Bateman, 2011).

2. *Reflect on feelings for the purpose of enhancing mentalization in group members.* One way that trauma victims survive complex trauma inflicted by an attachment figure is to shut down mentally and emotionally. By closing off their reflection about thoughts and feelings, they insulate themselves from the reality that the person who is supposed to care for them feels and acts hatefully

toward them (Bateman & Fonagy, 2003; Fonagy & Bateman, 2006). As a result, insecurely attached trauma group members may be quick to mentally shut down at any time they sense a potential recapitulation of their trauma experience in the group, real or imagined. Group leaders should help these members to identify, explore, and understand the emotions that arise in their relationships with other members to better identify the interpersonal interactions that trigger their traumatic reactions and reduce mentalization (Bateman & Fonagy, 2003; Karterud & Bateman, 2011).

3. *Structured or integrated groups may be more appropriate for trauma victims with high attachment avoidance.* Given that some studies have found poorer outcomes for group members with a dismissing-avoidant attachment in trauma groups (Muller & Rosenkranz, 2009; Saunders & Edelson, 1999), cognitive behavioral therapy or dialectical behavioral therapy groups may be more appropriate for these members. Both of these group treatments are structured and teach particular skill sets that may directly facilitate emotion regulation and indirectly improve attachment (Fonagy & Bateman, 2006). For example, dialectical behavioral therapy groups emphasize mindfulness, which is related to improved mentalization (Fonagy & Bateman, 2006; Wallin, 2007).

CONCLUSION

The common thread across all of these special populations is that these patients' attachments not only play a role in developing their symptoms but also can have a powerful influence on the group treatment process and outcome. Regardless of whether a member has an eating disorder, has a history of trauma, or relies on alcohol to cope, his or her level of attachment anxiety and avoidance is relevant to the group treatment and can be useful to group leaders working with members who share a common issue: difficulty regulating emotions and maintaining intimate relationships.

10

DIVERSITY IN GROUP PSYCHOTHERAPY: ATTACHMENT, ETHNICITY, AND RACE

Many group members enter group psychotherapy with the same plaguing questions and doubts about whether they will feel a sense of safety, acceptance, and belonging in the group. The way in which a group member initially answers these questions is likely to be influenced by his or her attachment history with significant others and with groups. Furthermore, all of these relational experiences occur within a specific context known as *culture*. One's personal relationship history is shaped and defined by one's political, social, and cultural histories, all of which influence how group members think about and behave in relationships. Accordingly, recent research has begun to explore differences in adult attachment styles that exist between people of diverse backgrounds. The first part of this chapter briefly reviews the research on how adult attachment orientations relate to ethnicity and culture. To demonstrate how culture influences the group therapy process and group therapist, the chapter focuses on three broad

http://dx.doi.org/10.1037/14186-011
Attachment in Group Psychotherapy, by C. L. Marmarosh, R. D. Markin, and E. B. Spiegel
Copyright © 2013 by the American Psychological Association. All rights reserved.

ethnic groups, recognizing that there is much more diversity within these groups that we cannot fully address. Special attention is given to how cultural context may affect group members' dyadic and group attachment internal working models.

DYADIC AND GROUP ATTACHMENTS AND RACIAL–ETHNIC DIFFERENCES: RESEARCH AND CLINICAL APPLICATION

Only a few studies have examined adult attachment styles in close relationships among different racial–ethnic groups in the United States. Wei, Russell, Mallinckrodt, and Zakalik (2004) conducted the first study that compared adult attachment in close relationships among four U.S. racial–ethnic groups in the same investigation, including African American, Hispanic American (the term used in their research to describe Latin American and individuals from Latino backgrounds), Caucasian, and Asian American college students in their sample, using the Experiences in Close Relationship Scale (Brennan, Clark, & Shaver, 1998; described in Chapter 3, this volume) to measure attachment. Wei et al. (2004) described several important findings. First, the constructs of attachment avoidance and anxiety were equivalent for the ethnically diverse college students in this study. Wei et al. (2004) suggested that perhaps the ethnically diverse students in their sample were highly acculturated and, as a result, held a common view of attachment anxiety and avoidance. This may be a limitation because they did not explore attachments in less acculturated individuals.

Although individuals from different racial–ethnic groups conceptualized avoidance and anxiety similarly in this study, group differences in attachment style and the associations between attachment and negative mood were found (Wei et al., 2004). Specifically, although African American and Asian Americans reported higher avoidance than Caucasians, avoidance was not related to negative mood for these two groups. Avoidance was related to mood for Hispanic Americans and Caucasians. Asian American and Hispanic Americans also reported greater attachment anxiety compared with Caucasians. However, attachment anxiety was associated with negative mood for all four racial–ethnic groups, consistent with previous research on attachment and mental health with Caucasian samples (e.g., Lopez & Brennan, 2000). However, the relationship between attachment anxiety and negative mood was significantly stronger for Asian Americans than for Caucasians or African Americans. In other words, Asian Americans with more attachment anxiety were more likely to report negative moods than were Caucasians or African Americans with more attachment anxiety. Wei et al.'s (2004) work represents a significant contribution to the literature in that their study specifically examined differences in adult attachment across four racial–ethnic groups living in the United States, although their sample was a highly educated college population, and it may not represent more diverse members of these groups. The results of their study are discussed here in the context of other research on attachment and race–ethnicity.

ATTACHMENT ORIENTATION AND HISPANIC AND LATINO CULTURE

Hispanic and Latino Americans in Wei et al.'s (2004) study reported more attachment anxiety than did their Caucasian peers, consistent with previous research and Hispanic cultural norms. Although Caucasian adults classified as secure tend to be more independent and less likely to rely on others to meet their needs (Bartholomew & Shaver, 1998), Hispanic and Latin American cultures value interdependence and a family orientation (D. W. Sue & Sue, 2003). They are more likely to depend on others to meet their needs and seek social approval (Gloria & Segura-Herrera, 2004). Consistent with this, previous research has also found that Latino adults (Mickelson, Kessler, & Shaver, 1997) score higher on preoccupation. When working with Hispanic and Latino American group members, it is important for group leaders not to overpathologize these group members' attachment-seeking behaviors and instead to understand these behaviors within the cultural context. The following clinical vignette illustrates how Hispanic cultural norms and expectations can influence Hispanic American group members' attachment orientations to dyads and groups.

Case Example: Hispanic Cultural Norms and Attachment Orientations

Maria is a 20-year-old Hispanic American college student who came to group therapy to address depression and self-esteem issues. Maria's parents are first-generation immigrants, and she is the first member of her family to attend college. She describes coming from a tight-knit extended family and ethnic community in which she felt a sense of belonging, comfort, and connection. However, Maria and her mother continually clashed over Maria's desire to go away to school, a wish that left Maria's mother feeling betrayed and abandoned. Maria described her mother as very depressed, with a history of sexual abuse and poverty. Maria was often the one who took care of her mother, and she was the one who maintained the household and cooked for the family. Shortly after they moved to the United States, her mother became more incapacitated and struggled with leaving her homeland. Maria said her mother would lock herself in her room for hours, leaving Maria alone to care for her siblings because her father worked two jobs and was focused on supporting the family.

The conflict that Maria experienced with her mother over going away to college is not uncommon within Latin cultures that are family oriented. However, Maria's reaction to this conflict—namely, intense anxiety and depression—is better understood when considering the chaotic and unpredictable atmosphere in which she was raised. Maria's experiences related to poverty and immigrating to a new and unfamiliar country led to helpless feelings of being out of control, alone, and unprotected. Maria's mother, because of her depression and history of sexual abuse, was not consistently available to help Maria through these threatening and scary situations because she had difficulty coping herself, vacillating between extreme mood swings. Maria's experience of not knowing what to expect, whether her mother would be in a good mood or a depressed mood or even where her next real meal would come from, influenced her attachment internal working models of others as inconsistent and unavailable. Consequently, as a group member, Maria was clingy with other members, fearing that she could not predict their reactions to her or when they would or would not be available to meet her attachment needs.

Although Maria struggled with her attachment to her mother, Maria's ethnic community responded to her needs, providing a sense of support and mirroring and even celebrating her college admission. As a matter of fact, Maria's church collected money and financed part of her college tuition. Because of Maria's positive attachment experiences with her ethnic group but inconsistent attachment experiences with her caregivers, in the therapy group, Maria demonstrated a secure group attachment but a more preoccupied dyadic attachment given her elevated attachment anxiety and minimal attachment avoidance. Maria experienced the therapy group as a safe haven, where she could turn in times of distress. She demonstrated a strong allegiance to the group and strong group identity, and she perceived the group to be cohesive and caring. However, Maria had a difficult time forming attachments to individual members and would often try to form "special" relationships with individuals in the group by taking care of them. This hyperactivating strategy was seen as an attempt to gain self-worth in one-on-one relationships, stemming from her early role as a caregiver to her mother and family. Maria believed that she had to earn her self-esteem through giving to others. Regardless of how much others liked her, Maria never felt that she was truly accepted by them.

Maria's attempts to form close or special relationships with particular members usually resulted in them pulling away. When these repeated interactions were processed in the group, members revealed that they sometimes felt suffocated by Maria's need to take care of them and her continued pursuit of their affection. They also felt that Maria was focusing on them to get what she needed and that she was not always honest about her feelings of frustration or anger. Although Maria felt hurt by this feedback, she was able to remain engaged and explore these reactions within the safety of the group because of her secure group attachment style. With the help of the members, Maria eventually was able to link her within-group behaviors to her fears of being rejected and disappointed in relationships. She was also able to start to understand how her mother's depression and history of trauma affected her own perceptions of herself and others.

Commentary

The case of Maria highlights the complexity of the attachment system and how an individual can have a secure group attachment that is based on his or her ethnic identity while also having a more preoccupied attachment to a primary caregiver. In this case, Maria formed a secure attachment to the therapy group based on her experiences with her ethnic community but struggled with dyadic relationships within the group because of her more preoccupied attachment to her mother. There are several main points that group leaders can take from the case of Maria and apply to their work with diverse group members.

1. Maria was from a more collectivistic culture, was strongly identified with that culture, and was able to rely on a secure group attachment to engage in the group and to explore her attachment fears in dyadic relationships. More generally, because Hispanic culture values interdependence and collectivism (D. W. Sue & Sue, 2003), Hispanic/Latin American group members who are not conflicted with their culture may have a relatively positive internal working model of groups and actively seek proximity from the group, experiencing it as a secure base.

2. In general, racial–ethnic minority group members' expectations of the group leader may vary depending on their attachment avoidance or anxiety. For instance, because Latino and Hispanic American adults have been found to score higher on attachment anxiety (Mickelson, Kessler, R. C., & Shaver, 1997; Wei, Russell, Mallinckrodt, & Zakalik, et al., 2004), Hispanic American group members may actively seek the approval of the group leader and be concerned with the leader's rejection. The challenge for group leaders is to tease apart which aspects of these types of group member attachment behaviors, typically referred to as hyperactivating behaviors, are culturally normative and which aspects represent past attachment traumas.

Suggestions for Group Leaders

Identify the Impact of Culture on Perceived Threats to Attachment Ties and How Members Respond to These Threats

There are likely to be cultural differences pertaining to what is perceived as a threat to one's attachment bonds and what are considered to be adaptive ways of responding to these threats. To Maria, coming from a Hispanic culture that emphasizes family, loyalty, and interdependence, behaviors that prioritize individual autonomy at the expense of the family (or group) are likely to feel like, and even be, a threat to her attachment relationships. Hispanic cultural norms related to dependency and community have a significant role in shaping self–other boundaries, making them less differentiated, in dyadic and group relationships. Less psychological space exists between caregiver and infants, extended family and individuals, and the ethnic community and individuals, relative to European American culture. Because of these differences in the quality of attachment bonds in Hispanic cultures, compared with European American culture, behaviors that prioritize the self and one's own autonomy, which are seen as signs of a healthy adult attachment in European American culture, can be experienced as threats to attachment bonds in Hispanic cultures. For example, whereas Maria's decision to go away to college would be considered a healthy expression of autonomy in European American culture, in cultures that value family loyalty and interdependency, this decision is more likely to be experienced as an attachment loss to both Maria and her mother.

Focus on Both Dyadic and Group Attachments

Group members from collectivistic cultures are likely to internalize their ethnic group or community as a group attachment object that guides expectations of new groups. Maria had a strong attachment to her ethnic community, which guided her expectations of the therapy group. It is important for group leaders to understand how members' past experiences with groups affect the ways in which they perceive, internalize, and respond to the therapy group. For example, Maria's secure attachment to groups helped her use the therapy group to explore her feelings and the internal conflicts underlying her depression and low self-esteem.

Although Maria had a history of positive experiences with groups that helped her to use the therapy group as a source of support, mirroring, and emotional regulation, she was in the process of forming multiple group attachments that sometimes conflicted with one another. Maria's conflict with her mother, and within herself, over attending college away from home can be in least partly attributed to differences in acculturation, because Maria was more acculturated than her mother. Maria wrestled with the desire to express her autonomy and pursue college and the wish to please her mother and stay close to home and help run the family business, clearly reflecting a conflict between different cultural expectations and norms. This can be understood in as a clash between two group attachments. She felt a strong ethnic group attachment that she relied on for support, mirroring, and a sense of self. At the same time, she had an emerging group attachment to Western individualistic culture. Balancing these two attachments without feeling like ties to one had to be severed to keep ties to the other engendered much grief and conflict for Maria. The group's tolerance for accepting differences in others was crucial for Maria to eventually learn to accept different parts of herself.

Explore Majority–Minority Subgrouping

As alluded to in the clinical vignette, Maria wanted to form special and close relationships with certain members at the exclusion of others. When she tried to establish intimacy with Caucasian group members in the ways she was accustomed to in her own culture, she was called "clingy" and meddlesome, and others withdrew from her. However, subgrouping with other minority members who shared a more collectivist view of relationships naturally felt safer and more accepting for Maria. Group leaders should help members explore the function of these majority–minority subgroups and appreciate the cultural differences among them so subgrouping is no longer necessary.

ATTACHMENT ORIENTATION AND AFRICAN AMERICAN CULTURE

Two separate studies have found that African American college students report greater attachment avoidance than their Caucasian peers (Lopez, Melendez, & Rice, 2000b; Wei et al., 2004). Other research using a more representative sample has also found that dismissiveness and avoidance are more common among African Americans than European American adults (Griffin & Bartholomew, 1994; Leerkes & Siepak, 2006; Magai et al., 2001; Mickelson, Kessler, & Shaver, et al., 1997; Montague, Magai, Consedine, & Gillespie, 2003).

There are several possible reasons why African Americans overall tend to score higher on attachment avoidance. First, in general, greater instability in the family of origin, lower socioeconomic status, and financial adversity predict lower levels of security in young and middle-age adults (Mickelson et al., 1997; Schmitt et al., 2004). Given the results of this research, it may be that socioeconomic status directly predicts attachment avoidance, although being African American in and of itself does not make one more likely to be classified as dismissing-avoidant. Second, experiences with prejudice and racism may breed a sense of cultural mistrust and avoidance among minorities in a majority culture (Terrell & Terrell, 1981). Experiences of being discriminated against and marginalized not only by individuals but also by groups on a systemic level would make most people feel wary of new individuals and groups, expecting them to be hostile, uncaring, and even aggressive. Last, adult attachment avoidance among African Americans may be a result of group differences in early socialization practices and parental style. Specifically, African American parents tend to use harsher discipline than European American parents (e.g., Deater-Deckard, Dodge, Bates, & Pettit, 1996), and their parenting style has been characterized as "no-nonsense," classified between "authoritarian" and "authoritative" (Brody & Flor, 1998). In turn, parenting style has a clear relationship to attachment patterns (Collins, 1996; Magai, 1999). This has led some authors (e.g., Consedine, Magai, & Bonanno, 2002) to speculate that these kinds of discipline and socialization practices are partially responsible for the greater prevalence of dismissing-avoidant attachment (Magai et al., 2001; Mickelson et al., 1997), emotional inhibition (Consedine & Magai, 2002), and reluctance to self-disclose (Plasky & Lorion, 1984) among African Americans.

Although some studies suggest that African American parents tend to rely on harsh discipline when socializing their children, these practices may be adaptive within a certain cultural context (Montague, Magai, Consedine, & Gillespie, 2003). Parents may adopt this style for the purpose of helping their children adapt to challenging, unsafe, and discriminatory environments (Brody & Flor, 1998). Because these parenting practices occur within a specific cultural context, they may not have the same effect on internal working models for African Americans compared with other ethnic groups (Montague et al., 2003). Montague et al. (2003) found that caregivers' punitive responding during childhood affects adult attachment patterns differently for African Americans and European Americans in later life. Specifically, punitive emotional socialization predicted dismissing-avoidant attachment dimensions for African Americans, whereas such practices predicted the fearful-avoidant attachment dimension among European Americans. These findings suggest that punitive parenting practices lead to African American adults developing a more negative internal working model of others, whereas European Americans develop a more negative model of self and others. This is consistent with research that African Americans tend to have better self-esteem than do European Americans (Gray-Little & Hafdahl, 2000). Developing a negative internal working model of others may help African Americans cope with racism and discrimination while maintaining their self-esteem. Although this has never been empirically tested, individuals who experience group discrimination, racism, or group hatred may learn that groups can be threatening, dangerous, and even aggressive, suggesting that African Americans may also score higher on group attachment avoidance in certain situations.

African American families have been characterized as extended, and children often have multiple caregivers (Howes, 1999). The extended family, community, and multiple caregivers may all serve as multiple dyadic and group attachment objects. How these nonparental figures and groups help or hinder attachment security has yet to be investigated. It may be that individuals possess multiple attachment schemas that become activated depending on the traits of new people and groups (see Mikulincer & Shaver, 2001). For example, an avoidant schema of groups may develop as a result of experiences with group hatred and discrimination, whereas simultaneously a secure schema of groups may also develop as a result of experiences with one's church, extended family, and racial–ethnic community. The clinical vignette that follows illustrates how experiences with racism and discrimination can impact dyadic and group attachments within the therapy group.

Case Example: The Impact of Racism on Attachment Orientations

Pete and Steve are group members in a diverse group for veterans with a dual diagnosis of posttraumatic stress disorder and substance abuse. Pete is a 35-year-old African American man with a dismissing-avoidant attachment style to the group, as demonstrated by his denial of a group identity and attribution of hostile intentions to the group as a whole. However, he formed bonds with some of the other members within the group, seeking support from these individual members and reciprocating this support as well. Steve, a 50-year-old White man, demonstrated a dismissing-avoidant attachment to both the group and individuals within the group. He acted superior to the other members and said that he was too advanced in his sobriety for this group. He rarely self-disclosed and often showed contempt for other members, especially for Pete and the other two Black group members.

Pete unexpectedly missed two group sessions with no explanation or warning. When Pete returned to the group, some of the other members confronted him about his unexplained absences and expressed genuine concern for him and his sobriety. Pete grew defensive and angry with the group, protesting that although he felt close to some of the other members, he didn't need or care about the group. The group leader asked Pete, "It seems hard for you to believe that this group really cares about you. I wonder what feels hard about that?" Pete disclosed that he was shuffled between his grandmother and foster care, where he was physically abused, and he has never felt connected to or safe within a family or community. He enlisted in the army at 18, and upon his return home, he could not find employment and became homeless. Pete felt like society had largely forgotten him because he was a Black man but also a war veteran. The group leader wondered out loud, "Pete, given your experiences, it would make sense to me that you may have decided not to come to group last week because it was hard to know if you could trust the closeness that the group felt the week before. Given what you've been through, I would understand why you would want to protect yourself from being hurt again." Most of the group members gave Pete support and validation, saying that he put words to some of their own experiences and feelings. In return, Pete slowly began to self-disclose more and began to access more emotional parts of himself that were previously walled off.

However, during this group encounter, Steve was quiet for most of the group session and kept shaking his leg and looking at the clock. When the group leader asked what Steve's reactions were, he exploded with rage, "I think this damn group is being way too easy on Pete! It's obvious he didn't come to group last week because he was drunk. He's a liar, and he should not be allowed back in the group." At this point, the group leader intervened and asked Steve to explain what his anger was about. With help and input from the group, Steve eventually revealed that he was having his own impulses to use drugs again, and Pete's absence last week reminded him of his own desire to not show up for group and "use" instead. Steve had projected his own desire to use drugs onto Pete because he felt inadequate and ashamed of his own addictions.

Once Steve was able to recognize his own feelings, the group leader normalized feelings of wanting to use drugs and alcohol (differentiating between the wish to use and the action or behavior) and helped Steve, along with the rest of the group, share their experiences of longing for the emotional numbness that comes from drugs and alcohol. Steve was able to recognize that Pete served as a symbol for his own impulses and desires and that his desire to expunge Pete from the group was an unconscious attempt to deny his own shame about wanting to use again.

When another group member asked if there was something about Pete that provoked Steve, Steve mumbled something under his breath and, after much prodding, revealed that his father held the view that Black people were just liars. Steve minimized the impact of his comment. Immediately many White members confronted Steve, but Steve was initially not able to acknowledge his own racism and discrimination toward Pete in the group. As the members confronted Steve, Pete's body language changed, turning toward the other members and relaxing, rather than his usual stance of looking away from the members and tensing his muscles, as if he were awaiting an attack. The group leader asked Pete what he was feeling right now, and Pete replied that hearing the other White group members confront Steve made him feel supported and more trusting of the group. He said that no group of people, White or Black, has ever cared enough to stick up for him like this. Pete was able to express to the other members how much their support meant to him, and the other members expressed to Pete that they valued and respected him and that he deserved to be treated with respect and dignity.

When Pete was asked the same question about Steve, Pete revealed experiences of racism and discrimination (especially with White men in a position of power) that made it hard to trust Steve, who was the only older White male member in the group. Pete revealed a history of discrimination and even violence related to the color of his skin and expressed how this influenced his perceptions of members in the group. Without warning, Steve became bright red and slowly revealed a history of emotional and physical abuse at the hands of an older White man, his father. The experience of abuse and humiliation was familiar to both Pete and Steve. Steve eventually revealed shame at his White identity, and this led to group members sharing their own painful pasts and how their experience of race and hatred influences their attitudes and feelings about their own race and what they project on other members.

Commentary

The group process, described in this clinical vignette, helped to facilitate changes in Pete's internal representations of self, others, and groups. Through the other White members confronting Steve about the impact of his racist attitudes, Pete learned that sometimes other people and groups will support him regardless of the color of his skin and that not all White people will treat him as he has been treated in the past by individuals from the dominant culture. Also, because Steve ultimately acknowledged his own projections and stopped placing unwanted aspects of himself onto Pete, rather than Pete internalizing Steve's negative projections, Pete developed a more positive view of himself. Because of these experiences, over time, Pete was able to develop a more secure attachment to other individuals and groups. More general expectations of African American group members' internal working models are as follows.

1. Because African Americans have been found to score higher on attachment avoidance (e.g., Griffin & Bartholomew, 1994; Leerkes & Siepak, 2006), African American group members may possess a positive internal working model of self but a negative internal working model of others and of the group itself, especially if the group comprises mostly members and leaders from the dominant culture. Instances of oppression, marginalization,

and discrimination by individuals and groups may make it difficult for these group members to trust the group, self-disclose, and
generally to use the group as a secure base.

2. If a group member's internal working model of others is negative, then this group member is more likely to see the group
leader as rejecting, unavailable, and unempathic. For example,
because of Pete's past experiences with White people in positions of power who marginalized and humiliated him, his internal working model of others (particularly of others in positions
of power) led him to expect the group leader to also be rejecting, shaming, and uncaring. To protect himself from being
hurt, Pete initially put the group leader down and rejected the
leader before the leader could reject him. Furthermore, consistent with a dismissing-avoidant attachment style, Pete had a
positive internal working model of himself as self-sufficient and
independent (Bartholomew & Horowitz, 1991). Group members like Pete with a positive internal working model of self as
too self-sufficient and strong to need others are likely to see the
group leader as incompetent or in some way not able to meet
his or her needs. A dismissing-avoidant member is likely to see
the self as independent and strong to cope with the pain and
loss over not having one's attachment needs met yet again by
someone in a caregiving role, such as the group leader.

Suggestions for Group Leaders

*Explore Sociocultural as Well as Familial Experiences That Contribute
to an Insecure Attachment Style*

Whereas traditional attachment theory focuses on individual dynamics, experiences with racism and oppression may contribute to a dismissing-
avoidant attachment style for minorities. Negative internal working models
of groups that result from neglectful, hostile, and even aggressive experiences
with groups can be activated when encountering new and unknown groups,
especially groups with majority White group members and/or leaders. It is
reasonable to assume that Pete's experiences with caregivers contributed to
his attachment avoidance, his experiences with discrimination and oppression also significantly contributed to his distrust and avoidance of groups. In
essence, society as a whole acted as a poor attachment object, reflecting back
to Pete that he is not a person of value and that his needs and feelings are
not important enough to respond to adequately. He had reason to experience
groups as uncaring, hostile, and even aggressive. Key for him, however, was
the ability to recognize when it was safe to trust new groups and individuals

and when avoidant behaviors served as an adaptive coping strategy. For Pete to develop more positive internal working models of others and groups, the therapy group had to address his underlying feelings of loss and rage toward individuals and groups that made him feel powerless and marginalized.

Examining the sociocultural factors that contribute to an insecure attachment style is important not only for minorities but also for White group members. Steve experienced his father as dogmatic and authoritarian and his mother as passive and distant. As a child, his attachment needs were likely either neglected by his mother or criticized by his father, leading to his avoidance in relationships as an adult. Steve's racist views can be seen as a way of projecting the rage he felt toward his parents, especially his father, onto another, less powerful group, enabling him to avoid the overwhelming feelings he experienced as a child.

Recognize That Group Therapy Can Help Group Members Heal From the Effects of Racism and Discrimination

Failing to address racism and discrimination in the group may retraumatize marginalized group members and reinforce avoidant attachment patterns (Eason, 2009). Process-oriented groups evoke powerful forces that create a social microcosm of racism, oppression, and exclusion within the group just as they exist in society at large. Thus, these groups have the potential to help clients heal from the effects of oppression and exclusion (C. V. Johnson, 2009), but also, either consciously or unconsciously, they may reinforce feelings of oppression and exclusion in a group (Billow, 2005; Eason, 2009). A dismissing-avoidant attachment to groups or individuals can be viewed as one effect of racism, exclusion, and oppression that can be subject to either healing or reinforcement in the therapy group. Marginalized group members need to ultimately feel a sense of power, validation, and attunement they have not previously experienced, and group members holding racist attitudes or beliefs need to accept their own feelings rather than projecting them on to individuals with less power.

Cheng, Chae, and Gunn (1998) offered four steps that need to occur in the therapy group to address instances of racism and exclusion. In their model, individuals (or group) that hold racist attitudes move from (a) a position of limited insight, based on splitting and projective identification, as manifested in prejudicial attitudes and feelings; (b) to a deeper awareness of their own split-off and projected feelings and attitudes; (c) to identification of split-off parts as a defense originally devised to avoid earlier pain and trauma; resulting in (d) a fuller acceptance of themselves and of the people on whom they had projected their negative feelings. In the clinical vignette we just considered, Steve went from feeling rage toward Pete, wanting to expunge him from the group, to a deeper awareness that Pete merely served as a symbol for his own "unacceptable" desires and unwanted feelings. Addressing racism in the therapy group is good therapeutic work for everyone, not just marginalized members. Steve could not fully work through his own dismissing-avoidant attachment until he came to terms with the rage and loss he felt in his relationship with his father, and in turn, he could not realistically examine his relationship with his father until he fully understood how his racist attitudes and feelings served to avoid the trauma he felt as a child. Pete also had several experiences in the therapy group that helped him trust the group more. For instance, the group empathized with Pete feeling as if he needed to protect himself from the therapy group, based on his experiences feeling marginalized and discriminated against in other groups, and other members shared similar stories easing Pete's feeling of isolation and normalizing his experiences.

Process-oriented groups have the potential to help members heal from instances of oppression and racism, but these groups can also unintentionally reinforce these same power dynamics of oppression and exclusion. It is essential for group leaders to recognize and understand dominant–minority dynamics and how they relate to the unconscious as well as the often covert nature of modern racism (Eason, 2009). If the group leaders and/or the majority of the members are White, then the group structure is highly vulnerable to recapitulating dominant–minority power dynamics. Minority group members may feel powerless, invisible, and pressured to comply and represent one's minority group (Eason, 2009). For example, Steve, as the older and more experienced White group member, clearly had more power than Pete. If Steve's attitudes and feelings were left to fester under the surface, then Pete may have eventually become the group's scapegoat for unwanted feelings and impulses, reinforcing his dismissing-avoidant attachment internal working models that groups cannot be trusted.

Recognize That Multiple Dyadic and Group Attachment Figures May Lead to Multiple Internal Working Models

Although attachment style is often conceptualized as a global orientation toward close relationships, there is reason to believe that individuals possess multiple attachment styles that correspond to a complex array of cognitive networks that form on the basis of specific instances and relationships in a person's life (Mikulincer & Shaver, 2003). Research suggests that reports of attachment orientations can change depending on the context and recent experiences (for a review, see Pietromonaco, Laurenceau, & Barrett, 2002). Other research suggests that people possess multiple attachment schemas (e.g., Baldwin, Keelan, Fehr, Enns, & Koh Rangarajoo, 1996) and that actual or imagined encounters with supportive or nonsupportive others can activate similar attachment orientations (e.g., Mikulincer & Shaver, 2001), even if they are incongruent with a person's global attachment style.

Individuals who identify with a minority ethnic community and are raised by multiple caregivers within an extended family may develop multiple attachment figures early on and develop multiple attachment internal working models. Relatively more or less positive experiences with these multiple attachment objects may give rise to more or less positive internal working models of other individuals and groups. African Americans who have more positive ingroup experiences than outgroup experiences may develop a more secure group attachment to new groups with minority members but a dismissing-avoidant attachment to groups with mostly White members. In the clinical vignette, while Pete began group feeling distrustful of the group as a whole and the White members within it in particular, he formed relationships with several of the other minority members around his age. These more secure attachments enabled him to stay in the group despite not trusting the group as a whole.

ATTACHMENT ORIENTATION AND ASIAN AMERICAN CULTURE

In one research study, Asian Americans reported significantly greater attachment avoidance and anxiety than Caucasians (e.g., Wei et al., 2004). The attachment avoidance may be due to racism or discrimination, similar to the experience of African Americans, or it may relate to cultural norms regarding emotional self-control. Although emotional self-control is culturally normative and valued in Asian cultures (Kim, Atkinson, & Yang, 1999; Tsai & Levenson, 1997), emotional inhibition is a sign of attachment avoidance for Caucasians from Western cultures (Wei, Vogel, Ku, & Zakalik, 2005). Because Asian cultures reinforce emotional inhibition to maintain social harmony and Western culture reinforces emotional expression to encourage individualism, it is not surprising that Asian Americans have been found to score higher on attachment avoidance than Caucasians (see Rothbaum, Weisz, Pott, Miyake, & Morelli, 2000; Wei et al., 2004). Persons from Asian cultures do not tend to express their emotions in relationships directly (Kim et al., 1999; Tsai & Levenson, 1997). This lack of emotional expression may not be a function of negative internal working models of others as unreliable or hostile, but rather an indication that Asian Americans prefer less direct ways of establishing intimacy in relationships.

In addition to reporting greater attachment avoidance, research on attachment classification in Asian countries and with Asian Americans consistently finds that these groups score higher on attachment anxiety then their Caucasian peers (DiTommaso, Brannen, & Burgess, 2005; Malley-Morrison, You, & Mills, 2000; Schmitt et al., 2004; Wei et al., 2004; You & Malley-Morrison, 2000). Given Asian cultural values regarding social harmony and interdependence, persons from Asian cultures are more likely to seek approval in relationships (see Rothbaum et al., 2000), cognitions and behaviors that are classified as reflecting a preoccupied attachment in the West.

Interestingly, whereas Wei et al. (2004) found that avoidance was not related to negative mood for Asian Americans, attachment anxiety was significantly associated with negative mood for Asian Americans more so than for Caucasians or African Americans. These results are consistent with previous research on primarily Caucasian samples that have found attachment anxiety to be associated with depression and anxiety (e.g., Lopez & Brennan, 2000). The exact reason for why the relationship between attachment anxiety and negative mood was stronger for Asian Americans than other ethnic–racial groups in Wei et al. (2004) is not clear. These researchers pointed out that Asian Americans tend to score higher on measures of depression and anxiety in general compared with their Caucasian peers (e.g., Chang, 1996; D. Sue, Ino, & Sue, 1983) and the association between attachment anxiety and negative mood may be particularly strong for Asian American college students, who are separated from their family and ethnic community and placed within a predominantly White university that may stress an Individualistic culture over collective support and identity.

Because individuals from Asian cultures tend to report more behaviors typically associated with attachment anxiety and avoidance in the West, they may have a difficult time with key components of the group process that are inconsistent with their cultural norms and expectations, such as direct feedback, self-disclosure, and interpersonal process comments. In other words, group therapists typically encourage group members to use direct *low-context* language, whereas individuals from Eastern cultures are accustomed to using languages that are indirect and rely on *high-context*, or common ingroup experiences, to "say" the unspoken (see Hall, 1976). Because of these cultural differences, Asian American group members may appear "resistant" and insecurely attached. The following case vignette highlights how cultural differences can be misinterpreted as attachment orientations and how this can have a negative impact on members with different cultural backgrounds.

Case Example: Misunderstanding Cultural Differences and Attachment

Amy was a 23-year-old Taiwanese American graduate student, referred to group therapy for depression and anxiety as well as somatic symptoms by the University Counseling Center. One of the other members in Amy's therapy group was Joy, an Asian American college student who had entered the group 3 months before Amy. Joy was a productive member of the group who held a strong group identity and positive attitudes toward the group, and she often sought out comfort from the other members in times of distress.

According to Berry's (1980) acculturation model, Joy fell into the integrationist stage of acculturation because she identified with both American and Asian cultures. In contrast, Amy, who was a first-generation Asian American and grew up in a predominantly Asian community, better fit into the separation stage of acculturation; she maintained contact with her Asian culture but was not assimilated into American culture.

Amy attended two group sessions in total. During this time, she seldom spoke and generally seemed uncomfortable in the group. The group members asked Amy about her feelings of depression and anxiety and about her family of origin. However, Amy disclosed little and instead focused on asking the group leader for direct advice. The group leader was forming a conceptualization of Amy as dismissing-avoidant because she self-disclosed little, seemed disconnected from her affect, and did not readily use the group for support. The leader said to Amy, "I'm noticing that you haven't shared your feelings about what brings you here with the group. I wonder if there is something hard about trusting the group with your feelings?" Amy responded that there was nothing she could do to change her feelings, so there was no point dwelling on them.

During the subsequent group session, another group member was discussing the pressure he felt from his parents to declare a business major, although he wanted to study music. Amy told this member that he should listen to his parents or he would come to regret it. The other group members quickly pounced on Amy's advice and encouraged the troubled group member to "listen to his heart," stand up to his parents, and declare music as his major. Joy came to Amy's rescue and told the group that in their culture, people don't question authority, nor do they freely share their emotions. Joy explained that it would be considered immature not to obey your parents' advice. Sadly, Amy did not return to the therapy group after these series of empathic ruptures. However, this experience opened the door for Joy to discuss some of the ways in which the group norms conflicted with her Asian cultural values. As the minority in the group, when her own values conflicted with those of the groups, Joy felt like she could not speak up out of fear of losing the groups' approval. This led her to show her "American side" and hide her "Asian side," as Joy put it. This discussion encouraged other group members to openly discuss how they also sometimes conceal parts of themselves that conflict with group norms out of fear that the group will not accept their differences.

Commentary

This clinical vignette demonstrates how essential it is for group leaders to be sensitive to cultural differences pertaining to how individuals are socialized to relate to other individuals and groups. In particular, Eastern cultural values emphasizing social harmony and collectivism may be misinterpreted by Western group leaders as reflecting an insecure attachment style. As seen in Amy's case, misinterpreting cultural differences can lead to empathic ruptures with minority group members who often enter the group already feeling marginalized and misunderstood, ultimately leading to their premature termination of therapy. It is important to train group leaders to be sensitive to cultural differences and how these differences can be misinterpreted and affect the therapy group (DeLucia-Waack, 2011). It is also essential to prepare new group members for group therapy because many of the group norms common to therapy groups are dramatically different across cultures (DeLucia-Waack, 2011). Last, group leaders must also pay attention to group members' acculturation status. Asian group members who are more acculturated to Western individualistic culture are more likely to engage in the group processes of self-disclosure, intrapsychic exploration, and honest feedback. At the same time, as seen in the case of Joy, group leaders must be careful not to unintentionally reinforce only those aspects of Asian group members that are more Western and familiar to the leaders, sending the message to these members that their cultural differences should be hidden or minimized. Some guiding principles pertaining to Asian American group members' internal working models of self and other in the group therapy context are offered here.

1. Asian American group members' internal working models of self, other, and groups are difficult to define in Western terms because the cultural conception of the self and of others is fundamentally different. Asian Americans are more likely to define the self in terms of their group memberships and have early attachment experiences in which interdependence, rather than individualism, was met with proximity to caregivers and groups (see Rothbaum et al., 2000). Thus, an internal working model that clearly distinguishes between self and other may not apply to Asian American group members. Instead, Asian American group members' internal working models may guide them to inhibit their own emotions for the sake of social harmony, value the group over the self, and be concerned with what other members think of them, because these are the kinds of behaviors and norms that have gained proximity to caregivers and groups in the past (see Kim et al., 1999; Rothbaum et al., 2000). Essentially, Asian American group members are likely to have a positive internal working model of groups, consistent with cultural norms that value the collective. Furthermore, depending on past experiences of feeling a sense of belonging and acceptance by groups, Asian American

members may develop a positive internal working model of the self in relation to the group as someone worthy of group membership, or a negative internal working model of the self as someone unworthy of group membership.

2. Because Asian American culture values respect for authority, Asian American group members are likely to have a positive internal working model of the group leaders as wiser and available in the sense that they know what is best for the group and the members (see Kinzie et al., 1988). However, if an Asian American group member has a negative internal working model of the self as unlovable or selfish and unworthy of group membership, then he or she may perceive the group leader as rejecting and hostile. However, these group members may blame themselves for this perceived rejection and feel shame around disappointing the group leader and perhaps the group.

Suggestions for Group Leaders

Do Not Place Western Assumptions About Attachment Onto Group Members From Eastern Cultures

Group leaders schooled in attachment theory are taught that certain group member behaviors indicate an insecure attachment style. From this perspective, it is understandable that the group leader in the clinical vignette just offered conceptualized Amy as dismissing-avoidant and framed interventions to address obstacles to trusting the group and experiencing affect. Unfortunately, interpreting Amy's ingroup behavior through a Western perspective set the stage for Amy to feel marginalized and misunderstood, ultimately leading to her premature termination. Free participation, exchange of ideas, individualism, and directness of communication are all quintessential expectations of process-oriented therapy groups that are in conflict with Asian cultural norms and expectations (Chung, 2004). For Amy, to directly express her feelings, as the group asked of her, would seem immature and selfish. Additionally, whereas Joy's wish for the group's approval might be interpreted as a sign of a more preoccupied attachment, her concern about maintaining the group's acceptance reflects Asian cultural norms. It is important to notice that although Joy was more acculturated than Amy, at times, she participated in the group process at the expense of hiding parts of herself that identified with Asian cultural values. Just as children learn to deactivate their attachment needs if those needs are rejected by their caregiver, minority group members like Joy may learn to hide or compartmentalize the more "ethnic" parts of themselves if these parts are not accepted by the group.

TRAINING MULTICULTURALLY COMPETENT GROUP LEADERS: APPLYING ATTACHMENT THEORY

DeLucia-Waack and Donigian (2004) offered four steps to training multiculturally competent group leaders. In what follows, we outline these four steps and expand on them for group leaders working from an attachment perspective.

Step 1: Examine your own culture, ethnic values, and racial identity to understand who you are as a person. When working with group member attachment issues, it is important for the group leader to examine his or her cultural, ethnic, and personal values regarding relationships. Specifically, culture influences one's beliefs about how one is expected to show emotions in relationships, the degree to which one is expected to depend on others in relationships, and the degree of autonomy that is considered "normal" in relationships (see Rothbaum et al., 2000).

Step 2: Examine your beliefs about group work and the inherent assumptions within the Eurocentric view of group work. Group leaders trained in the European American interpersonal process therapy group model are typically taught to stress certain group processes and values that may be inconsistent with other cultures, such as open self-disclosure, a focus on universality over differences, group member direct feedback and confrontation of the group leader, as well as the idea that group therapy is appropriate for all clients (see Chung, 2004). Group leaders should examine their assumptions about group work and how they may not fit for certain group members from diverse backgrounds. When group members do not fit the group leader's assumptions, the leader may mistakenly classify the member as insecurely attached or unable to feel safe to self-disclose or give direct feedback, for example, when in reality, this poor fit may be related it differences in cultural norms.

Step 3. Learn about other cultures in terms of what they value and how these values may affect group work. It is particularly important for group leaders to learn what other cultures value in terms of the ideal relationship or ideal romantic partner when it comes to understanding the attachment of diverse group members. For example, Wang and Mallinckrodt (2006) found that the ideal person for Asian participants was significantly more anxious and avoidant than for Caucasian participants.

Step 4: Develop your personal plan for group work that emphasizes and uses cultural diversity guidelines for leading effective multicultural groups. For group leaders trained in attachment theory, it is important to reflect on how their theoretical orientation and personal and cultural beliefs about attachment and relationships in general may conflict with those of group members from diverse backgrounds, rather than unintentionally forcing diverse group members to fit into their theoretical model.

CONCLUSION

Universality, the notion that there are elements of the human experience that are common to every living person, is considered to be a key therapeutic factor in group psychotherapy (Yalom & Leszcz, 2005). Yalom and Leszcz (2005) wrote that many group members enter group therapy feeling as if they are "unique in their wretchedness" and that "the disconfirmation of a patient's feelings of uniqueness is a powerful source of relief" (p. 6). Yet among all of our within- and between-cultural differences, what is truly universal to all human beings and by default all group members? Arguably, part of the appeal of attachment theory is that it offers an answer to this perplexing question—that is, we all share biological hardwiring to love and to be loved and to be cared for by a more competent other. Despite this similarity, this chapter reviewed important racial–ethnic differences in how individuals seek and experience intimacy and attachment bonds to individuals and to groups that must not be forgotten amid the allure of universal phenomena. In their discussion of universality, Yalom and Leszcz (2005) wrote,

> Cultural minorities in a predominantly Caucasian group may feel excluded because of different attitudes toward disclosure, interaction, and affective expression. Therapists must help the group move past a focus on concrete cultural differences to transcultural—that is, universal—responses to human situations and tragedies. (p. 8)

Attachment researchers have the daunting task of unraveling which aspects of attachment theory are transcultural and which are culture-specific to better help group leaders conceptualize and treat diverse group members.

11

ATTACHMENT, LOSS, AND TERMINATION IN GROUP PSYCHOTHERAPY

Every group leader understands that loss is an inevitable part of every group therapy experience. From the moment the group begins, the group tolerates the potential for members to leave, leaders to retire or move on, and the group itself to end. The group members will eventually have to say goodbye. Attachment theory is one theoretical lens that can help guide our interventions when these losses emerge in group treatment.

This chapter first reviews Bowlby's (1980) contribution to understanding how attachment styles influence reactions to loss. It focuses on the growing number of empirical studies linking attachment to bereavement and mourning loss and concludes with the applications of this literature to group psychotherapy. Specifically, we review how group therapists can be sensitive to attachment-related issues that emerge during different experiences of loss within the therapy group. Case examples highlight the powerful ways that group therapy can help members navigate intense emotional experiences such as termination from group.

http://dx.doi.org/10.1037/14186-012
Attachment in Group Psychotherapy, by C. L. Marmarosh, R. D. Markin, and E. B. Spiegel

Bowlby (1980) addressed two types of grief reactions that are relevant to therapists working with patients. The first is *protracted grief*, a grief that does not abate over time and is all consuming for the individual. He described adults who suffer this type of grief as individuals chronically grieving and unable to move on with their lives after the loss. These individuals spend significant time ruminating about their lost loved ones and reacting to the loss as if they have lost a part of themselves. One 40-year-old patient described her experience a year after her father suddenly died:

> I still live in a haze. It is as if he died yesterday, and I have lost my anchor in the world. He was my soul mate. There is no reason for me to get out of bed anymore. All I do is think of him and wish he was still here. I feel empty.

Bowlby (1980) believed that individuals who struggle with this type of loss are more likely to have an anxious attachment to their early caregivers because they are currently preoccupied with the lost loved one and unable to cope with the separation. These individuals are inclined to engage in hyper-activating attachment strategies, struggle to tolerate the separations and feelings of aloneness, and continue to seek out the attachment figure years after the individual is gone.

On the opposite extreme are patients who fail to exhibit any significant signs of grief after a loss. They do not overtly express sadness, anger, or distress. They may seek little solace from friends and go on with life as if nothing has happened or changed. One patient described her experience a year after her daughter died:

> I felt sad, but you have to move on. I went to work and focused on the things I usually do. My husband could not understand me; he thought I was cold and callous. We ended up separating soon after. I just did not want to wallow in it the way he did.

Bowlby (1980) argued that these individuals are more inclined to have avoidant attachment styles, and they have learned early on how to deactivate their distress responses and mobilize defenses that split off expressions of longing and despair. He described this process as defensive exclusion. Fraley and Shaver (1997) argued that defensive exclusion is an adaptive strategy for these individuals because it diverts attention away from experiences that threaten self-sufficiency and emotion regulation, such as the loss of a beloved attachment figure. In essence, the more dismissing-avoidant individual is able to bypass thoughts and feelings that would lead to vulnerability, anxiety, and dependency. Rather than feeling overwhelmed with sadness, the individual feels nothing and is able to resume life activities without the experience of emotional pain. Whether these individuals actually cope better has been debated in the literature. Some argue that the avoidance of grief leads to complicated mourning later (Lindemann, 1994), whereas others believe that the avoidance of grief is adaptive and not necessarily pathological (Bonanno, Keltner, Holen, & Horowitz; 1995; Wortman & Silver, 1989).

What has not been debated is the advantage that securely attached individuals seem to have when faced with loss. Secure individuals, unlike insecure individuals described earlier, experience the loss of a loved one and are better able to experience the pain of the loss, are more able to seek soothing from other people, and can rely on internal memories of the deceased person that allow them to remain connected to the individual despite the person being physically gone. This internal connection allows secure individuals to redefine their relationship from one that was tangible to one that is now representational, allowing them to still experience a continued connection and a secure attachment, despite the physical absence of the person. According to some, without this secure internal representation of the lost loved one, the risk of complicated bereavement increases (Stroebe, 2002). Many theorists would argue that individual and group therapies facilitate the internalization of a secure base, and this process enables patients both to cope with loss and to move on to positive relational experiences.

ACUTE GRIEF AND ATTACHMENT

Shear et al. (2007) developed a model of bereavement based specifically on attachment theory. These authors integrated adult attachment research, adult bereavement studies, and clinical observations of individuals with complicated grief. They have emphasized the importance of the death of an attachment figure setting in motion a challenging situation for all bereaved individuals, even more secure individuals. After the immediate death of an attachment figure, the physical relationship with the individual no longer exists, but the internal mental representation of the loved one remains, active and unrevised—the way it was when the attachment figure was alive. The authors have argued that this unresolved situation is the root of acute grief symptoms that occur in most individuals, securely attached or insecurely attached. Grief symptoms develop because the internal model continues to activate a sense that the individual is present or exists in the physical world. To make matters worse, the pain of the loss activates the attachment proximity-seeking system and promotes the longing for that attachment figure, but that person is no longer there. The internal working model that facilitated self-soothing has been disrupted, leading to challenges regulating emotional pain. The authors argued that this experience of acute grief is all consuming, disorganizing, and painful, leaving the bereaved initially disengaged from everyday life. Although it is difficult, once the loss is metabolized and integrated, life resumes, and sadness, preoccupying thoughts of the bereaved, and grief abate. For some individuals, the relentless loss and agony continue, and they are unable to resume healthy relationships.

ATTACHMENT AND CHALLENGES TO SAYING GOODBYE

For those who struggle with complicated mourning, the grief persists for years without lessening. The prolonged suffering leads to diminished relationships, maladaptive coping strategies, avoidant behaviors, and an inability to return to preloss functioning (Rando, 1993). According to Shear et al. (2007), complicated mourning is linked to having an insecure attachment style. Specifically, those with more attachment anxiety exhibit chronic forms of mourning, whereas those with more attachment avoidance demonstrate less overt symptoms (Hazan & Shaver, 1992; Shaver & Tancredy, 2001; Wayment & Vierthaler, 2002). Parkes (2003) interviewed 181 individuals with complicated bereavement and explored the link between their attachment styles and grief reactions. He found that attachment anxiety was related to clinging to the deceased individuals, conflicted relationships with the deceased, and lengthier grief reactions.

Fraley and Bonanno (2004) set out to study empirically how attachment styles relate to different grief patterns by studying 59 bereaved individuals. Individuals were assessed at two time points so the researchers could determine grief symptoms that abate, grief symptoms that are chronic, and grief symptoms that have a delayed onset. They found that securely attached individuals were similar to dismissing-avoidant individuals. Their anxiety decreased over time, and they revealed less grief at the second time point—what the authors termed a *resilient pattern*. Preoccupied and fearful-avoidant individuals demonstrated increases in anxiety over time, greater depression over time, and unresolved grief. These findings support the link between attachment anxiety and unresolved grief, and they shed light on how different dismissing-avoidant and fearful-avoidant styles are.

According to attachment theorists, a dismissing-avoidant style evolves over years of coping with loss and splitting off emotional needs. Individuals with this type of style cope easily with the physical loss of an attachment figure because they have already experienced the emotional loss of an attachment figure years earlier. According to Fraley and Shaver (1997), these individuals already protect themselves from attachment-related injuries and do not tend to allow themselves to become as attached to people. In the event of a loss, they are already less attached and therefore more protected from the pain of grief.

Wayment and Vierthaler (2002) found that bereaved individuals who reported a closer attachment to the individual who died reported greater grief compared with individuals who were not as attached. They also found that preoccupied individuals reported the greatest levels of grief and depression, whereas securely attached individuals reported the least grief and depression. Interestingly, these authors also found that individuals with dismissing-avoidant styles reported more somatic symptoms compared with other styles. In essence, they expressed physical symptoms of loss (e.g., headaches, stomach pains, body aches) instead of emotional expressions of grief. It is possible that these individuals expressed grief physically due to their difficulty experiencing and tolerating painful emotional states.

Securely attached individuals have the capacity to express grief and share their experience of the loss without becoming too overwhelmed with emotion and losing their ability to cope (Parkes, 2001; Stroebe, 2002). These findings shed light on what might be helpful to patients who are suffering a loss or terminating from treatment and have insecure attachment styles. Psychotherapists may need to help these insecure patients develop a cohesive and meaningful way of making sense of the loss, to facilitate an internal representation of the attachment figure that also acknowledges the physical absence of the attachment figure, and to assist them in coping with the emotional deregulation that may feel unbearable.

Most patients come to treatment with some significant losses that have had an impact on them, and all will have to cope with the eventual loss of the psychotherapist who has functioned as a secure base. We can rely on the literature describing the link between attachment and bereavement to understand how patients and therapists respond to the ending of the therapy relationship.

ATTACHMENT AND TERMINATION

Yalom and Leszcz (2005) described termination in therapy groups as the "microcosmic representation of some of life's most crucial and painful issues" (p. 387). Because saying goodbye can be so powerful, it is not uncommon for it to activate previous losses and the coping mechanisms used to cope with or avoid grief. We have already reviewed how adult attachments influence coping with loss, tolerating emotions, and the development of complicated mourning. Now we explore how both group members' and leaders' attachments influence termination in group therapy. We conclude the chapter with clinical examples of how hyperactivating and deactivating strategies emerge during termination and how group leaders can understand these reactions and facilitate meaningful endings.

The Client's Contribution to the Ending of Treatment

According to Holmes (1997), secure patients not only cope better with grief in general, they also cope better with termination of therapy. They tend to approach the ending of treatment with an appreciation of both the gains and losses of treatment, are better able to regulate the emotions they experience, and have a larger coping repertoire when dealing with distress. Secure individuals are also better at seeking social support outside of treatment and have more resources to rely on when losing a secure base, such as the therapist. Shulman (1999) found that secure patients in individual therapy experienced more positive affect and less anxiety and depressive affect in response to termination.

More preoccupied patients tend to struggle more with the loss of a therapist. Similar to their difficulty regulating emotions when grieving (Stroebe, 2002; Wayment & Vierthaler, 2002), they often engage in coping strategies that create more emotional deregulation, such as ruminating about the ending or making attempts to gain others' attention by reengaging in self-destructive behaviors. Pistole (1999) described how more preoccupied patients often display protest behaviors (e.g., missing appointments, reemergence of symptoms, increased anger and anxiety) in response to termination. During termination, these patients may also become clingy or symptomatic in an attempt to reduce feelings of abandonment by engaging caretaking from others. Cognitively, they may become preoccupied with thoughts of being helpless, alone, and unwanted. The distress may be so overwhelming that more preoccupied patients may delay termination to avoid the distress of the loss (Holmes, 1997). They may also prematurely end treatment to regulate their distress and regain a sense of control. According to Holmes (1997), therapists need to help these individuals understand the meaning behind their experience of the ending, identify their motives behind these maladaptive coping strategies, establish internal resources to cope with feelings, and develop outside support systems.

Patients with more dismissing-avoidant attachments are also likely to end treatment prematurely but deny the importance of the relationship (Holmes, 1997). Similar to the way more dismissing-avoidant adults deal with the death of a loved one, they are likely to deal with the ending of psychotherapy treatment. They engage in deactivating strategies that limit their experience of emotional pain and tend to rely on themselves during endings. Turning inward allows them to preserve their sense of self-sufficiency and facilitates their detachment from the relationship.

The Therapist's Contribution to the Ending of Treatment

As we have learned in previous chapters, the therapist's contribution to the therapy process is critical, and this is equally true when it comes to therapy termination. Much research has addressed therapists' countertransference reactions to termination and how these reactions can influence the ending of treatment. It is not hard to imagine how a therapist's attachment style will influence the experience of guilt and the termination process.

According to Holmes (1997), therapists with a more dismissing-avoidant attachment style are likely to minimize the importance of therapy relationships because they are inclined to minimize dependency. These therapists may end treatment too soon in order to avoid the patients', and their own, longings for the relationships. Because they have split off their own grief, they may not be aware of their patients' grief. If the patient brings up the ending of treatment, the more dismissing-avoidant therapist may focus on the positive aspects of the ending, the future treatment, or intellectually summarizing treatment progress that was made. The reactions of fear, sadness, gratitude, and love are more likely to be glossed over or avoided completely.

More preoccupied therapists, in contrast, may be overly sensitive to the ending and feel a sense of abandonment, perceiving that he or she is deserting the patient. If the more preoccupied therapist is overly concerned with avoiding conflict and reducing guilt, he or she may be more inclined to avoid talking about the ending, fail to acknowledge the patient's anger and disappointment, and try to focus overly on the positive aspects of the transfer or termination. These therapists may even try and avoid the ending of the treatment. Boyer and Hoffman (1993) were among the first to study empirically the link between a therapist's history of loss and anxiety during termination. They found that the therapists' loss histories predicted their anxiety during termination. Not only did having histories of loss predict their anxiety, it also predicted their depression during the termination phase of treatments. In essence, the terminations with their patients likely stirred up their own experiences of loss and affected their own sense of well-being during the endings.

Strategies for Facilitating Endings in Group Psychotherapy

Yalom and Leszcz (2005) described the importance of addressing endings in group therapy. They highlighted how, similar to individual therapy, the loss in the group can stir up previous losses, causing some members to pull away to protect themselves from the painful affect that is provoked. The authors recommended challenging the members' avoidance of termination and endings, and they warned that "without proper separation, that process will be compromised and the client's future growth constricted" (p. 384). Yalom and Leszcz did not explore which group members might be more vulnerable to loss and why they might be inclined to engage in more avoidant behaviors or in more care-seeking ways.

The authors could not find empirical studies that explored how attachment styles influenced clients' or therapists' experiences of termination in group therapy, but they did find one theoretical paper that focused on bridging group member attachment style to the complex experience of losing the group leaders. Hammond and Marmarosh (2011) compared the transfer process for members of an interpersonal process group who had either more preoccupied or more dismissing-avoidant styles and identified the deactivating and hyperactivating strategies they engaged in during the transfer of the leaders. The deactivating strategies that more dismissing-avoidant members engaged in included minimizing the importance of the leaders, denying any negative feelings about the transition, and dismissing the reactions of members who were reporting distress about the loss of the leaders. One dismissing-avoidant member described a history of relationship difficulties. When describing her childhood, she minimized her chaotic upbringing and had difficulty describing her childhood in detail. She avoided her own emotional needs and struggled to maintain attachments. Despite her devaluation of relationships, she expressed suicidal thoughts linked to feelings of isolation and loneliness.

At the start of the group, this member said to the others:

Okay, interpersonal relationships, let's see. . . . Well, I don't have a relationship, I'm not good at relationships, they only ever last for 6 months and then I give up. That always happens. Usually it's me that gets tired of them. I just get irritated after awhile and don't want to stick around. I didn't get a very good model of what a relationship should be from my parents. . . . (later after some others talked about their own relationship patterns) If you're a boring person, I don't make the effort to get to know you. I can extend myself only so much before it's just not worth it. (p. 604)

During the transition of the leaders, this same group member said the following to a fellow group member, who had just revealed sadness about the transition:

[laughing] I just don't feel sad at all. I mean, what's the big deal? You guys aren't really part of the group anyway, are you? [stares at leader, waiting for an answer]

Leader: What do you think?

Group Member: I mean, you don't really participate fully. You're pretty removed from it all. I mean, you're like furniture [everyone laughs nervously]. I mean, you're like functional furniture I guess, like ottomans or something [giggling]. (pp. 610–611)

During this interaction, she minimized the emotional experience of the therapists, leaving with sarcasm and hostile humor. She also downplayed the loss for others in the group who are experiencing their sadness about the ending.

A few members were more preoccupied and engaged in hyperactivating strategies during the transition. These members started to reveal an increase in symptoms such as substance abuse outside of the sessions, feelings of being abandoned and betrayed by the leaders, and difficulty trusting the group to be there for them during the transition. One member said,

> I've started to feel in the last week like I'm just not making a very valuable contribution to the group. I used to think I was really good at this, that I was a good group member, but lately I haven't been feeling that way at all. Maybe I shouldn't be a member if I can't contribute right. (p. 608)

This group member was trying to elicit reassurance from the group by putting himself down and sharing his thoughts of leaving the group.

The observational data suggest that attachment style is an important contributor to members' ability to cope with leader transitions. One can imagine similar reactions if the one who is leaving is dropping out. What is most important is that in group therapy, there are multiple perspectives and potential endings that can facilitate members' curiosity about their own attachment-based reactions. The group leader is able to use members' diverse reactions to these endings by exploring members' here-and-now reactions in the group, which can help them process unresolved issues related to grief.

A Case Example: Hyperactivating and Deactivating Strategies During Termination

Yalom and Leszcz (2005) described members who "experience a brief recrudescence of their original symptomatology shortly before termination" (p. 385), similar to individual therapy. It is as if they are protesting the upcoming separation and ending. Although these authors did not reference attachment theory, they did use Bowlby's notion of protest and recommended that leaders help members understand the behaviors as a "protest against termination" (p. 385). They also advocated that returning to earlier issues can help prepare these members for experiences outside the group after termination.

The following case vignette is an example of how a more preoccupied member, Mary, engages in hyperactivating strategies as the group is approaching termination, whereas Dave engages in more deactivation. More important, it demonstrates how other group members, with both different and similar attachment styles, cope with the upcoming ending and facilitate the group's ability to begin to say goodbye.

Mary: [*more preoccupied member*]	I was feeling that panicky feeling this weekend and had those thoughts again. Like I wanted to just crawl in a hole and die. I was thinking about things we talked about in group—things I could think about to feel better, but it just was not helping me. I just can't take that feeling anymore.
Tonya: [*more secure member*]	I remember when you used to feel that way all the time. Were you feeling more alone now this weekend? I know that we are talking about the end of group in a few weeks. I was thinking about us ending and it stirred up a lot of feelings in me.
Mary:	I was not thinking about the group ending, so I'm not sure.
John: [*more secure member*]	That would make sense. I recall last time you had that feeling in here, and it was after you and your boyfriend broke up. You had a lot of panic back then.
Dave: [*more dismissing-avoidant member*]	I think she [*to Mary*] will be fine everyone. [*Turns to Mary*] You will be fine, Mary [*smiles*]. You have beaten these panic feelings before . . . try focusing on the good things in your life.
Mary:	There you go again, you are doing what we talked about in here. I know you are probably trying to make me feel better, but that is not helping at all. It is making me feel worse [*getting agitated and frustrated*]. You should know that by now. Why can't you just listen?
Dave:	Look, I just was trying to help, I apologize. You don't need to bite my head off.
Mary:	I didn't bite your head off. You just don't get it.
Dave:	Get what?
Leader:	I can see you're both getting upset. Dave, I imagine you were trying to be helpful. I wonder what it was like for you to hear that Mary was feeling panicky again as we are ending group?

Dave:	I don't know. I didn't mean to piss anyone off [*disengaging and looking frustrated*].
Leader:	It is clear you did not intend to piss anyone off. I imagine you were having some type of feeling or reaction that led you to tell Mary to look for the positive. What were you feeling immediately before you responded? Right before you tried to help her?
Dave:	I'm not sure . . . what was I feeling? [*long pause*] I guess, I don't want her to be upset. She sounded like she was feeling bad again.
Leader:	How do you imagine you felt when you thought about her feeling badly again . . . as she was saying she felt more alone and panicky as group is ending?
Dave:	You know I have a hard time with feelings. [*silence*] I guess, maybe I felt something . . . [*hesitatingly*] I don't know [*stops suddenly*] . . . maybe, I felt a little frustrated . . . but just a little.
Mary [jumps in]:	What? Why would you feel frustrated with me? [*annoyed and with an angry tone*]
Dave:	I felt frustrated because . . . well you have worked so hard to feel better and I guess I want you to be OK, Mary.
Tonya:	You say you want her to be OK, but you do sound annoyed with Mary. Why?
Dave [looking at Mary]:	Mary, I do care, and sometimes I do get angry because it is hard to see you suffer like this. It is easier to get mad than sit there with these feelings . . . I just want all of us to end in a good place . . . with the things we want in life. I think we deserve those things. We are going to say goodbye in a few weeks, and I want to feel good.
Leader:	It would be so much easier to end the group feeling as though there were no worries, disappointments, or unresolved issues. That everyone is in a good place. Mary is in a good place. You want to be in a good place.

Dave [nods his head yes]:	I hate that.
Steve:	Hate what?
Dave:	I hate bringing up things from the past. I've been feeling better and don't want to go backward. I do want to end in a good place.
John:	So when you hear Mary talking about her feelings of panic as the group is ending, it triggers your own worries about feeling bad again?
Dave:	I guess it does. I don't want to worry about that, but if I am honest with myself, I don't want to be in that place again. It was such a long road to finally start feeling better. It's always there in the background.
John:	I can relate to that as well. I would never have guessed that from you, Dave.
Mary: *[looking much less angry at Dave and more open]*	It's hard for me to believe you worry about your depression coming back too. Sometimes I go back to the way I used to see myself, as someone weaker than others in the group. I see everyone else as strong and independent—especially you, Dave. It feels so much better to know others feel the same.
Tonya:	I feel that way too. As I was sitting here, I started to think about what it will be like without you all in my life. I will miss this group. It is not easy to say goodbye when we have shared so much with each other. You have all been there for me. I actually thought about not coming today, but I knew I had to. I didn't want to deal with it. You *[turning to the leader]* mentioned that we would start saying goodbyes in the next few weeks. I just do not want to do it. Actually, I don't know where to begin.

As demonstrated in the case material, one of the priorities for the group leader was exploring how the group could explore the upcoming ending. Rather than avoiding the loss or simply reassuring the members that it would be fine, it was important to link the internal experience of Mary's abandonment with the increase in symptoms at termination; help the members express the diverse emotional reactions to the group ending that includes sadness, anger, and disappointment; and help the members move out of positions in which they could get stuck (deactivation in the face of hyperactivation).

The group leader facilitated an important repair of a rupture that could have led to Mary's continued attack and Dave's withdrawal, as well as the avoidance of the underlying issues that started to emerge. The group leader was quick to intervene before Mary or Dave were unable to continue exploring their reactions due to emotional overload or complete withdrawal (Wallin, 2007). The leader redirected them to focus on the underlying dynamic that was activating them—the experience of the group ending. This was something a secure group member, Tonya, raised in the group. The open questions, facilitating comments, and supportiveness of the leader and members encouraged members to resume their exploration of their reactions and feelings about the upcoming ending. The leader was also able to reengage Dave by inquiring about his withdrawal and acknowledging his efforts to help, which the other members were not recognizing.

The leader was attuned to the disappointment associated with ending, and the group started to help Mary link her increased symptoms to the upcoming termination and feelings of abandonment. When the group functioned as a secure base, Mary's own curiosity facilitated her exploration of her emotional reactions, and she was able to understand how the group ending was influencing her panic. Dave, a more dismissing-avoidant member, was able to gain insight into how his deactivation in the group was due to his own fears of weakness. Initially, he focused on wanting Mary to feel better as the group ended, but he later recognized that he was activated by his own fears of his depression returning. The secure member, Tonya, was able to link group members' reactions to the upcoming loss and to explore more vulnerable feelings of sadness and grief. She was instrumental in helping group members talk more openly about saying goodbye.

The leader was able to tolerate the member's diverse reactions to the ending, visualize and actively explore the underlying motivations of group members, and speak to the anxiety and feelings about ending without becoming overwhelmed or detached. Not all leaders are able to engage in this way. Leaders who are insecurely attached may have more difficulty tolerating the experiences of loss in the group.

Hyperactivating Strategies in the Leader at Termination

Just as a preoccupied group member is activated during losses in group, a preoccupied group leader can also be affected. During a supervision session, a group leader with a history of sexual trauma presented her tape of the termination session. During the last session, it became clear that she was uncomfortable with the ending. Instead of exploring the discomfort and awkward silences, she jumped to take control of the group and decided to go around the group reciting a laundry list of nice things to each of the members, one by one. She gave glowing feedback to all of them, and some looked pressured to give her positive feedback in return. Because the feedback felt contrived, it was painful to watch the video of the session. It was obvious that the feedback was more about the leader's need to alleviate her feelings of discomfort than about helping the members process their reactions to the ending. When the supervisor asked the group leader why she decided to engage in that intervention, the latter answered that she had felt consumed with anxiety and pressure. The group leader had decided to do "something" and try and get through the last session. Although it was unclear what attachment style this leader actually had, her anxiety about the ending influenced her ability to stay attuned to the group members and help them identify and express what was difficult for all of them.

Deactivating Strategies in the Leader at Termination

There is a wonderful example of leader avoidance in *Complex Dilemmas in Group Psychotherapy: Pathways to Resolution*. Motherwell and Shay (2005) described several dilemmas that group therapists experience. One of the dilemmas concerns a leader's uncertainty about self-disclosure during the termination of a group. The case example starts by describing one of the members of the group who requested personal information from the leader during the termination session; the member asked, "Do you have children?" The leader refused to answer because she said she was concerned that other members did not want to know this personal information. She felt it was crossing a boundary.

The curious member, who had asked the personal question, became frustrated when the leader refused to answer the question, and the situation escalated and was not resolved before the group ended. More important, the leader said that she was upset that this tension was developing just as she was saying goodbye to someone she had grown fond of. The leader blamed the group member, saying that the member needed to end in an angry way to leave. Although the leader attempted to minimize her responsibility for the unresolved rupture, she was left feeling badly about how the relationship ended because she genuinely liked the group member.

It is possible that the personal question to the leader could have many meanings, not simply an attempt to pick a fight, and the therapist may have been colluding with the group members who were all struggling to say goodbye. The leader, similar to the members, was overly focusing on disclosure rather than the underlying feelings about the ending. Although the attachment style of the leader is unclear, the leader's avoidance, especially in the face of pursuit, inhibited her ability to explore the underlying meaning behind the question and link it to the possible issues of loss in the group. She was also unable to express her own sadness at the end of the group or her feelings of closeness to the member, and she was unable to repair a rupture with a member whom she had grown to care about. From an attachment perspective, this enactment reveals an interaction between hyperactivating strategies—members challenging boundaries and seeking out information at termination to deal with the upcoming loss—and deactivating strategies— therapists' avoidance of vulnerability and withdrawal from the emotional experience of the group.

The Secure Leader: Loss and Termination in Group Therapy

Fieldsteel's (2005) article "When the Therapist Says Goodbye" describes the leader's process of retiring and how she struggled with her group through termination. During the termination, she was able to question the impact of her interventions and explored the underlying emotions with which she and her group members struggled. More important, she was able to address her mistakes when countertransference led her to invite group members to continue the group in another format rather than move deeper into the reality of the ending. The leader is able to stop herself and examine her desire to avoid emotions triggered by the upcoming ending, and she is able to facilitate the expression of members' sadness, anger, love, and hope. The leader is not afraid to reveal appropriate parts of herself during the termination process and is able to facilitate a meaningful experience for the group members.

CONCLUSION

A microcosm of life, group therapy forces members and leaders to experience both the sudden unexpected losses and those anticipated endings. These transitions within the group can often trigger earlier losses and expose group members' difficulties dealing with endings. We see how preoccupied members and leaders can become flooded with emotions, whereas their more dismissing-avoidant counterparts deactivate and withdraw from affect. The secure group members and leaders often facilitate the process of saying goodbye and are better able to identify, manage, and empathize with the emotions that are triggered in the group. Although these members have different attachment styles, one of the benefits of group psychotherapy is having these individuals interact and push each other to experience diverse reactions to losses. Those with more preoccupied attachments, like Mary in our example, tend to push the group to explore painful feelings and fears that many circumvent. In contrast, those with more dismissing-avoidant attachments, like Dave, tend to be experts at letting go and force the group to explore the desire to compartmentalize painful emotions and move on. The secure group members, such as Tonya and John, have the ability to empathize with members' sadness, loss, and anger and can link outside experiences to the group ending. Group leaders can embrace all of these attachment-based reactions to facilitate meaningful conversations that bring members closer together. It offers us an opportunity to confront some of our most basic existential anxieties and to learn an invaluable lesson about life—about the importance of embracing relationships with those we care about while we still can.

12

IN-DEPTH CLINICAL CASE STUDIES: ATTACHMENT THEORY AND GROUP PSYCHOTHERAPY

The two clinical cases featured in this chapter highlight the importance of group member attachment and how members' attachment styles influence group preparation, process, and dropout. The first example focuses on the preparation and initial group therapy experience of an individual patient. The case of Jenny emphasizes the many issues the individual therapist who is also the group leader addresses as he invites a more preoccupied individual patient, Jenny, into his therapy group.

The second clinical example highlights the impact that a member's attachment style has on the group process. The case of Molly demonstrates how a more fearful-avoidant group member can stir up intense conflict in the group and how the rupture can lead to dropout but also to increased cohesion. The case material highlights the importance of assessing new members' interpersonal histories, abilities to regulate emotions, and toleration of conflict before they are invited to join an existing therapy group.

http://dx.doi.org/10.1037/14186-013
Attachment in Group Psychotherapy, by C. L. Marmarosh, R. D. Markin, and E. B. Spiegel
Copyright © 2013 by the American Psychological Association. All rights reserved.

JENNY: THE PREPARATION OF A
MORE PREOCCUPIED GROUP MEMBER

Jenny was a 35-year-old White woman whom the group leader had been working with in individual therapy for a year. Jenny had originally sought out individual therapy to help her address the strong ambivalent feelings she experienced in a romantic relationship. Her boyfriend was 10 years younger than she was, and Jenny worried that their differences in age, life experiences, and personality styles would prevent the relationship from working. Although she struggled to trust the relationship with her boyfriend, she had a long history of difficulties trusting people and feeling safe and secure in relationships.

When describing her childhood, Jenny said that her mother often seemed emotionally overwhelmed and distracted by her marital problems and that it took a lot of effort to get her attention. She said it was "frustrating" growing up with a depressed and agitated mother and an engaging (when he was present) but absent father. She said she had to work hard to get her emotional needs met and often felt like her needs were insignificant. Although she felt emotionally abandoned by her mother, Jenny felt both a desire and sense of obligation to take care of her mother, often at her own expense. Jenny's self-deprecation, intense emotional reactions, fears of engulfment, and ambivalence about being in close relationships suggest that she has an attachment style characterized by high anxiety and low avoidance, a more preoccupied attachment style.

During the year of individual therapy, the therapist focused on enhancing Jenny's ability to step back and observe her emotions with diminished reactivity. She often experienced a sense of "smothering" and codependency in her relationships, which felt exciting but too intense. She often felt a wish to flee these relationships a sense of relief after ending them. In sessions, Jenny would experience strong feelings of anxiety when she described a sense of being "trapped" in relationships.

The individual therapist, who was also the group leader, began assembling an interpersonal process group addressing relationship themes for adult patients. Jenny seemed like an excellent fit for the group because she was bright and moderately well functioning, and despite a year of therapy continued to struggle with a pattern of interpersonal difficulties outside of treatment. Interestingly, Jenny had never revealed much negative transference toward the male therapist despite her long history of anger and mistrust of men. The therapist wondered if she might have some idealizing transference towards him (e.g., putting him on a pedestal and seeing him as different from other men). It is also possible that Jenny's inability to access negative feelings for fear of rejection or abandonment led her to avoid important aspects of herself in the individual treatment.

Given her more preoccupied attachment style, the therapist expected her to have some ambivalence and/or conflict with the other group members around intimacy, despite her ability to mask her anger so well in treatment. The leader expected that their therapeutic alliance in the individual treatment would serve as an anchor for her in the group work. As this was to be an interpersonal process group, which would involve therapist process self-disclosures and numerous group member transferences, the leader anticipated that Jenny's idealizing transference towards the leader could very well be challenged and that this would be an important aspect of the treatment. The rupture in the alliance could facilitate Jenny being more genuine and honest about all of her reactions to the leader that included confrontation, disappointment, and anger.

The therapist raised the idea of group with her early in the group formation process, and Jenny was curious about it. They spent part of two sessions discussing how the group would operate, how it could be of help to her, and potential therapeutic issues that it might stimulate for her. As part of the informed consent process, the leader addressed various group rules around confidentiality, subgrouping, and attendance (including a five-session minimum commitment, designed to help group members work through withdrawal or inclination to prematurely drop out). The leader also used the group contract, which she was required to sign. Doing so allowed her to engage in simultaneous auditory and visual processing of these rules and norms.

Jenny joined the group, which consisted of six members (three men, three women), ranging in age from 20 to 38. In addition to Jenny (age 35), Michael and Katie, the two youngest group members, were college upperclassmen; Tina was a 30-year-old pediatrician; John a 34-year-old architect; and Allen a 38-year-old photographer. The first group therapy session appeared to run remarkably well. The group began by reviewing the group structure and rules and processing reactions. The members then shared and related common relationship attitudes and experiences. Members spoke about how they were similar to and different from one another. Overall, the leader was pleased with the group's ability to process the anxiety about the first session in the "here and now."

That evening, shortly after the conclusion of the group, Jenny called her therapist, and the leader, to express her concern that the group was not a good fit for her because of the members' age differences. The leader had an individual therapy session scheduled with Jenny before the next group meeting, so he encouraged her to discuss this in person during the session.

After getting off the phone, the leader wondered how her attachment style was influencing this ambivalence as well as the timing of her expressing it (almost immediately after the first group session ended). During the session she had appeared fine, but it occurred to the leader that her fears of rejection and abandonment, her attachment anxiety, must have been activated during the process. It is possible that sharing her individual therapist with other patients for the first time stimulated fears of abandonment and loss. Although Jenny did not speak to those fears, the leader knew that the preoccupation with age was symbolic of a deeper issue, which he hoped to uncover with Jenny in their individual and group work.

Although the leader was frustrated that Jenny was already considering leaving group after the first session, he was encouraged that she contacted him to tell him about her ambivalence rather than acting it out. During the individual session, she revealed that she was worried that the developmental differences associated with age would interfere with her ability to get the help that she needed from the group. Interestingly, this was a similar concrete fear that she had expressed about her younger boyfriend. Jenny seemed to believe that the differences between people would hinder them from being able to understand her. In essence, she feared she would be alone again. The sense of being alone was something Jenny had experienced as a child when her parents were unable to acknowledge or understand her emotional needs. The terror of being alone again was too frightening for her. Although she could not fully articulate this during the session, she was able to reveal the fears that she would be alone in the group. This was an important revelation because Jenny's fears can be true for many group members.

Upon deeper exploration, Jenny said she was uncomfortable because she firmly believed that Katie and Michael could not help her because of their age, yet she felt invested in the group and afraid to leave because doing so could hurt the other group members. When the leader questioned her about her feelings regarding his referral of her to group, she was able to express her anger at him. She blamed the leader for putting her in the situation and said she felt "misled" by him for not giving her more information about the composition of the group. Finally, Jenny was able to express her anger at the leader and begin to explore her feelings of betrayal. This was an extremely important process.

The leader encouraged Jenny to express her anger to him. He said he thought it was important for her to be able to express her feelings about the situation, including her anger toward him for not preparing her in the way she needed. He wondered what it had been like for her to tell him this. Jenny stated that there was not much she could say to describe her feelings beyond what she had already disclosed. She looked drained and depleted, sitting slumped in her chair.

The leader wondered about her strong reaction to being in the group and her rage at and disappointment in him. What was behind her feeling unsafe in group, and what triggered her feeling betrayed? He also wondered whether there was underlying anger toward him that had been avoided in their individual treatment that was now surfacing in the group. The leader responded by saying he felt concerned and wanted to process the meaning behind her experience. Even if her disappointment about the age gap between her and the two youngest members was real, what about the other three group members who were in their 30s? She began listing reasons why these fellow "thirty-somethings" would not be able to relate to her either—gender difference with Allen and John, age difference with Tina.

The leader empathized with Jenny's perception that she would be alone again in the group, and he also noted the intensity of her emotion and how quickly it had arisen. Had she ever had this kind of intense feeling come up in such a rapid manner before? Jenny's eyes teared up, and she said that she had spent too much time in her life taking care of other people and had not looked after herself enough. She said she was afraid that if she was too different from the other group members, then she wouldn't be able to focus on herself enough in group. The leader said that this sounded like an important feeling and fear, one she should honor and they could explore together.

It became apparent that Jenny had found herself in the same bind she experienced in all of her relationships when she entered the group. The group had activated what Jenny dreaded most: being stuck in relationships in which she would have to sacrifice herself to avoid hurting others while squelching her own pain and feelings. Interestingly, Jenny appeared to hold on to age as the one thing that would concretely keep her from sinking into a frightening relationship situation in which she would be overwhelmed by the other. With her current boyfriend, she also feared their age difference despite his caring and loving nature. With the group, she feared the age difference would again lead to despair, despite the fact that from an outside perspective, it appeared age was not really what was keeping Jenny from committing to relationships that could provide more intimacy and caring for her.

It was as if age was the one thing she could hold on to that could protect her from the fears and anxieties that were triggered in the group session. Fortunately, the group policy was developed to keep people like Jenny in the group for enough time to deal with some of the issues that threaten members' commitment to the group. After processing Jenny's feelings, the leader reminded her of the attendance policy of waiting five sessions before making any decisions about leaving the group. The leader connected this rule to her situation by explaining that in group, it can take time for members' issues to come to the forefront in the group process. Before this can happen, the group members must develop rapport and trust. The leader said, "Until this happens, perhaps we can use the safety and security of our established relationship to help you imagine what it would be like to share these concerns you've mentioned to me today with the group." "OK," Jenny said, "but before we do that, I need to tell you how embarrassed I feel right now." She said that she was still upset with her therapist for not helping her anticipate more clearly the way in which she would be different from the other group members but that mostly now she just felt embarrassed for "freaking out" on the phone and in the session. She became quiet; when the leader noted this silence, Jenny said she felt herself "shutting down." She realized that she had been disappointed before and that shutting down was her way of "protecting" herself and getting "space" as well as "punishing" the other person. To the leader, this sequence of the session indicated a contextual shift in her attachment pattern. Unlike past developmental disappointments with her mother and father, she was able to express her rage without overwhelming anyone. This struck the therapist as a fuller and courageous expression of her attachment needs.

Ultimately, having the opportunity to repair this empathic rupture was helpful to their therapeutic relationship in the individual treatment. This moment also allowed the leader to make the important link about her ability to have ruptures and possibly repair them in the group as well. The leader used the remaining time in the session to anticipate the thoughts, feelings, and reactions that might emerge in group when Jenny shared her concerns with the group, imagining what it would be like for her to raise these issues, how others might react, and how she might react to their reactions.

During the following group session, Jenny did raise the issue of age with the other group members. Jenny seemed more nervous and less composed than she had in the previous session. She stated that she was concerned about hurting the other group members' feelings, but she also felt that this issue was an important one to address. As she did with the leader, Jenny expressed concern that the two younger group members would not be able to relate to and help her. Allen, the oldest group member, did not empathize and simply responded that he did not feel age was as prominent an issue for him. He felt there was enough in common with the other group members for the experience to be worthwhile. Michael, one of the younger group members, said he felt a little offended that Jenny automatically assumed he would have no life experiences that could be of value to her. Jenny became flustered and replied that she hadn't meant to hurt his feelings but wondered how he could possibly empathize with some of her developmental life concerns, such as being unmarried and without children in her mid-30s. Michael responded that although that might be true, he still might be able to help her cope with her feelings about these issues. John, also in his mid-30s, said somewhat casually with a smile, "I'm young at heart. Age is what you make it to be." The lack of support in the group angered Jenny, and she replied to John, "That's easy for you to say . . . you're a man . . . men have that luxury in our society. Women have to balance having children and a career, if that is important to them, which it is to me." Jenny was experiencing in the group exactly what she had feared. She would not be understood and she would feel alone. Her face was flushed, and her hands appeared to be trembling as she spoke.

The group was still focusing on the concrete question about age rather than exploring the deeper meaning behind Jenny's fears, such as "Do I belong here?" "Will I get what I need?" and "Will you understand me or will I be alone again?" The leader chose to empathize with Jenny's comment, in order to model empathy to the group and to prevent Jenny from being left out in the cold after taking the risk in group. "It sounds like being both a working professional and a mother is important to you, and you are aware of the fragility of this balance, particularly at your age." At this point, Tina said,

> Jenny, I'm a few years younger than you, so I can't say that I'm exactly in your situation . . . but every day I feel like I need 25 hours in the day . . . it scares me . . . I'm not ready to have kids yet, but I worry about how I will juggle everything when I am. It's also been really tough to date while in medical school and residency. Now that I'm out, my hours are better, but sometimes I worry it's too late. I hear my biological clock ticking and wonder if I will meet a guy by the time I'm ready to have kids.

"Yeah, it's hard," Jenny replied, and her voice trailed off. She seemed emotionally spent and disconnected.

The leader decided to process what had transpired in the group. "Something very important just happened," he said. "I noticed that although Tina's situation is not identical to Jenny's, Tina was able to use her own experience to imagine being in Jenny's shoes . . . and then share the feelings that came up from doing that with Jenny and the group. Did anybody else notice that?" Allen said that he had and was glad the leader had mentioned it. He said he had been thinking that Jenny sounded lonely, and it had reminded him of times where he had felt misunderstood but was afraid to speak up because he didn't know if his experience as a man would matter to Jenny. Tina turned to Allen and said, "I felt afraid too . . . this whole group experience is so new to me, and I didn't want to say the wrong thing . . . but I guess I wanted Jenny to know that she wasn't alone."

"Can you say that directly to Jenny?" asked the leader.

Looking Jenny in the eye, Tina said, "Jenny, you're not alone."

Jenny's face became flushed and tears welled up in her eyes. "I guess I've been so worried about having to take care of other people that I never saw people trying to look after me." This was a pivotal moment in Jenny's participation, and it allowed enough of her ambivalence about staying in the group to dissipate for her to participate more meaningfully in future group sessions.

From an attachment perspective, what was significant about this final series of interchanges was that they challenged Jenny's internal working models of attachment relationships. Although Jenny initially responded with fears of being misunderstood and alone, she received "layers" of empathic responses. First Tina empathized with Jenny's concerns about age, and later Allen empathized with her experience of being alone in the group. The manner of the last response by Tina, delivered directly to Jenny in a way that she could not miss despite her intensified affect and reduced coherence of mind, pierced Jenny's attachment-related defenses. This was immediately apparent in Jenny's verbal and nonverbal responses, which indicated that she finally heard Tina's empathy and felt understood. This was a corrective emotional experience for Jenny because she did not have to sacrifice her own needs to attend to the needs of another, and the group demonstrated to her that they could understand her and have compassion for her even if she was disagreeing and especially if she expressed anger at them.

LESSONS FROM JENNY'S CASE

Many important lessons can be drawn from this case example. The first is the role that an individual orientation session(s) can play in preparing a group member for group and disarming any attachment-related defenses. Jenny's subjective sense of not feeling fully informed about what the group would be like is important and should not be dismissed. Her surprise at arriving to the first group and finding that it was different from what she was expecting seems associated with her history of attachment-related anxiety. On a dyadic attachment level, she seems to have feared being pulled into relationships with individual group members in which she would have served in a caregiver role and had her own needs go unseen and misunderstood. In this respect, her anticipation of what dyadic relationships in the group might be like was clearly influenced by her own dyadic attachment history. Because it was most likely inevitable that Jenny's attachment patterns would be stimulated by any group composition (if she hadn't focused on age differences, she probably would have focused on some other way in which she was different from other group members), this would have been an opportunity to connect her fears to her attachment history and help her imagine how the group could be helpful over time in working through these issues. In addition, the leader might have considered Jenny's attachment anxiety and how her history of emotional neglect by a father who cheated on her mother could be activated by seeing her individual therapist with fellow patients in the group. One could imagine that Jenny felt the need to engage the leader in some way after feeling threatened by having to share the leader (her therapist) with other patients for the first time. Calling the leader outside the session and threatening to leave the group could be seen as a hyperactivating strategy to stimulate caring from the leader.

At the group attachment level, Jenny could have feared a re-creation of her family dynamic in which she was the different one, being rejected by and feeling left out of the group. As an only child, she was by default different from her parents, with the difference interestingly being one of age (they were adults, she was a child). She was also abandoned by her father, who had his business travel girlfriends, and abandoned by her mother, who withdrew into herself. Thus, Jenny was on the outside of her family system and may have anticipated being on the outside of this group system. As part of the mentalization process that Fonagy and colleagues (2002) described, it would have been important to help Jenny imagine a different kind of dyadic and group attachment experience through group therapy. This could have been facilitated in part by helping Jenny ponder how she might mentally know that she was in other group members' thoughts. One reason that the end of the second group session was so pivotal, from an attachment perspective, is that some of the other group members did this for her. Both Allen and Tina told Jenny that they were thinking of her and feeling empathy toward her; thus, she could know that not only did they have minds separate from their behaviors but she mattered enough to be included in their thoughts.

Additionally, in this case example, we see the important role that individual therapy can play as a supplement for addressing the emerging attachment issues in the group therapy. Segalla, Wine, and Silvers (2000) recommended concurrent individual and group therapy to help patients understand and integrate their internal reactions. In this case, the individual therapy session between the first and second group sessions was a particularly significant moment to deal with the emergent dyadic and group attachment issues that had arisen. As Jenny made clear in the session, a rupture had emerged in the therapeutic relationship. It was important to repair this rupture first to strengthen the secure dyadic attachment between Jenny and the leader. Both Jenny's sharing her feelings and the leader's acknowledging and validating them were important parts of this repair, and something that her parents had not done with her. With the secure base reestablished, the second half of the individual therapy session used the dyadic relationship as a foundation for engaging the mentalizing functions necessary for secure group attachment. First, bearing in mind Tasca, Balfour, Ritchie, and Bissada's (2007b) recommendations for preparing preoccupied group members, the leader reminded Jenny of her five-session commitment while encouraging her to be patient with the initial alliance and trust-building developmental stage of group. The leader wanted Jenny to realize that it might take more time than she would prefer to discover that the other group members were not so different from her. Next, keeping in mind the literature on cognitive preparation (Yalom & Leszcz, 2005) and mentalization (Fonagy, Gergely,

Jurist, & Target, 2002), the leader used her forthcoming self-disclosure in group about age to imagine this experience from start to finish and from a range of perspectives. Thus, Jenny was able to prepare for the larger process of building secure group attachment.

Finally, the leader used the first and particularly the second group sessions to prepare group members to deal with the emergent dyadic and group attachment issues in the group process. This occurred in several ways. First, understanding that the expressed individual anxieties of many of the group members (Jenny, Katie, Michael, Allen, Tina) was partially eliciting a fight-or-flight anxious group response (Bion, 1974), the leader structured many of his interventions to provide affect containment for the group.

On a related note, Tasca, Foot, and colleagues (2011) described a therapeutic technique of "downregulating" (p. 251) affect with highly preoccupied group members. (This is explained in more detail in Chapter 6.) In their description of this technique, they proposed that the therapist facilitate awareness in the group members of when their emotions are hyperactivated and then develop strategies for distancing from those emotions in the moment. This was the leader's intention when, toward the end of the second group session, he highlighted his observation of Tina's empathic attunement to Jenny's fears and described how the leader noticed her empathizing. By discussing his observation of this encounter, the leader was signaling to the other group members that this was something they should be aware of. In addition, by describing what he was noticing, he was teaching the members how one empathizes with another. This manner of describing empathy in the group would most likely promote the distancing from the intense emotions and encourage a more self-reflective stance (Wallin, 2007) for those with higher attachment anxiety. Last, the leader was facilitating mentalization in the group members. By describing the mental process of empathy, the leader was helping them understand how they existed in one another's minds, which is the crux of Fonagy and colleagues' (2002) definition of mentalization.

As this example illustrates, in the initial group sessions, the leader was active in connecting group members' experiences and intentional in making these linkages known to the group. Part of this connecting and linking work included providing repetition of pivotal group member comments to further establish their resonance with members and penetrate any attachment anxiety or avoidance that would diminish their internalization. Or if it seemed more appropriate, the leader encouraged group members to repeat their comments directly to one another, as with his final intervention with Tina. In that case, seeing Tina look Jenny in the eye and hearing her say, "Jenny, you're not alone" gave Jenny a new experience that was different from her mental representations of others and herself.

MOLLY: WHEN ATTACHMENT LEADS
TO RUPTURE, DROPOUT, AND REPAIR

The previous case reveals how a more preoccupied client can join a group with the help of the secure base of the individual therapist. Once Jenny was able to express and tolerate her anger and her fear of joining, she was able to take the risk of opening up to the group and disclose her struggles with intimacy. This courageous act elicited a corrective emotional experience for Jenny. Unfortunately, this successful outcome does not always occur. Sometimes insecurely attached clients join a therapy group and are unable to tolerate the group process. Unlike Jenny, who was able to process her reaction with her individual therapist and return to the group, some group members drop out prematurely. The following case example describes how a new member, Molly, influences the rupture in the group and the group's ability to facilitate a repair.

After 1 month of weekly group meetings, the group leader was looking to add a new member. Molly had been referred from her individual therapist in the counseling center, and her therapist said he enjoyed working with her but was not able to help her address this issue with which she continued to struggle. When asked what the issue was, he said she got into frequent conflicts with others that ended with her leaving the relationship. When the leader asked if she had ever had conflict with him, he said, "No . . . we have a great relationship."

The leader met with Molly for a group intake, and Molly appeared to be a bright graduate student with a pleasant disposition. The leader could understand her colleague's confusion and was also surprised to hear of her frequent relational troubles. Although Molly was pleasant, there were red flags that she would likely struggle in the group. What was most notable was that she minimized her relationship conflicts and seemed to answer questions vaguely, in a way that appeared to mask her true feelings and thoughts. The leader had the sense that Molly wanted to avoid talking about relationship difficulties and instead wanted to impress the leader with her many achievements and her strengths. There was little detail about her childhood, she reported an idealized relationship with her parents, and she seemed to focus her attention on wanting to find "better partners," without much insight about her own contribution to her difficulties. When the leader asked about her relationship struggles, she seemed sincerely confused as to why she frequently found herself in these conflicted situations. Despite having reservations, the leader accepted Molly into the group.

When Molly joined, she was engaging and open with group members, similar to how she presented herself during the group intake. Her integration into the group appeared seamless. Three weeks into the group process, however, things shifted dramatically. Mike, a more dismissing-avoidant group member who often found it difficult to be open in the group, disclosed something he was struggling with. He said that a former girlfriend, one who had suddenly broke up with him a year ago, had recently sent him an e-mail. Although he was unsure what to do, he had a huge smile on his face. When asked by another group member how he felt, Mike said the e-mail made him feel confused because he was not sure whether he should ignore it or reach out to her again. He could not decide, and left it for the group to mull over.

Group members immediately jumped at the opportunity to respond, and most of their reactions mirrored their own feelings of being rejected or hurt in relationships and their struggles to forgive or end those attachments. After many members expressed their thoughts and feelings, one more securely attached group member, Joy, the youngest and most inexperienced with dating, smiled, and said enthusiastically, "That sounds great. I think you should definitely call her! Why not?" Joy's vigor and innocence made some group members smile. Her affect also expanded on Mike's restrained affect.

Molly did not feel positive about this feedback, and she let out a loud groan of disgust, which the others ignored. Another, more secure member jumped in to restore the hopeful energy and said, "That's a good point. What do you have to lose?" Molly, who had attempted to be restrained, could not take it any longer and blurted out to Mike,

> This is just ridiculous. She [pointing to Joy] has probably never even been on a date before. So, how can you listen to her? What the hell does she know? I know for a fact that you need to just forget this ex-girlfriend and never look back. Didn't you say that she left you?! You walk away! I cannot believe you are all even discussing this bullshit. I have been sitting here and just listening, and I don't think I can get anything from this group if you are all dumb enough to wonder if you should contact this idiot. The answer is so obvious!

The group members looked stunned. The immediacy of her attack and devaluation of the members left them speechless and afraid of her. In that moment, as Molly was ranting, the leader managed to cope with her own shock to look below Molly's defensiveness to its motivation. It was obvious that the group had walked into a land mine.

The leader realized that Molly could not tolerate being a part of a group that was willing to forgive or express hope in the face of loss, disappointment, and pain. She also could not tolerate others feeling differently. The leader said,

> Molly, from your experience, you should never forgive someone who has hurt you. Hearing the group members even entertain the possibility of contacting this person seems ridiculous, if not crazy, to you. It makes

you so angry that is hard even to sit here and believe the group can be of any help to you. I think this is an important experience where you become so angry that you have a hard time staying engaged. You need to write them off.

Molly gave a snide acknowledgment, but she continued to look away. Molly continued to withdraw despite multiple efforts to help her examine what was happening in the group. Group members' reactions and attempts to empathize failed. Nothing could remove the black hole that Molly's attack engendered, and she simply refused to engage with the members. Despite the many efforts to repair the rupture, the session came to an uncomfortable end. It was clear to the leader that Molly, who appeared outgoing and pleasant on the surface, was struggling with a significant amount of pain.

Without a doubt, the leader was concerned about the group's cohesion and specifically how some of the group experienced the attack and the subsequent withdrawal. Unfortunately, Molly had no idea that her own suffering left her as abusive as those who must have betrayed and hurt her. She was not aware of her own destructiveness and how her devaluation was a protective shield from more excruciating underlying emotions and vulnerabilities. After this session, it was clear why she was in frequent conflicts in relationships and why she was alone. Unfortunately, Molly coped with this enactment the exact way she recommended in the group: You leave and never look back.

Despite multiple attempts to talk with her by phone and one cheerful phone message saying she would return to the group, Molly dropped out. What was even more surprising was her individual therapist's reaction. Unlike Jenny's therapist, who helped Jenny sort out her reactions in the group, Molly's therapist did not want to explore what happened in the group during the individual sessions. He too made the unilateral decision to end the process, saying, "If she does not want to talk about the group, I am not going to make her talk about it. It is in the past now, and she has other things she wants to focus on."

The leader's concern immediately went to the group members who had welcomed Molly and were now dealing with her attack and sudden abandonment. Not surprisingly, the first thing the group members requested was closing the group to new members. This led to them revealing their feelings of being hurt and wanting to ensure their future safety in the group. Initially, group members minimized their feelings of anger, but eventually, with the leader's coaching, they expressed frustration with Molly, with each other, and eventually with the leader. This led to more honesty and engagement within the group. Mike, the dismissing-avoidant group member who disclosed his desire to contact his ex-girlfriend, revealed that the attack felt similar to how he experienced his father when he was growing up. He opened up about the humiliation that he experienced when he expressed his desire for something. The group focused on how these frequent degrading experiences left him mistrustful of others' opinion of him and afraid to open up about his feelings or desires. During the session, he revealed gaining more insight into his automatic withdrawal and need to protect himself when Molly attacked.

Group members shared a similar experience of fear and shame. Joy, the younger, more secure member, revealed surprise at Molly's reaction. She revealed confusion about how her own openness to the ex-girlfriend could elicit such rage in someone. It was initially challenging for her to comprehend Molly's anger and even her own anger after the attack. When asked if she ever experienced intense rage before, she first denied experiencing it but then disclosed that the most anger she ever felt was when she was seriously ill at age 10 and was hospitalized. She described a painful memory of how her mother would often try and prevent her from expressing any anger about her illness out of fear it would have a negative effect on her health or treatment. Her mother always said she had to be hopeful and positive despite painful treatments and serious losses. While processing her experience with her mother, she recalled how her mother's forced optimism would often leave her feeling alone, angry, and misunderstood. Suddenly, she wondered if this was how Molly felt in the group. Although the experience was challenging for Joy, it demonstrates how an insecure member like Molly can facilitate the exploration of a darker aspect of the human experience such as hate and aggression in a more secure group member. As a matter of fact, all of the remaining group members made an incredible use of the rupture, and it facilitated a deeper sense of intimacy and cohesion within the group. Unfortunately, Molly did not benefit from a process she inspired.

LESSONS FROM THE CASE OF MOLLY

When reviewing this case, it is helpful to consider some of the principles that might have received more attention and led to both deepening the group cohesion and retaining Molly's membership in the group. In the case of Molly, there are many things that the leader might have done to better prepare her for group treatment. First of all, the leader might have tried to determine Molly's attachment style from a more detailed history from the referring therapist or from a formal assessment of her attachment. Even without a more formal assessment, it is clear that Molly was frequently encountering conflicts that were not resolved in outside relationships, that she was not able to present a more cohesive picture of her relationships with her early caregivers, and that she was not insightful about her contribution to problems. This information alone gives us important information about her interpersonal style that has both avoidant and anxious elements. In group therapy and in outside relationships, she alternated between intense rage or aggressive outbursts and complete withdrawal. More important, she was able to avoid these alternating expressions within individual therapy, in which she had been able to complain about others and maintain a committed relationship devoid of conflict with her therapist. Because the therapist making the group referral had not experienced her rage, he was baffled that her relationship problems were not resolving. However, it was likely that the conflicts occurring outside the group were going to play out within the group over time as well.

During the group intake, the leader could have focused more on the likelihood that this would happen in the group, even conveying that this would be a desirable situation because it would offer insight into Molly's struggles outside of the group. Setting the expectation for some type of conflict would have better prepared both Molly and her individual therapist for what was to come, especially because this was Molly's presenting problem in the group. The leader might have set the expectation that Molly might experience emotionally unpleasant reactions in the group, similar to those in outside relationships, and find a way to help her cope with these feelings as they developed in the group, possibly using her individual therapist as a secure base. The leader could also have set the stage with the referring individual therapist so that both were on the same page when attachment issues became enacted in the group.

With regard to Molly, one wonders whether less damage would have resulted if the group leader had interrupted the process sooner and taken control of the situation. Molly started to express her agitation subtly, non-verbally, before fully blowing up and attacking members. If the group leader could have intervened sooner, it might have been possible to help Molly experience her reactions in the here and now before it was too overwhelming, striking when the iron is cold. Because Molly became enraged and then disengaged, it was difficult to process her and the other members' reactions or for any feedback to be digested.

If the referring individual therapist had been prepared for the likelihood that Molly would struggle in the group, maybe he would have been more supportive of helping her work through her reaction and facilitate insight into her anger and detachment. Although it does not appear that Molly benefitted from the group process, it is clear that the group members were able to express deeper emotions, gain insight into their own reactions, express more trust in each other, and feel greater intimacy in the group after the conflict.

CONCLUSION

The two in-depth clinical case studies of Jenny and Molly highlight the impact that attachment styles have on the referral, screening, and preparation for group; the impact of conflict on group cohesion; and the different outcomes that can occur, including premature termination. In the case of Jenny, we see the helpful role that combined individual and group therapy can offer members who are coping with the activation of insecure attachments. This case contrasts with that of Molly, whose referring individual therapist missed an important opportunity to use the rupture in the group to facilitate the treatment.

Although the outcomes differ, in both cases, the group provokes something within the person that is not being expressed in individual treatment alone. Insecure attachments are quickly activated in group settings, and the group leaders help their respective groups address the conflicts in the group while also building cohesion. We are able to gain insight into how the group process can have a powerful impact on members with both secure and insecure attachments even when a group member prematurely leaves the group.

AFTERWORD: CLOSING REFLECTIONS ON ATTACHMENT AND GROUP PSYCHOTHERAPY

In our closing reflections, we review the application of attachment theory to group therapy and highlight the ways that researchers, group therapists, and those training and supervising future group therapists can make use of what has been done and move the field forward. We also want to conclude with some of the topics that we were not able to fully delve into but that certainly influence group therapy. The literature is constantly growing, replete with interesting and relevant research studies and clinical applications that we are not able to explore in more depth.

After reviewing the clinical and empirical literature applying attachment theory to psychotherapy and the empirical research in social psychology, we have a better understanding of how important the attachment styles of members and leaders are to the process and outcome of group treatment. The research has taught us that attachment patterns influence the group even before it starts through the expectations and attitudes people have about group therapy. Patients with more attachment avoidance reported more fears of humiliation and shame related to group therapy (Marmarosh et al., 2009), and clinicians with more avoidance toward their own personal groups tend to project these negative attitudes about group therapy onto their patients (Marmarosh et al., 2006). These studies suggest that dimensions of attachment anxiety and avoidance influence referrals to group and patients' perceptions of group therapy before they even step into a group session. Once the group therapy process begins, researchers have taught us much about how attachments influence the process.

WHAT WE KNOW ABOUT THE GROUP MEMBER AND ATTACHMENT

Group members' attachments influence how well they disclose, empathize, and make use of the group sessions (Shechtman & Dvir, 2006; Shechtman & Rybko, 2004). Securely attached group members are most likely to be able to engage in a variety of productive ingroup behaviors, whereas insecure group members struggle with overwhelming emotions, ineffective self-disclosures, and misattuned reactions in the group. For those who are high on attachment avoidance, their perceptions of the group alliance tend to decrease over time (Kanninen, Salo, & Punamaki, 2000). Those who are high on attachment anxiety often feel overwhelmed with conflict and struggle with interpersonal feedback. These insecure members are most at risk of dropping out of group (Hummelen, Wilberg, & Karterud, 2007; Tasca, Taylor, Bissada, Ritchie, & Balfour, 2004).

Given these findings, group therapists may need to pay more attention to insecure group members and how they often struggle with the group process. Specific screenings, preparation, and group interventions are needed to facilitate their ability to use the group to promote change. We described in Chapter 2 how group therapists can assess members' attachments, at both the individual and group levels. Once leaders are familiar with their group members' attachment-based strategies, we believe there is great hope for these patients in group treatment. Researchers have shown that members with more attachment avoidance value the group therapists' emotional presence and acceptance when describing group factors that were effective (Kirchmann et al., 2009). Although they may avoid affect and deactivate during the group, they value the group's ability to help them cope with emotions and feel understood. Those members with more attachment anxiety also value the group and come to learn how to manage their emotions and maintain more close relationships, which is what they are hungry for.

Perhaps the most useful study was done more than a decade ago. Kilmann and colleagues (1999) developed a manualized attachment-focused group treatment. Unlike other group approaches based on attachment theory (Kahn & Feldman, 2011; McClusky, 2002, 2008), Kilmann and colleagues empirically compared their treatment with another form of group therapy and found that group participants in the attachment-focused treatment reported higher self-esteem, less anger, and greater management of emotions. Having a comparison treatment group allows us to identify what specific interventions facilitate change. Specifically, we learned that focusing on group members' attachments in treatment facilitates their perceived ability to cope with anger and increases their sense of self-worth.

Although we now know that attachment-based interventions facilitate change in groups, we do not know how this plays out in different types of group therapies for various types of patients. Tasca and colleagues (Tasca, Balfour, Ritchie, and Bissada, 2006, 2007a, 2007b; Tasca, Foot, et al., 2011) are among the few researchers who are exploring the differences between cognitive behavioral and interpersonal psychodynamic group treatment for patients with eating disorders while taking into account patient attachment styles. Future studies like this are needed to fully understand how specific types of group treatments and their interventions address specific types of patient issues.

WHAT WE KNOW ABOUT THE GROUP LEADER AND ATTACHMENT

We know much less about the leaders' attachment styles and how they influence group therapy. We can speculate on the basis of social psychological research that the leaders' attachments influence how they are able to manage emotions within the group and ultimately facilitate safe interactions that lead to corrective emotional experiences. Although there has yet to be any empirical research exploring group therapist attachment and group process or outcome, social psychologists have demonstrated the importance of the leader's attachment style and how it can have a significant impact on the functioning and well-being of a group. Specifically, they have found that dismissing-avoidant leaders have the worst impact on insecure group members, but they can also erode the well-being of secure members over time (Mikulincer & Shaver, 2007b). This is probably one of the most important areas needing future attention from both researchers and professionals involved in training and supervision.

Empirical studies are needed to explore how leader attachments influence coleadership, group climate, emotion regulation, conflict resolution, cohesion, disclosure, and treatment outcome. Similar to attachment research within individual therapy, research is needed to explore the interaction between the leader and member attachment styles. Once we have this information, we can help group therapists gain insight into how they may be influencing the group process by avoiding emotions (having a dismissing-avoidant attachment) or avoiding conflict to be liked (having a more preoccupied attachment). This is probably one of the most important underdeveloped areas in both group treatment research and practice.

DYADIC ATTACHMENTS AND THE GROUP AS A WHOLE: IMPLICATIONS FOR FUTURE RESEARCH

One of the important topics we did not fully explore is the influence of individual attachments on the overall group climate and attachment to the group. Researchers have focused on how individuals' attachments influence personal perceptions of group climate (Kirchmann et al., 2009) but not how it influences the overall group atmosphere. As a professor who teaches group psychotherapy, the first author is often asked, "How many insecurely attached individuals should one include in a group?" To this, she often answers, "It depends on the group." We touched on this in Chapter 4, but there is much research needed to fully explore how dyadic attachments influence the group as a whole. How does having a group with many members with more preoccupied attachment influence the group process? Is it much different if there are many secure members or the rest of the group members are more dismissing-avoidant? How do dyadic and group attachment interactions (e.g., Markin & Marmarosh, 2009) influence the group process? In essence, when developing heterogeneous groups, how does one select group members and consider different attachment styles?

This question is often addressed in textbooks with regard to selecting members who may be in a minority group, as we described in Chapter 10. The response is often to ensure that one group member has someone else in the group to relate to or identify with and to ensure the individual does not become a scapegoat (DeLucia-Waack, 2011). It is wise to include more than one more preoccupied or dismissing-avoidant member, as long as the individuals have the capacity to tolerate the type of group the leader is implementing. Attachment strategies may be less important in structured groups (i.e., short-term cognitive behavioral groups) where there is less focus on the interpersonal process and more significant in long-term interpersonal or dynamic groups. These are speculations based on past research (Kivlighan, Coco, & Gullo, 2012; Tasca, Balfour, et al., 2006; Tasca et al., 2007a) and clinical work, and they need to be the focus of future research.

USING ATTACHMENT TO FOSTER TREATMENT GOALS

Not only is it helpful for group leaders to have a clear sense of group members' interpersonal functioning, it is also helpful for the group members to understand how they interact and how group therapy can facilitate change. Whittingham and his colleagues (Greening, Whittingham, & Yutrzenka, 2012; Yutrzenka, Whittingham, & Greening, 2012) have described how educating group members about their placement on the interpersonal circumplex can be used to help establish goals for group members. In two presentations, they reported that excessively needy (similar to preoccupied adults) and socially inhibited group members (similar to dismissing-avoidant adults) have different change patterns in group therapy and can benefit from learning about their interpersonal style during the preparation for group treatment. This research is impressive and could be applied to attachment theory.

It is possible for group leaders to assess group members' attachment dimensions of anxiety and avoidance during the screening process and explain to them where they fall along these dimensions. Group members can gain a better sense of how they engage with others and how this can be addressed in group treatment. For example, the leader could assess a member's elevated anxiety and lower avoidance and note that he or she falls within the more preoccupied attachment configuration. Once identifying the individual's attachment style, the leader could help the individual understand how the person's self-devaluation, fears of rejection, and idealization of others influences his or her relationships and how group therapy can be a place to address these issues. Although we have focused mainly on how insecure attachments can hinder the group process and how group treatment can facilitate more security, it is important to note that there is value to all group members, including more insecurely attached group members.

THE VALUE OF INSECURE ATTACHMENTS IN GROUP THERAPY

Ein-Dor, Mikulincer, Doron, and Shaver (2010) presented an interesting argument that there is an evolutionary advantage to having insecurely attached people in a society given the large percentage of insecure individuals. They argued that preoccupied individuals act as sentinels in the group, warning other members of potential threats, whereas dismissing-avoidant individuals act as catalysts to move on and escape from potentially dangerous situations. This is an interesting perspective and can be applied to group therapy as well.

It is possible that preoccupied group members push the group to explore dependency, self-hatred, and overwhelming emotions such as aggression, envy, and rage. They may be the first to detect anger and conflict in the group and to perceive problems that are emerging in the group process. In Chapter 12, we saw how Jenny's anxiety about being different and alone pushes the group to explore their differences related to gender and age. Her revelation about her fears exposes the more dismissing-avoidant members' inability to empathize, and it fosters opportunities for the members to struggle with who they are and how they will relate to one another in the group.

Group members who are more dismissing-avoidant, in contrast, push the group to explore denial, repression, and projection of unwanted parts of the self onto others. They may be the first to express the need to withdraw and push the group to struggle with autonomy and separation. In Chapter 7, we saw how a more dismissing-avoidant member, Raj, pushed the group to explore how withdrawal affects intimacy and how underneath the facade of superiority lurks the terror and longings of a small boy. In Chapter 8, we saw how John pushed the group to tolerate conflict and explore how the same interaction in the group can trigger complex and diverse reactions in the members.

Often we tend to focus on the many ways secure group members facilitate the group process for insecure group members. However, secure members may benefit from insecure ones as well. Secure group members, unlike insecurely attached group members, may not be prepared for oppression or hatred in groups (Mikulincer & Shaver, 2007b). They may have been sheltered from neglect, abuse, discrimination, and trauma. In Chapter 12, we saw how Joy was unable to experience her aggression in the group and how the conflict in the group instigated by an insecure group member's attack facilitates her exploration of forced optimism. It is the insecurely attached group member's rage that pushes Joy to look at her own anger and how she dealt with her own feelings as a child. The therapy group may be the first place where secure members like Joy are exposed to their own destructive impulses and the conflict between trust and self-protection. Group therapy may be preparing these more secure patients for the painful experiences that we may all face in today's society (Mikulincer & Shaver, 2007b).

GROUP ATTACHMENTS: ANOTHER PATH TO CHANGE

Although the attachment literature focuses on the importance of multiple types of dyadic relationships, from early caregivers to adult romantic partners, there is much less attention on attachments to groups. We believe that this is an important area for both research and clinical intervention. Keating et al. (in press) addressed the influence that group therapy attachments have on changing dyadic attachments. Specifically, they found preliminary evidence that increasing a secure attachment to the therapy group can influence a movement toward secure dyadic attachments outside the group. In essence, helping group members develop a trusting relationship with the therapy group in which they can express vulnerability, experience intimacy, and feel a sense of connection and belonging can facilitate secure attachments in personal dyadic relationships outside of the group.

Bowlby knew long ago that a secure relationship was critical early in life because it was the foundation for future experience. He also understood that these implicit attachment processes were accessible for change and one force that could facilitate change was psychotherapy treatment. Although Bowlby was clear that therapists could provide this felt security, he may have overlooked one of the most powerful facilitators of security: the groups we belong to. We hope that we have demonstrated how the relationships people have with one another via the groups they join can foster the development of more secure dyadic and group attachments, reduce symptoms, and facilitate healthy intimacy in relationships.

APPENDIX:
GROUP THERAPY QUESTIONNAIRE–S

The Group Therapy Questionnaire is designed to help you learn more about how you might profit from group therapy and how we might be better able to help you. There are no right or wrong answers. Please respond to the questions as honestly and clearly as you can.

Counseling:

1. Have you had previous counseling of any type? Yes____ No____
    A. If yes, what type?
*Individual therapy_____ *Group therapy_____
    *Family therapy_____ *Other_____

	(Not at all)					(Very much)
2. I look forward to beginning group therapy.	1	2	3	4	5	6 7
3. I hope this group will meet my needs.	1	2	3	4	5	6 7
4. I suspect that I will be like other group members.	1	2	3	4	5	6 7
5. I expect I will stay with the group at least eight weeks.	1	2	3	4	5	6 7

Family:

1. How did your parents show their caring for you?
2. Children play different roles in their family. What role did you play in your family?
3. How did your parents show their anger at you?
4. How did you express your anger toward your parents?

"Group Therapy Questionnaire." Copyright 2004 by Rebecca MacNair-Semands. Reprinted with permission. Dr. MacNair-Semands extends special appreciation to the late John G. Corrazini.

5. Diagram your family. It can be helpful if you use placement to depict closeness and size to reflect status.

[ ]

6. What, if any, conflicts are arising in work or school relationships?
7. What role do you play in your current family or intimate relationships that contributes to difficulties?

Health:

1. Check any of the following you experience:
   □ vomiting
   □ difficulty swallowing
   □ pain in legs, arms, back, joints, during urination
   □ shortness of breath when not exerting oneself
   □ painful menstruation
   □ amnesia
   □ burning sensation in sexual organs (other than intercourse)

2. Do you have friends? (Check one)   □ None   □ Few   □ Many

3. Are you feeling suicidal?   □ No   □ Yes, with thoughts only
   □ Yes, with intent/plan

4. Are you feeling homicidal/wanting to kill someone?
   □ No   □ Yes, with thoughts only   □ Yes, with a plan

5. Please check the interpersonal problems you experience:
   □ excessive arguments
   □ physical fights with partner
   □ physical fights with others
   □ divorce
   □ verbal abuse to people I care about
   □ physical fights with family
   □ separation

- [ ] feeling too dependent on others
- [ ] shyness
- [ ] not being assertive
- [ ] lose my temper frequently
- [ ] unstable relationships
- [ ] lack of control of my anger
- [ ] feel empty and bored
- [ ] constantly need reassurance, approval and praise
- [ ] avoid social activities
- [ ] allow others to make my important decisions
- [ ] often feel uncomfortable or helpless when alone
- [ ] easily hurt by criticism or disapproval
- [ ] procrastinate
- [ ] often unaware of feelings or numb
- [ ] feel isolated and lonely
- [ ] difficulty socializing
- [ ] loneliness
- [ ] difficulty trusting others
- [ ] do not enjoy or desire close relationships
- [ ] moods change quickly
- [ ] lack of personal identity
- [ ] feel abandoned
- [ ] preoccupied with feelings of envy
- [ ] unable to make decisions without reassurance from others
- [ ] difficulty initiating things on my own
- [ ] feel devastated when close relationships end
- [ ] perfectionism that interferes with task completion

6. Are you in any kind of crisis right now?
   - [ ] Yes
   - [ ] No

Therapy Considerations:

1. What are you most afraid of about group therapy?
2. If you could change something about yourself as a result of group therapy, what would you change?
3. Specify what *you believe* to be your difficulties.
4. What are your goals for group therapy?
5. What might prevent you from reaching your goals?
6. Is there anything you have not told us that you believe might be helpful

REFERENCES

Abouguendia, M., Joyce, A. S., Piper, W. E., & Ogrodniczuk, J. S. (2004). Alliance as a mediator of expectancy effects in short-term group psychotherapy. *Group Dynamics: Theory, Research, and Practice, 8,* 3–12. doi:10.1037/1089-2699.8.1.3

Ainsworth, M. D., Blehar, M. C., Waters, E., & Wall, S. (1978). *Patterns of attachment: A psychological study of the Strange Situation.* Hillsdale, NJ: Erlbaum.

Alexander, F., & French, T. M. (1946). *Psychoanalytic therapy: Principles and application.* New York, NY: Ronald Press.

Allen, J., Hauser, S., & Borman-Spurrell, E. (1996). Attachment theory as a framework for understanding sequelae of severe adolescent psychopathology: An 11-year follow-up study. *Journal of Consulting and Clinical Psychology, 64,* 254–263.

Alonso, A., & Rutan, S. (1984). The impact of object relations theory on psychodynamic group therapy. *The American Journal of Psychiatry, 141,* 1376–1380.

American Psychiatric Association. (2000). *Diagnostic and statistical manual of mental disorders* (4th ed., text revision). Washington, DC: Author.

Andersen, S. M., Reznik, I., & Glassman, N. S. (2005). The unconscious relational self. In R. Hassin, J. S. Uleman, & J. A. Bargh (Eds.), *The new unconscious* (pp. 421–481). New York, NY: Oxford University Press.

Bakermans-Kranenburg, M. J., & Van IJzendoorn, M. H. (1993). A psychometric study of the Adult Attachment Interview: Reliability and discriminant validity. *Developmental Psychology, 29,* 870–879.

Baldwin, M. W., Keelan, J. P. R., Fehr, B., Enns, V., & Koh Rangarajoo, E. (1996). Social-cognitive conceptualization of attachment working models: Availability and accessibility effects. *Journal of Personality and Social Psychology, 71,* 94–109. doi:10.1037/0022-3514.71.1.94

Barone, L., & Guiducci, V. (2009). Mental representations of attachment in eating disorders: A pilot study using the Adult Attachment Interview. *Attachment & Human Development, 11,* 405–417. doi:10.1080/14616730902814770

Bartholomew, K., & Allison, C. J. (2006). An attachment perspective on abusive dynamics in intimate relationships. In M. Mikulincer & G. S. Goodman (Eds.), *Dynamics of romantic love* (pp. 102–127). New York, NY: Guilford Press.

Bartholomew, K., & Horowitz, L. M. (1991). Attachment styles among young adults: A test of a four-category model. *Journal of Personality and Social Psychology, 61,* 226–244. doi:10.1037/0022-3514.61.2.226

Bartholomew, K., & Shaver, P. R. (1998). Methods of assessing adult attachment: Do they converge? In J. A. Simpson & W. S. Rholes (Eds.), *Attachment theory and close relationships* (pp. 25–45). New York, NY: Guilford Press.

Bateman, A. W., & Fonagy, P. (2003). The development of an attachment-based treatment program for borderline personality disorder. *Bulletin of the Menninger Clinic, 67,* 187–211. doi:10.1521/bumc.67.3.187.23439

Beebe, B. (2005). Mother–infant research informs mother–infant treatment. *The Psychoanalytic Study of the Child, 60,* 7–46.

Beebe, B., & Lachmann, F. (2002). *Infant research and adult treatment: Co-constructing interactions.* Hillsdale, NJ: Analytic Press.

Beebe, B., & Lachmann, F. M. (1988). The contribution of mother–father influence to the origins to self and other object representations. *Psychoanalytic Psychology, 5,* 305–337. doi:10.1037/0736-9735.5.4.305

Behrends, R. S., & Blatt, S. J. (1985). Internalization and psychological development throughout the life cycle. *The Psychoanalytic Study of the Child, 40,* 11–39.

Ben-Ari, A., & Lavee, Y. (2005). Dyadic characteristics of individual attributes: Attachment, neuroticism, and their relation to martial quality and closeness. *American Journal of Orthopsychiatry, 75,* 621–631. doi:10.1037/0002-9432.75.4.621

Benoit, D., & Parker K. (1994). Stability and transmission of attachment across three generations. *Child Development, 65,* 1444–1456.

Berk, M. S., & Andersen, S. M. (2000). The impact of past relationships on interpersonal behavior: Behavioral confirmation in the social-cognitive process of transference. *Journal of Personality and Social Psychology, 79,* 546–562. doi:10.1037/0022-3514.79.4.546

Bernard, H., Burlingame, G., Flores, P., Greene, L., Joyce, A., Kobos, J., . . . Feirman, D. (2008). Clinical practice guidelines for group psychotherapy. *International Journal of Group Psychotherapy, 58,* 455–542. doi:10.1521/ijgp.2008.58.4.455

Bernier, A., & Dozier, M. (2002). The client counselor match and the corrective emotional experience: Evidence for interpersonal and attachment research. *Psychotherapy: Theory, Research, Practice, Training, 39,* 32–43. doi:10.1037/0033-3204.39.1.32

Berry, J. W. (1980). Acculturation as varieties of adaptation. In A. Padilla (Ed.), *Acculturation: Theory, models and some new findings* (pp. 9–25). Boulder, CO: Westview.

Billow, R. M. (2005). The two faces of the group therapist. *International Journal of Group Psychotherapy, 55,* 167–187. doi:10.1521/ijgp.55.2.167.62190

Bion, W. R. (1961). *Experiences in groups.* New York, NY: Basic Books. doi:10.4324/9780203359075

Bion, W. R. (1974). *Experiences in groups and other papers.* Oxford, England: Ballantine.

Bonanno, G. A., Keltner, D., Holen, A., & Horowitz, M. J. (1995). When avoiding unpleasant emotions might not be such a bad thing: Verbal-autonomic response dissociation and midlife conjugal bereavement. *Journal of Personality and Social Psychology, 69,* 975–989. doi:10.1037/0022-3514.69.5.975

Boon, S. D., & Griffin, D. W. (1996). The construction of risk in relationships: The role of framing in decisions about intimate relationships. *Personal Relationships, 3,* 293–306. doi:10.1111/j.1475-6811.1996.tb00118.x

Bowden, M. (2002). Anti-group attitudes at assessment for psychotherapy. *Psychoanalytic Psychotherapy, 16,* 246–258. doi:10.1080/14749730210163453

Bowlby, J. (1969). *Attachment and loss: Vol. 1. Attachment.* New York, NY: Basic Books.

Bowlby, J. (1973). *Attachment and loss: Vol. 2. Separation: Anxiety and anger.* New York, NY: Basic Books.

Bowlby, J. (1980). *Attachment and loss: Vol. 3. Loss: Sadness and depression.* New York, NY: Basic Books.

Bowlby, J. (1982). *Attachment and Loss: Vol. 1. Attachment* (2nd ed.). New York, NY: Basic Books.

Bowlby, J. (1988). *A secure base: Clinical applications of attachment theory.* London, England: Routledge.

Boyer, S. P., & Hoffman, M. A. (1993). Therapists' affective reactions to termination: The impact of therapist loss history and client sensitivity to loss. *Journal of Counseling Psychology, 40,* 271–277. doi:10.1037/0022-0167.40.3.271

Brennan, K. A., Clark, C. L., & Shaver, P. R. (1998). Self-report measurement of adult romantic attachment: An integrative overview. In J. A. Simpson & W. S. Rholes (Eds.), *Attachment theory and close relationships* (pp. 46–76). New York, NY: Guilford Press.

Brennan, K. A., & Morris, K. A. (1997). Attachment styles, self-esteem, and patterns of seeking feedback from romantic partners. *Personality and Social Psychology Bulletin, 23,* 23–31. doi:10.1177/0146167297231003

Briere, J., & Scott, C. (2006). *Principles of trauma therapy.* New York, NY: Sage.

Brody, G. H., & Flor, D. L. (1998). Maternal resources, parenting practices, and child competence in rural, single-parent African American families. *Child Development, 69,* 803–816.

Brumbaugh, C. C., & Fraley, R. C. (2007). The transference of attachment patterns: How parental and romantic relationships influence feelings toward novel people. *Personal Relationships, 14,* 513–530. doi:10.1111/j.1475-6811.2007.00169.x

Budman, S. H., Soldz, S., Demby, A., Davis, M., & Merry, J. (1993). What is cohesiveness? An empirical examination. *Small Group Research, 24,* 199–216. doi:10.1177/1046496493242003

Burlingame, G. M., Fuhriman, A., & Johnson, J. (2001). Cohesion in group psychotherapy. *Psychotherapy: Theory, Research, and Practice, 38,* 373–379. doi:10.1037/0033-3204.38.4.373

Burlingame, G. M., Fuhriman, A. F., & Mosier, J. (2003). The differentiated effectiveness of group psychotherapy: A meta-analytic review. *Group Dynamics: Theory, Research, and Practice, 7,* 3–12. doi:10.1037/1089-2699.7.1.3

Burlingame, G. M., & Krogel, J. (2005). Relative efficacy of individual versus group psychotherapy. *International Journal of Group Psychotherapy, 55,* 607–611. doi:10.1521/ijgp.2005.55.4.607

Burlingame, G. M., MacKenzie, K. R., & Strauss, B. (2004). Small group treatment: Evidence for effectiveness and mechanisms of change. In M. Lambert (Ed.), *Bergin and Garfield's handbook of psychotherapy and behavior change* (5th ed., pp. 647–696). New York, NY: Wiley.

Burlingame, G. M., Strauss, B., Joyce, A., MacNair-Semands, R., MacKenzie, K. R., Ogrodniczuk, J., & Taylor, S. (2006). *CORE Battery—Revised: An assessment tool kit for promoting optimal group selection, process, and outcome*. New York, NY: American Group Psychotherapy Association.

Cassidy, J. (1994). Emotion regulation: Influences of attachment relationships. *Monographs of the Society for Research in Child Development, 59,* 228–249. doi:10.2307/1166148

Cassidy, J., & Kobak, R. R. (1988). Avoidance and its relationship with other defensive processes. In J. Belsky & T. Nezworski (Eds.), *Clinical implications of attachment* (pp. 300–323). Hillsdale, NJ: Erlbaum.

Castonguay, L. G., Pincus, A. L., Agras, W. S., & Hines, C. E. (1998). The role of emotion in group cognitive-behavioral therapy for binge-eating disorder: When things have to feel worse before they get better. *Psychotherapy Research, 8,* 225–238.

Chang, E. C. (1996). Cultural differences in optimism, pessimism, and coping: Predictors of subsequent adjustment in Asian American and Caucasian American college students. *Journal of Counseling Psychology, 43,* 113–123. doi:10.1037/0022-0167.43.1.113

Chen, E. C., & Mallinckrodt, B. (2002). Attachment, group attraction and self-other agreement in interpersonal circumplex problems and perceptions of group members. *Group Dynamics: Theory, Research and Practice, 6,* 311–324. doi:10.1037/1089-2699.6.4.311

Cheng, W. D., Chae, M., & Gunn, R. W. (1998). Splitting and Projective Identification in Multicultural Group Counseling. *Journal for Specialists in Group Work, 23,* 372–387. doi:10.1080/01933929808411408

Chung, R. C. (2004). Group counseling with Asians. In J. L. DeLucia-Waack, D. A. Gerrity, C. R. Kalodner, & M. Riva (Eds.), *Handbook of group counseling and psychotherapy* (pp. 200–212). Thousand Oaks, CA: Sage.

Clarkin, J. F., Levy, K. N., Lenzenweger, M. F., & Kernberg, O. F. (2004). The Personality Disorders Institute/Borderline Personality Disorder Research Foundation randomized control trial for borderline personality disorder: Rationale, methods, and patient characteristics. *Journal of Personality Disorders, 18,* 52–72. doi:10.1521/pedi.18.1.52.32769

Clarkin, J. F., Yeomans, F. E., & Kernberg, O. F. (2006). *Psychotherapy for borderline personality: Focusing on object relations*. Washington, DC: American Psychiatric Publishing.

Clulow, C. (2001). *Attachment theory and the therapeutic frame in adult attachment and couple psychotherapy: The secure base in practice and research*. Philadelphia, PA: Brunner Routledge.

Collins, N. L. (1996). Working models of attachment: Implications for explanation, emotion and behavior. *Journal of Personality and Social Psychology, 71,* 810–832. doi:10.1037/0022-3514.71.4.810

Collins, N. L., & Feeney, B. C. (2004). An attachment theory perspective on closeness and intimacy. In D. J. Mashek & A. Aron (Eds.), *Handbook of closeness and intimacy* (pp. 163–187). Mahwah, NJ: Erlbaum.

Collins, N. L., & Read, S. J. (1990). Adult attachment, working models, and relationship quality in dating couples. *Journal of Personality and Social Psychology, 58*, 644–663. doi:10.1037/0022-3514.58.4.644

Connelly, J. L., Piper, W. E., DeCarufel, F. L., & Debanne, E., G. (1986). Premature termination in group psychotherapy: Pretherapy and early therapy predictors. *International Journal of Group Psychotherapy, 36*, 145–152.

Connors, M. E. (2011). Attachment theory: A "secure base" for psychotherapy integration. *Journal of Psychotherapy Integration, 21*, 348–362. doi:10.1037/a0025460

Consedine, N. S., & Magai, C. (2002). The uncharted waters of emotion: Ethnicity, trait emotion and emotion expression in older adults. *Journal of Cross-Cultural Gerontology, 17*, 71–100. doi:10.1023/A:1014838920556

Consedine, N. S., Magai, C., & Bonanno, G. A. (2002). Moderators of the emotion inhibition-health relationship: A review and research agenda. *Review of General Psychology, 6*, 204–228. doi:10.1037/1089-2680.6.2.204

Corey, G. (2008). *Theory and practice of counseling and psychotherapy.* Belmont, CA: Thomas/Brooks/Cole.

Corey, M. S., & Corey, G. (1997). *Group process and practice* (5th ed.). Pacific Grove, CA: Brooks/Cole.

Cortina, M., & Marrone, M. (2003). *Attachment theory and the psychoanalytic process.* London, England: Whurr.

Cozolino, L. (2002). *The neuroscience of psychotherapy: Building and rebuilding the human brain.* New York, NY: Norton.

Crowell, J., Treboux, D., & Waters, E. (1993, April). *Alternatives to the Adult Attachment Interview? Self-reports of attachment style & relationships with mothers and partners.* Presented at the biennial meeting of the Society for Research in Child Development, New Orleans, LA.

Crowell, J. A., Fraley, R. C., & Shaver, P. R. (1999). Measurement of individual differences in adolescent and adult attachment. In J. Cassidy & P. R. Shaver (Eds.), *Handbook of attachment: Theory, research, and clinical applications* (pp. 434–465). New York, NY: Guilford Press.

Crowell, J. A., & Treboux, D. (1995). A review of adult attachment measures: Implications for theory and research. *Social Development, 4*, 294–327. doi:10.1111/j.1467-9507.1995.tb00067.x

Cyranowski, J. M., Bookswala, J., Feske, U., Houck, P., Pilkonis, P., Kostelnik, B., & Frank, E. (2002). Adult attachment profiles, interpersonal difficulties, and response to interpersonal Psychotherapy in women with recurrent major depression. *Journal of Social and Clinical Psychology, 21*, 191–217. doi:10.1521/jscp.21.2.191.22514

Daniel, S. I. F. (2006). Adult attachment patterns and individual psychotherapy. A review. *Clinical Psychology Review, 26*, 968–984. doi:10.1016/j.cpr.2006.02.001

Davidovitz, R., Mikulincer, M., Shaver, P., Ijzsak, R., & Popper, M. (2007). Leaders as attachment figures: Leaders' attachment orientations predict leadership-related mental representations and followers' performance and mental health. *Journal of Personality and Social Psychology, 93*, 632–650. doi:10.1037/0022-3514.93.4.632

Davila, J., & Levy, K. N. (2006). Introduction to the special section on attachment theory and psychotherapy. *Journal of Consulting and Clinical Psychology, 74*, 989–993. doi:10.1037/0022-006X.74.6.989

Deater-Deckard, K., Dodge, K. A., Bates, J. E., & Pettit, G. S. (1996). Physical discipline among African American and European American mothers: Links to children's externalizing behaviors. *Developmental Psychology, 32*, 1065–1072. doi:10.1037/0012-1649.32.6.1065

de Carufel, F. L., & Piper, W. E. (1988). Group psychotherapy or individual psychotherapy: Patient characteristics as predictive factors. *International Journal of Group Psychotherapy, 38*, 169–188.

De Dreu, C. K. W., Greer, L. L., Handgraaf, M. J., Shalvi, S., Van Kleef, G. A., Baas, M., . . . Feith, S. W. (2010). The neuropeptide oxytocin regulates parochial altruism in intergroup conflict among humans. *Science, 328*, 1408–1411. doi:10.1126/science.1189047

DeLucia-Waack, J. (2011). Diversity in groups. In R. K. Conyne (Ed.), *The Oxford handbook of group counseling* (pp. 83–101). New York, NY: Oxford Press.

DeLucia-Waack, J., & Donigian, J. (2004). *The practice of multicultural group work: Visions and perspectives from the field.* Pacific Grove, CA: Wadsworth Press.

de Zulueta, F., & Mark, P. (2000). Attachment and contained splitting: A combined approach of group and individual therapy to the treatment of patients suffering from borderline personality disorder. *Group Analysis, 33*, 486–500. doi:10.1177/05333160022077542

Diamond, D., Clarkin, J. F., Levine, H., Levy, K., Foelsch, P., & Yeomans, F. (1999). Borderline conditions and attachment: A preliminary report. *Psychoanalytic Inquiry, 19*, 831–884. doi:10.1080/07351699909534278

Diamond, D., Clarkin, J. F., Stovall-McClough, K. C., Levy, K. N., Foelsch, P. A., Levine, H., & Yeomans, F. E. (2003). Patient–therapist attachment: Impact on the therapeutic process and outcome. In M. Cortina & M. Marrone (Eds.), *Attachment theory and the psychoanalytic process* (pp. 127–178). London, England: Whurr.

Diamond, D., Stovall-McClough, C., Clarkin, J., & Levy, K. (2003). Patient–therapist attachment in the treatment of borderline personality disorder. *Bulletin of the Menninger Clinic, 67*, 227–259. doi:10.1521/bumc.67.3.227.23433

Diener, M. J., Hilsenroth, M. J., & Weinberger, J. (2009). A primer on meta-analysis of correlation coefficients: The relationship between patient-reported therapeutic alliance and adult attachment style as an illustration. *Psychotherapy Research, 19*, 519–526. doi:10.1080/10503300802491410

Diener, M. J., & Monroe, J. M. (2011). The relationship between adult attachment style and therapeutic alliance in individual psychotherapy: A meta-analytic review. *Psychotherapy: Theory, Research, Practice, Training, 48*, 237–248. doi:10.1037/a0022425

Dierick, P., & Lietaer, G. (2008). Client perception of therapeutic factors in group psychotherapy and growth groups: An empirically-based hierarchical model. *International Journal of Group Psychotherapy, 58,* 203–230. doi:10.1521/ijgp.2008.58.2.203

Dinger, U., & Schauenburg, H. (2010). Effects of cohesion and patient interpersonal style on outcome in psychodynamically oriented inpatient group psychotherapy. *Psychotherapy Research, 20,* 22–29. doi:10.1080/10503300902855514

Dion, K. L. (2000). Group cohesion: From "field of forces" to multidimensional construct. *Group Dynamics: Theory, Research, and Practice, 4,* 7–26. doi:10.1037/1089-2699.4.1.7

DiTommaso, E., Brannen, C., & Burgess, M. (2005). The universality of relationship characteristics: A cross-cultural comparison of different types of attachment and loneliness in Canadian and visiting Chinese students. *Social Behavior and Personality, 33,* 57–68. doi:10.2224/sbp.2005.33.1.57

Dozier, M. (1990). Attachment organization and treatment use for adults with serious psychopathological disorders. *Development and Psychopathology, 2,* 47–60. doi:10.1017/S0954579400000584

Dozier, M., Stovall, K. C., & Albus, K. E. (1999). Attachment and psychopathology in adulthood. In J. Cassidy & P. R. Shaver (Eds.), *Handbook of attachment: Theory, research, and clinical applications* (pp. 497–519). New York, NY: Guilford Press.

Eames, V., & Roth, T. (2000). Patient attachment orientation and the early working alliance: A study of patient and therapist reports of alliance qualities and ruptures. *Psychotherapy Research, 10,* 421–434. doi:10.1093/ptr/10.4.421

Eason, E. A. (2009). Diversity and group theory, practice and research. *International Journal of Group Psychotherapy, 59,* 563–574. doi:10.1521/ijgp.2009.59.4.563

Ein-Dor, T., Mikulincer, M., Doron, G., & Shaver, P. R. (2010). The attachment paradox: How can so many of us (the insecure ones) have no adaptive advantages? *Perspectives on Psychological Science, 5,* 123–141. doi:10.1177/1745691610362349

Fairbairn, W. R. D. (1952). *An object-relations theory of personality.* New York, NY: Basic Books.

Feeney, J. A. (1995). Adult attachment and emotional control. *Personal Relationships, 2,* 143–159. doi:10.1111/j.1475-6811.1995.tb00082.x

Feeney, J. A. (2005). Hurt feelings in couple relationships: Exploring the role of attachment and perceptions of personal injury. *Personal Relationships, 12,* 253–271. doi:10.1111/j.1350-4126.2005.00114.x

Feeney, J. A., & Noller, P. (1990). Attachment style as a predictor of adult romantic relationships. *Journal of Personality and Social Psychology, 58,* 281–291. doi:10.1037/0022-3514.58.2.281

Fieldsteel, N. D. (2005). When the therapist says goodbye. *International Journal of Group Psychotherapy, 55,* 245–279. doi:10.1521/ijgp.55.2.245.62191

Flores, P. J. (2001). Addiction as an attachment disorder: Implication therapy. *International Journal of Group Psychotherapy, 51*, 63–81. doi:10.1521/ijgp.51.1.63.49730

Flores, P. J. (2004). *Addiction as an attachment disorder*. Lanham, MD: Jason Aronson.

Flores, P. J. (2010). Group Psychotherapy and Neuro-Plasticity: An Attachment Theory Perspective. *International Journal of Group Psychotherapy, 60*, 546–570. doi:10.1521/ijgp.2010.60.4.546

Fonagy, P. (2000). Attachment and borderline personality disorder. *Journal of the American Psychoanalytic Association, 48*, 1129–1146. doi:10.1177/00030651 000480040701

Fonagy, P. (2001). *Attachment theory and psychoanalysis*. New York, NY: Other Press.

Fonagy, P., & Bateman, A. (2006). Mechanism of change in mentalization based treatment of borderline personality disorder. *Journal of Clinical Psychology, 62*, 411–430. doi:10.1002/jclp.20241

Fonagy, P., Gergely, G., Jurist, E. L., & Target, M. (2002). *Affect regulation, mentalization, and the development of the self*. New York, NY: Other Press.

Fonagy, P., Leigh, T., Steele, M., Steele, H., Kennedy, R., Mattoon, G., . . . Gerber, A. (1996). The relation of attachment status, psychiatric classification, and response to psychotherapy. *Journal of Consulting and Clinical Psychology, 64*, 22–31. doi:10.1037/0022-006X.64.1.22

Fonagy, P., Steele, H., & Steele, M. (1991). Maternal representations of attachment during pregnancy predict the organization of infant mother attachment at one year of age. *Child Development, 62*, 891–905. doi:10.2307/1131141

Fonagy, P., Steele, H., & Steele, M. (1992, July). *A prospective longitudinal study of adult attachment of infant attachment and child development*. Presented at the XXV International Congress of Psychology, Brussels, Belgium.

Fonagy, P., Steele, M., Steele, H., Leigh, T., Kennedy, R., Mattoon, G., & Target, M. (1995). Attachment, the reflective self, and borderline states. In S. Goldberg, R. Muir, & J. Kerr (Eds.), *Attachment theory: Social, developmental, and clinical perspectives* (pp. 233–278). Hillsdale, NJ: The Analytic Press.

Fonagy, P., Steele, M., Steele, H., Moran, G. S., & Higgitt, A. C. (1991). The capacity for understanding mental states: The reflective self in parent and child and its significance for security of attachment. *Infant Mental Health Journal, 12*, 201–218. doi:10.1002/1097-0355(199123)12:3<201::AID-IMHJ2280120307>3.0.CO;2-7

Fonagy, P., & Target, M. (2008). Attachment, trauma, and psychoanalysis: Where psychoanalysis meets neuroscience. In E. Jurist, A. Slade, & S. Bergner (Eds.), *Mind to mind: Infant research, neuroscience, and psychoanalysis* (pp. 15–49). New York, NY: Other Press.

Fonagy, P., Target, M., Gergely, G., Jurist, J. G., & Bateman, A. W. (2003). The developmental roots of borderline personality disorder in early attachment relationships: A theory and some evidence. *Psychoanalytic Inquiry, 23*, 412–459. doi:10.1080/07351692309349042

Fonagy, P., Target, M., Steele, H., & Steele, M. (1998). *Reflective functioning manual, version 5. For application to Adult Attachment Interviews.* Unpublished manuscript, Subdepartment of Clinical Health Psychology, University College London.

Fosha, D. (2000). *The transforming power of affect: A model for accelerated change.* New York, NY: Basic Books.

Fosha, D. (2003). Dyadic regulation and experiential work with emotion and relatedness in trauma and disorganized attachment. In M. F. Solomon & D. J. Siegel (Eds.), *Healing trauma: Attachment, mind, body, and brain* (pp. 221–281). New York, NY: Norton.

Fraley, R. C., & Bonanno, G. A. (2004). Attachment and loss: A test of three competing models on the association between Attachment-related avoidance and adaptation to bereavement. *Personality and Social Psychology Bulletin, 30,* 878–890. doi:10.1177/0146167204264289

Fraley, R. C., & Shaver, P. R. (1997). Adult attachment and the suppression of unwanted thoughts. *Journal of Personality and Social Psychology, 73,* 1080–1091. doi:10.1037/0022-3514.73.5.1080

Fraley, R. C., & Shaver, P. R. (2000). Adult romantic attachment: Theoretical developments, controversies, and unanswered questions. *Review of General Psychology, 4,* 132–154. doi:10.1037/1089-2680.4.2.132

Fraley, R. C., & Waller, N. G. (1998). Adult attachment patterns: A test of the typological model. In J. A. Simpson & W. F. Rholes (Eds.), *Attachment theory and close relationships* (pp. 77–114). New York, NY: Guilford Press.

Gallagher, M. E., Tasca, G. A., Ritchie, K., Balfour, L., Maxwell, H., & Bissada, H. (2013). Interpersonal learning is associated with improved self-esteem in group psychotherapy for women with binge eating disorder. *Psychotherapy.* Advance online publication. doi:10.1037/a0031098

Ganzarain, R. (1989). *Object relations group psychotherapy.* Madison, CT: International Universities Press.

Gaston, L., & Marmar, C. R. (1993). *Manual of the California Psychotherapy Alliance Scales (CALPAS).* Unpublished manuscript, Department of Psychiatry, McGill University, Montreal, Canada; University of California, Berkeley.

Gelso, C., & Hayes, J. A. (1998). *The psychotherapy relationship: Theory, research, and practice.* New York, NY: Wiley.

Gelso, C. J., & Harbin, J. (2007). Insight, action, and the therapeutic relationship. In L. Castonguay & C. Hill (Eds.), *Insight in psychotherapy* (pp. 293–311). Washington, DC: American Psychological Association. doi:10.1037/11532-014

George, C., Kaplan, N., & Main, M. (1985). *The Adult Attachment Interview.* Unpublished protocol, Department of Psychology, University of California, Berkeley.

George, C., Kaplan, N., & Main, M. (1996). *Adult attachment interview* (3rd ed.). Unpublished manuscript, Department of Psychology, University of California, Berkeley.

Gergely, G., & Unoka, Z. (2008). Attachment and mentalization in humans: The development of The affective self. In E. Jurist, A. Slade, & S. Bergner (Eds.), *Mind to mind: Infant research, neuroscience, and psychoanalysis* (pp. 50–87). New York, NY: Other Press.

Gloria, A. M., & Segura-Herrera, T. A. (2004). Somo! Latinas and Latinos in the United States. In D. R. Atkinson (Ed.), *Counseling American minorities: A cross-cultural perspective* (6th ed., pp. 279–299). Boston, MA: McGraw-Hill.

Gold, P. B., Patton, M. J., & Kivlighan, D. M., Jr. (2009). *The pattern of endorsement of therapeutic factors over time and change in group member interpersonal problems.* Unpublished manuscript, Department of Counseling and Personnel Services, University of Maryland, College Park.

Goldman, G. A., & Anderson, T. (2007). Quality of object relations and security of attachment as predictors of early therapeutic alliance. *Journal of Counseling Psychology, 54,* 111–117. doi:10.1037/0022-0167.54.2.111

Gray-Little, B., & Hafdahl, A. R. (2000). Factors influencing racial comparisons of self-esteem: A quantitative review. *Psychological Bulletin, 126,* 26–54. doi:10.1037/0033-2909.126.1.26

Greenberg, L. S., & Elliott, R. (1997). Varieties of empathic responding. In A. C. Bohart & L. S. Greenberg (Eds.), *Empathy reconsidered: New directions in psychotherapy* (pp. 167–186). Washington, DC: American Psychological Association.

Greening, K., Whittingham, M., & Yutrzenka, D. (2012, August). Assessing change patterns for the intrusively/needy subtype within focused brief group therapy: A mixed-methods approach. Poster presented at the American Psychological Association Annual Convention, Orlando, FL.

Griffin, D. W., & Bartholomew, K. (1994). The metaphysics of measurement: The case of adult attachment. In K. Bartholomew & D. Perlman (Eds.), *Advances in personal relationships: Vol. 5. Attachment processes in adulthood* (pp. 17–52). London, England: Jessica Kingsley.

Guerrero, L. K. (1996). Attachment-style differences in intimacy and involvement: A test of the four-category model. *Communications Monographs, 63,* 269–292.

Gunderson, J. G., & Sabo, A. N. (1993). The phenomenological and conceptual interface between borderline personality disorder and PTSD. *The American Journal of Psychiatry, 150,* 19–27.

Hall, E. T. (1976). *Beyond culture.* Oxford, England: Anchor.

Hammond, E. S., & Marmarosh, C. L. (2011). The influence of individual attachment styles on group members' experience of therapist transitions. *International Journal of Group Psychotherapy, 61,* 597–620. doi:10.1521/ijgp.2011.61.4.596

Hand, I., Lamontagne, Y., & Marks, I. M. (1974). Group exposure (flooding) in vivo for agoraphobics. *The British Journal of Psychiatry, 124,* 588–602. doi:10.1192/bjp.124.6.588

Harel, Y., Shechtman, Z., & Cutrona, C. (2011). Individual and group process variables that affect social support in counseling groups. *Group Dynamics: Theory, Research, and Practice, 15,* 297–310.251658240251658240 doi:10.1037/a0025058

Harwood, I. H. (1983). The application of self psychology concepts to group psychotherapy. *International Journal of Group Psychotherapy, 33,* 469–487.

Hazan, C., & Shaver, P. (1987). Romantic love conceptualized as an attachment process. *Journal of Personality and Social Psychology, 52,* 511–524. doi:10.1037/0022-3514.52.3.511

Hazan, C., & Shaver, P. R. (1992). Broken attachments: Relationship loss from the perspective of attachment theory. In T. L. Orbuch (Ed.), *Close relationship loss: Theoretical approaches* (pp. 90–108). New York, NY: Springer-Verlag. doi:10.1007/978-1-4613-9186-9_5

Herman, J. L. (1992). *Trauma and recovery.* New York, NY: Basic Books.

Hesse, E. (1999). The Adult Attachment Interview: Historical and current perspectives. In J. Cassidy & P. R. Shaver (Eds.), *Handbook of attachment: Theory, research, and clinical applications* (pp. 395–433). New York, NY: Guilford Press.

Höfler, D. Z., & Kooyman, M. (1996). Attachment transition, addiction and therapeutic bonding—an integrative approach. *Journal of Substance Abuse Treatment, 13,* 511–519. doi:10.1016/S0740-5472(96)00156-0

Holmes, J. (1996). *Attachment, intimacy, autonomy: Using attachment theory in adult psychotherapy.* Northvale, NJ: Jason Aronson.

Holmes, J. (1997). "Too early, too late": Endings in psychotherapy—an attachment perspective. *British Journal of Psychotherapy, 14,* 159–171. doi:10.1111/j.1752-0118.1997.tb00367.x

Holmes, J. (2004). Disorganized attachment and borderline personality disorder: A clinical perspective. *Attachment & Human Development, 6,* 181–190. doi:10.1080/14616730410001688202

Holtz, A. (2005). Measuring the therapy group attachment in group psychotherapy: A validation of the social group attachment scale. *Dissertation Abstracts International, 65,* 4832.

Hopper, E. (2001). Difficult patients in group analysis. *Group, 25,* 139–171. doi:10.1023/A:1012221300761

Horvath, A. O., & Bedi, P. B. (2002). The alliance. In J. C. Norcross (Ed.), *Psychotherapy relationships that work* (pp. 37–69). Oxford, England: University Press.

Howes, C. (1999). Attachment relationships in the context of multiple caregivers. In J. Cassidy & P. R. Shaver (Eds.), *Handbook of attachment: Theory, research, and clinical applications* (pp. 671–687). New York, NY: Guilford Press.

Hughes, D. A. (2007). *Attachment focused family therapy.* New York, NY: Norton.

Hummelen, B., Wilberg, T., & Karterud, S. (2007). Interviews of female patients with borderline personality disorder who dropped out of group therapy. *International Journal of Group Psychotherapy, 57,* 67–91. doi:10.1521/ijgp.2007.57.1.67

Illing, V., Tasca, G., Balfour, L., & Bissada, H. (2011). Attachment dimensions and group climate growth in a sample of women seeking treatment for eating disorders. *Psychiatry: Interpersonal and Biological Processes, 74,* 255–269. doi:10.1521/psyc.2011.74.3.255

Illing, V., Tasca, G. A., Balfour, L., & Bissada, H. (2010). Attachment insecurity predicts eating disorder symptoms and treatment outcomes in a clinical sample of women. *Journal of Nervous and Mental Disease, 198*, 653–659. doi:10.1097/NMD.0b013e3181ef34b2

Janzen, J., Fitzpatrick, M., & Drapeau, M. (2008). Processes involved in client-nominated relationship building incidents: Client attachment, attachment to therapist, and session impact. *Psychotherapy: Theory, Research, Practice, Training, 45*, 377–390. doi:10.1037/a0013310

Johnson, C. V. (2009). A process-oriented group model for university students: A semi-structured approach. *International Journal of Group Psychotherapy, 59*, 511–528.

Johnson, J. E., Burlingame, G. M., Olsen, J. A., Davies, D. R., & Gleave, R. L. (2005). Group climate, cohesion, alliance, and empathy in group psychotherapy: Multilevel structural equation models. *Journal of Counseling Psychology, 52*, 310–321. doi:10.1037/0022-0167.52.3.310

Johnson, S. M., & Whiffen, V. E. (2003). *Attachment processes in family and couple therapy.* New York, NY: Guilford Press.

Jones, B. A. (1983). Healing factors of psychiatry in light of attachment theory. *American Journal of Psychotherapy, 37*, 235–244.

Joyce, A. S., Piper, W. E., & Ogrodniczuk, J. S. (2007). Therapeutic alliance and cohesion variables as predictors of outcome in short-term group psychotherapy. *International Journal of Group Psychotherapy, 57*, 269–296. doi:10.1521/ijgp.2007.57.3.269

Jurist, E. L., & Meehan, K. B. (2008). Attachment, mentalization and reflective functioning. In J. H. Obegi & E. Berant (Eds.), *Clinical applications of adult attachment* (pp. 71–93). New York, NY: Guilford Press.

Kahn, G. B., & Feldman, D. B. (2011). Relationship-focused group therapy (RFGT) to mitigate marital instability and neuropsychophysiological dysregulation. *International Journal of Group Psychotherapy, 61*, 518–536. doi:10.1521/ijgp.2011.61.4.518

Kaitz, M., Bar-Him, Y., Lehrer, M., & Grossman, E. (2004). Adult attachment style and interpersonal distance. *Attachment & Human Development, 6*, 285–304. doi:10.1080/14616730412331281520

Kanninen, K., Salo, J., & Punamaki, R. L. (2000). Attachment patterns and working alliance in trauma therapy for victims of political violence. *Psychotherapy Research, 10*, 435–449. doi:10.1093/ptr/10.4.435

Karterud, S., & Bateman, A. (2011). Mentalization based treatment: Group therapy techniques. In A. Bateman & P. Fonagy (Eds.), *Mentalizing in mental health practice* (pp. 81–105). Washington, DC: American Psychiatric Publishing.

Keating, L., Tasca, G., Gick, M., Ritchie, T., Balfour, L., & Bissada, H. (in press). Change in attachment to the therapy group generalizes to change in individual attachment among women with binge-eating disorder. *Psychotherapy: Theory, Research, and Practice.*

Kilmann, P., Laughlin, J., Carranza, L., Downer, J., Major, S., & Parnell, M. (1999). Effects of an attachment-focused group preventive intervention on insecure women. *Group Dynamics: Theory, Research, Practice, and Training, 3,* 138–147. doi:10.1037/1089-2699.3.2.138

Kilmann, P. R., Urbaniak, G. C., & Parnell, M. M. (2006). Effects of attachment focused versus relationship skills-focused group interventions for college students with insecure attachment patterns. *Attachment & Human Development, 8,* 47–62. doi:10.1080/14616730600585219

Kim, B., Atkinson, D. R., & Yang, P. H. (1999). The Asian Values Scale: Development, factor analysis, validation and reliability. *Journal of Counseling Psychology, 46,* 342–352. doi:10.1037/0022-0167.46.3.342

Kinley, J. L., & Rayno, S. M. (2012). Attachment style changes following intensive short-term group psychotherapy. *International Journal of Group Psychotherapy, 63,* 53–75.

Kinzie, J. D., Leung, P., Bui, A., Ben, R., Keopraseuth, K. O., Riley, C., . . . Ades, M. (1988). Group therapy with Southeast Asian refugees. *Community Mental Health Journal, 24,* 157–166. doi:10.1007/BF00756658

Kirchmann, H., Mestel, R., Schreiber-Willnow, K., Mattke, D., Seidler, K. P., Daudert, E., . . . Strauss, B. (2009). Associations among attachment characteristics, patients' assessment of therapeutic factors, and treatment outcome following inpatient psychodynamic group psychotherapy. *Psychotherapy Research, 19,* 234–248. doi:10.1080/10503300902798367

Kirchmann, H., Steyer, R., Mayer, A., Joraschky, P., Schreiber-Willnow, K., & Strauss, B. (2012). Effects of adult inpatient group psychotherapy on attachment characteristics: An observational study comparing routine care to an untreated comparison group. *Psychotherapy Research, 22,* 95–114.

Kirkpatrick, L., & Hazan, C. (1994). Attachment styles and close relationships: A four year perspective study. *Personal Relationships, 1,* 123–142. doi:10.1111/j.1475-6811.1994.tb00058.x

Kivlighan, D. M., Jr., Coco, G. L., & Gullo, S. (2012). Attachment anxiety and avoidance and perceptions of group climate: An actor-partner interdependence analysis. *Journal of Counseling Psychology, 59,* 518–527.

Kivlighan, D. M., Jr., & Coleman, M. N. (1999). Values, exchange relationships, group composition, and leader–member differences: A potpourri of reactions to dose (1999). *Group Dynamics: Theory, Research, and Practice, 3,* 33–39. doi:10.1037/1089-2699.3.1.33

Kivlighan, D. M., Jr., Multon, K. D., & Brossart, D. F. (1996). Helpful impacts of group counseling: Development of a multidimensional rating system. *Journal of Counseling Psychology, 43,* 347–355. doi:10.1037/0022-0167.43.3.347

Kivlighan, D. M., Jr., Patton, M. J., & Foote, D. (1998). Moderating effects of client attachment on the counselor experience-working alliance relationship. *Journal of Counseling Psychology, 45,* 274–278. doi:10.1037/0022-0167.45.3.274

Kobak, R. R. (1989). *The Attachment Interview Q-Set*. Unpublished manuscript, University of Delaware, Newark.

Kobak, R. R., & Hazan, C. (1991). Attachment in marriage: Effects of security and accuracy of working models. *Journal of Personality and Social Psychology, 60*, 861–869. doi:10.1037/0022-3514.60.6.861

Kohut, H. (1971). *The analysis of the self*. New York, NY: International Universities Press.

Kohut, H. (1984). *How does analysis cure?* Chicago, IL: The University of Chicago Press.

Kohut, H., & Wolf, E. S. (1978). The disorders of the self and treatment: An outline. *The International Journal of Psychoanalysis, 59*, 413–425.

Korfmacher, J., Adam, E., Ogawa, J., & Egeland, B. (1997). Adult attachment: Implications for the therapeutic process in a home visitation intervention. *Applied Developmental Science, 1*, 43–52. doi:10.1207/s1532480xads0101_5

Kottler, J. A. (1994). *Advanced Group Leadership*. Pacific Grove, CA: Brooks/Cole.

Lachmann, F. (2008). *Transforming narcissism: Reflections on empathy, humor, and expectations*. New York, NY: The Analytic Press.

Lavy, S. (2006). *Expressions and consequences of intrusiveness in adult romantic relationships: An attachment theory perspective* Unpublished doctoral dissertation, Bar-Ilan University, Ramat Gan, Israel.

Leerkes, E. M., & Siepak, K. J. (2006). Attachment linked predictors of women's emotional and cognitive responses to infant distress. *Attachment & Human Development, 8*, 11–32. doi:10.1080/14616730600594450

Levy, K. N. (2005). The implications of attachment theory and research for understanding borderline personality disorder. *Development and Psychopathology, 17*, 959–986. doi:10.1017/S0954579405050455

Levy, K. N., Kelly, K. M., Meehan, K. B., Reynoso, J. S., Clarkin, J. K., & Kernberg, O. F. (2006). Change in attachment organization during the treatment of borderline personality disorder. *Journal of Consulting and Clinical Psychology, 74*, 1027–1040. doi:10.1037/0022-006X.74.6.1027

Lichtenberg, J. D., Lachmann, F. M., & Fosshage, J. L. (2011). *Psychoanalysis and motivational systems: A new look*. New York, NY: Routledge.

Lieberman, M. A., & Golant, M. (2002). Leader behaviors as perceived by cancer patients in professionally directed support groups and outcomes. *Group Dynamics: Theory, Research, and Practice, 6*, 267–276. doi:10.1037/1089-2699.6.4.267

Lieberman, M. A., Wizlenberg, A., Golant, M., & Di Minno, M. (2005). The impact of group composition on internet support groups: Homogeneous versus heterogeneous Parkinson's groups. *Group Dynamics: Theory, Research, and Practice, 9*, 239–250. doi:10.1037/1089-2699.9.4.239

Lindemann, E. (1994). Symptomatology and management of acute grief. 1944. *The American Journal of Psychiatry, 151*(Suppl. 6), 155–160.

Linehan, M. M. (1993). *Skills training manual for treating borderline personality disorder*. New York, NY: Guilford Press.

Linehan, M. M., Dimeff, L. A., Reynolds, S. K., Comtois, K. A., Welch, S. S., Heagerty, P., & Kiylahan, D. R. (2002). Dialectical behavior therapy versus comprehensive validation therapy plus 12-step for the treatment of opioid dependent women meeting criteria for borderline personality disorder. *Drug and Alcohol Dependence, 67*, 13–26. doi:10.1016/S0376-8716(02)00011-X

Linehan, M. M., Tutek, D. A., Heard, H. L., & Armstrong, H. E. (1994). Interpersonal outcome of cognitive–behavioral treatment for chronically suicidal borderline patients. *The American Journal of Psychiatry, 151*, 1771–1776.

Liotti, G. (2004). Trauma, dissociation, and disorganized attachment: Three strands of a single braid. *Psychotherapy: Theory, Research, Practice, Training, 41*, 472–486. doi:10.1037/0033-3204.41.4.472

Lopez, F. G., & Brennan, K. A. (2000). Dynamic processes underlying adult attachment organization: Toward an attachment theoretical perspective on the healthy and effective self. *Journal of Counseling Psychology, 47*, 283–300. doi:10.1037/0022-0167.47.3.283

Lopez, F. G., Melendez, M. C., & Rice, K. G. (2000). Parental divorce, parent-child bonds, and adult attachment orientations among college students: A comparison of three racial/ethnic groups. *Journal of Counseling Psychology, 47*, 177–186. doi:10.1037/0022-0167.47.2.177

MacKenzie, K. R. (1994). Group development. In A. Fuhriman & G. M. Burlingame (Eds.), *Handbook of group psychotherapy: An empirical and clinical synthesis* (pp. 223–268). New York, NY: Wiley.

MacKenzie, K. R., & Grabovac, A. D. (2001). Interpersonal psychotherapy group (IPT-G) for depression. *Journal of Psychotherapy Practice and Research, 10*, 46–51.

MacNair, R. R., & Corazzini, J. (1994). Client factors influencing group therapy dropout. *Psychotherapy: Theory, Research, Practice, Training, 31*, 352–362. doi:10.1037/h0090226

MacNair-Semands, R. R. (2002). Predicting attendance and expectations for group therapy. *Group Dynamics: Theory, Research, and Practice, 6*, 219–228. doi:10.1037/1089-2699.6.3.219

MacNair-Semands, R. R., & Corazzini, J. (1998). *Manual for the Group Therapy Questionnaire (GTQ)*. Richmond: Virginia Commonwealth University, Counseling Services; Charlotte: University of North Carolina at Charlotte Counseling Center.

Magai, C. (1999). Affect, imagery, and attachment: Working models of interpersonal affect and the socialization of emotion. In J. Cassidy & P. R. Shaver (Eds.), *Handbook of attachment: Theory, research, and clinical applications* (pp. 787–802). New York, NY: Guilford Press.

Magai, C., Cohen, C., Milburn, N., Thorpe, B., McPherson, R., & Peralta, D. (2001). Attachment styles in older European American and African American adults. *The Journals of Gerontology: Series B, Psychological Sciences and Social Sciences, 56*, S28–S35. doi:10.1093/geronb/56.1.S28

Main, M. (1991). Metacognitive knowledge, metacognitive monitoring, and singular (coherent) versus multiple (incoherent) models of attachment: Findings and directions for future research. In C. M. Parkes, J. Stevenson-Hinde, & P. Marris (Eds.), *Attachment across the life cycle* (pp. 127–159). New York, NY: Routledge.

Main, M. (1995). Recent studies in attachment: Overview, with selected implications for clinical work. In S. Goldberg, R. Muir, & J. Kerr (Eds.), *Attachment theory: Social, developmental and clinical perspectives* (pp. 407–474). Hillsdale, NJ: Analytic Press.

Main, M., Goldwyn, R., & Hesse, E. (2003). *Adult Attachment Classification System 7.2.* Unpublished manuscript, University of California, Berkeley.

Main, M., & Hesse, E. (1990). Parents' unresolved traumatic experiences are related to infant disorganized attachment status: Is frightened and/or frightening parental behavior the linking mechanism? In M. T. Greenberg, D. Cicchetti, & E. M. Cummings (Eds.), *Attachment in Preschool Years: Theory, Research, and Intervention* (pp. 161–182). Chicago, IL: Chicago University Press.

Main, M., & Hesse, E. (1992). Disorganized/disoriented infant behavior in the Strange Situation, lapses in the monitoring of reasoning and discourse during the parent's Adult Attachment Interview, and dissociative states. In M. Ammaniti & D. Stern (Eds.), *Attachment and Psychoanalysis* (pp. 86–140). Rome, Italy: Gius, Laterza, and Figli.

Main, M., Kaplan, N., & Cassidy, J. (1985). Security in infancy, childhood, and adulthood. *Monographs of the Society for Research in Child Development, 50,* 66–104. doi:10.2307/3333827

Main, M., & Weston, D. R. (1982). Avoidance of the attachment figure in infancy: Descriptions and interpretations. In C. Parkes & J. Stevenson-Hinde (Eds.), *The place of attachment in human behavior* (pp. 31–59). New York, NY: Basic Books.

Malley-Morrison, K., You, H. S., & Mills, R. B. (2000). Young adult attachment styles and perceptions of elder abuse: A cross-cultural study. *Journal of Cross-Cultural Gerontology, 15,* 163–184. doi:10.1023/A:1006748708812

Mallinckrodt, B., & Chen, E. C. (2004). Attachment and interpersonal impact perceptions of group members: A social relations model analysis of transference. *Psychotherapy Research, 14,* 210–230. doi:10.1093/ptr/kph018

Mallinckrodt, B., Coble, H., & Gantt, D. (1995). Working alliance, attachment memories, and social competencies of women in brief therapy. *Journal of Counseling Psychology, 42,* 79–84.

Mallinckrodt, B., Gantt, D., & Coble, H. (1995). Attachment patterns in the psychotherapy relationship: Development of the Client Attachment to Therapist Scale. *Journal of Counseling Psychology, 42,* 307–317. doi:10.1037/0022-0167. 42.3.307

Mallinckrodt, B., Porter, M., & Kivlighan, D. (2005). Client attachment to therapist, depth of in-session exploration, and object relations in brief psychotherapy. *Psychotherapy: Theory, Research, Practice, Training, 42,* 85–100. doi:10.1037/0033-3204.42.1.85

Manassis, K., Bradley, S., Goldberg, S., Hood, J., & Swinson, R. P. (1994). Attachment in mothers with anxiety disorders and their children. *Journal of the American Academy of Child & Adolescent Psychiatry, 33,* 1106–1113. doi:10.1097/00004583-199410000-00006

Markin, R. D., & Marmarosh, C. (2010). Application of adult attachment theory to group member transference and the group therapy process. *Psychotherapy: Theory, Research, Practice, Training, 47,* 111–121. doi:10.1037/a0018840

Marmarosh, C. L. (2009). Multiple attachments and group psychotherapy: Implications for college counseling centers. *International Journal of Group Psychotherapy, 59,* 461–490. doi:10.1521/ijgp.2009.59.4.461

Marmarosh, C. L., Bieri, K., Fauchi-Schutt, J., Barrone, C., & Choi, J. (in press). The insecure psychotherapy base: Using client and therapist attachment styles to understand the early alliance. *Psychotherapy.*

Marmarosh, C. L., & Corazzini, J. (1997). Putting the group in your pocket: Using the collective identity to enhance personal and collective self-esteem. *Group Dynamics: Theory, Research, Practice, Training, 1,* 65–74. doi:10.1037/1089-2699.1.1.65

Marmarosh, C. L., Franz, V. A., Koloi, M., Majors, R., Rahimi, A., Ronquillo, J., . . . Zimmer, K. (2006). Therapists' group attachments and their expectations of patients' attitudes about group therapy. *International Journal of Group Psychotherapy, 56,* 325–338. doi:10.1521/ijgp.2006.56.3.325

Marmarosh, C. L., Gelso, C., Majors, R., Markin, R., Mallery, C., & Choi, J. (2009). The real relationship in psychotherapy: Relationships to adult attachments, working alliance, transference, and therapy outcome. *Journal of Counseling Psychology, 56,* 337–350. doi:10.1037/a0015169

Marmarosh, C. L., & Markin, R. D. (2007). Group and personal attachments: Two is better than one when predicting college adjustment. *Group Dynamics: Theory, Research, and Practice, 11,* 153–164. doi:10.1037/1089-2699.11.3.153

Marmarosh, C. L., Whipple, R., Schettler, M., Pinhas, S., Wolf, J., & Sayit, S. (2009). Adult attachment styles and group psychotherapy attitudes. *Group Dynamics: Theory, Research, and Practice, 13,* 255–264. doi:10.1037/a0015957

Martin, D., Garske, J., & Davis, M. (2000). Relation of the therapeutic alliance with outcome and other variables: A meta-analytic review. *Journal of Consulting and Clinical Psychology, 68,* 438–450.

Marziali, E., & Blum, H. M. (1994). *Interpersonal group psychotherapy for borderline personality disorder.* New York, NY: Basic Books.

Maxwell, H., Tasca, G. A., Ritchie, K., Balfour, L., & Bissada, H. (in press). Change in attachment insecurity is related to improved outcomes one year post-group therapy in women with binge eating disorder. *Psychotherapy.*

McCluskey, U. (2002). The dynamics of attachment and systems-centered group psychotherapy. *Group Dynamics: Theory, Research, and Practice, 6,* 131–142.

McCluskey, U. (2008). Attachment-based therapy in groups: Exploring a new theoretical paradigm with professional care-givers. *Attachment: New Directions in Psychotherapy and Relational Psychoanalysis, 2*, 204–215.

McRoberts, C., Burlingame, G. M., & Hoag, M. J. (1998). Comparative efficacy of individual and group psychotherapy: A meta-analytic perspective. *Group Dynamics: Theory, Research, and Practice, 2*, 101–117. doi:10.1037/1089-2699.2.2.101

Meredith, P. J., Strong, J., & Feeney, J. (2007). Adult attachment variables predict depression before and after treatment for chronic pain. *European Journal of Pain, 11*, 164–170. doi:10.1016/j.ejpain.2006.01.004

Meyer, B., Pilkonis, P. A., Proitetti, J. M., Heape, C. L., & Egan, M. (2001). Attachment styles, personality disorders and response to treatment. *Journal of Personality Disorders, 15*, 371–389. doi:10.1521/pedi.15.5.371.19200

Mickelson, K. D., Kessler, R. C., & Shaver, P. R. (1997). Adult attachment in a nationally representative sample. *Journal of Personality and Social Psychology, 73*, 1092–1106. doi:10.1037/0022-3514.73.5.1092

Mikulincer, M. (1995). Attachment style and the mental representations of the self. *Journal of Personality and Social Psychology, 69*, 1203–1215. doi:10.1037/0022-3514.69.6.1203

Mikulincer, M. (1998). Attachment working models and the sense of trust: An exploration of interaction goals and affect regulation. *Journal of Personality and Social Psychology, 74*, 1209–1224. doi:10.1037/0022-3514.74.5.1209

Mikulincer, M., Birnbaum, G., Woddis, D., & Nachmias, O. (2000). Stress and accessibility of proximity-related thoughts: Exploring the normative and intra-individual components of attachment theory. *Journal of Personality and Social Psychology, 78*, 509–523.

Mikulincer, M., & Florian, V. (1997). Are emotional and instrumental supportive interactions beneficial in times of stress? The impact of attachment style. *Anxiety, Stress and Coping, 10*, 109–127.

Mikulincer, M., & Florian, V. (1998). The relationship between adult attachment styles and emotional and cognitive reactions to stressful events. In J. A. Simpson & W. S. Rholes (Eds.), *Attachment theory and close relationships* (pp. 143–165). New York, NY: Guilford Press.

Mikulincer, M., & Florian, V. (2001). Attachment style and affect regulation: Implications for coping with stress and mental health. In G. Fletcher & M. Clark (Eds.), *Handbook of social psychology: Interpersonal processes* (pp. 537–557). Malden, MA: Blackwell Publishers. doi:10.1002/9780470998557.ch21

Mikulincer, M., & Shaver, P. R. (2001). Attachment theory and intergroup bias: Evidence that priming the secure base schema attenuates negative reactions to out-groups. *Journal of Personality and Social Psychology, 81*, 97–115. doi:10.1037/0022-3514.89.5.817

Mikulincer, M., & Shaver, P. R. (2003). The attachment behavioral system in adulthood: Activation, psychodynamics, and interpersonal processes. In M. P. Zanna

(Ed.), *Advances in experimental social psychology* (Vol. 35, pp. 43–152). San Diego, CA: Elsevier Academic Press. doi:10.1016/S0065-2601(03)01002-5

Mikulincer, M., & Shaver, P. R. (2007a). Attachment, group-related processes, and psychotherapy. *International Journal of Group Psychotherapy, 57,* 233–245.

Mikulincer, M., & Shaver, P. R. (2007b). *Attachment in adulthood: Structure, dynamics, and change.* New York, NY: Guilford Press.

Mikulincer, M., & Shaver, P. R. (2007c). Boosting attachment security to promote mental health, prosocial values, and inter-group tolerance. *Psychological Inquiry, 18,* 139–156. doi:10.1080/10478400701512646

Mikulincer, M., Shaver, P. R., Bar-On, N., & Ein-Dor, T. (2010). The pushes and pulls of close relationships: Attachment insecurities and relational ambivalence. *Journal of Personality and Social Psychology, 98,* 450–468. doi:10.1037/a0017366

Mikulincer, M., Shaver, P. R., Gillath, O., & Nitzberg, R. A. (2005). Attachment, caregiving, and altruism: Boosting attachment security increases compassion and helping. *Journal of Personality and Social Psychology, 89,* 817–839. doi:10.1037/0022-3514.89.5.817

Mikulincer, M., Shaver, P. R., Sapir-Lavid, Y., & Avihou-Kanza, N. (2009). What's inside the minds of securely and insecurely attached people? The secure-base script and its associations with attachment-style dimensions. *Journal of Personality and Social Psychology, 97,* 615–633. doi:10.1037/a0015649

Mikulincer, M., Shaver, P. R., & Slav, K. (2006). Attachment, mental representations of others, and gratitude and forgiveness in romantic relationships. In M. Mikulincer & G. S. Goodman (Eds.), *Dynamics of romantic love: Attachment, caregiving, and sex* (pp. 190–215). New York, NY: Guilford Press.

Montague, D. P. F., Magai, C., Consedine, N. S., & Gillespie, M. (2003). Attachment in African American and European American older adults: The roles of early life socialization and religiosity. *Attachment & Human Development, 5,* 188–214. doi:10.1080/1461673031000108487

Mosheim, R., Zachhuber, U., Scharf, L., Hofmann, A., Kemmler, G., Danzl, C., . . . Richter, R. (2000). Bindung und Psychotherapie [Attachment and psychotherapy]. *Psychotherapeut, 45,* 223–229. doi:10.1007/PL00006719

Motherwell, L., & Shay, J. J. (2005). *Complex dilemmas in group therapy, pathways to resolution.* New York, NY: Brunner-Routledge.

Muller, R. T., & Rosenkranz, S. (2009). Attachment and treatment response among adults in inpatient treatment for posttraumatic stress disorder. *Psychotherapy: Theory, Research, Practice, Training, 46,* 82–96. doi:10.1037/a0015137

Muller, R. T., Sicoli, L. A., & Lemieux, K. E. (2000). Relationship between attachment style and posttraumatic stress symptomatology among adults who report the experience of childhood abuse. *Journal of Traumatic Stress, 13,* 321–332. doi:10.1023/A:1007752719557

Nichols, K. A., & Jenkinson, J. D. (2006). *Leading a support group: A practical guide.* Maidenhead, England: McGraw-Hill International.

Ogrodniczuk, J. S., & Piper, W. E. (2001). Day treatment for personality disorders: A review of research findings. *Harvard Review of Psychiatry, 9*, 105–117. doi:10.1080/10673220127889

Ornstein, A. (2012). Mass murder and the individual: Psychoanalytic reflections on Perpetrators and their victims. *International Journal of Group Psychotherapy, 62*, 1–20. doi:10.1521/ijgp.2012.62.1.1

Padykula, N., & Conklin, P. (2010). The self-regulation model of attachment trauma and addiction. *Clinical Social Work Journal, 38*, 351–360. doi:10.1007/s10615-009-0204-6

Paley, B., Cox, M. J., Burchinal, M. R., & Payne, C. (1999). Attachment and marital functioning: Comparison of spouses with continuous-secure, earned secure, dismissing, and preoccupied attachment stances. *Journal of Family Psychology, 13*, 580–597. doi:10.1037/0893-3200.13.4.580

Parker, M. L., Johnson, L. N., & Ketring, S. A. (2011). Assessing attachment of couples in therapy: A factor analysis of the experiences in close relationships scale. *Contemporary Family Therapy: An International Journal, 33*, 37–48. doi:10.1007/s10591-011-9142-x

Parkes, C. M. (2001). A historical overview of the scientific study of bereavement. In M. S. Stroebe, W. Stroebe, R. O., Hansson, & H. Schut (Eds.), *Handbook of bereavement research: Consequences, coping and care* (pp. 25–45). Washington, DC: American Psychological Association.

Parkes, C. M. (2003). *Attachment patterns in childhood: Relationships, coping, and psychological state in adults seeking psychiatric help after bereavement.* Unpublished manuscript, St. Christopher's Hospice, London, England.

Pearlman, L. A., & Courtois, C. A. (2005). Clinical applications of the attachment framework: Relational treatment of complex trauma. *Journal of Traumatic Stress, 18*, 449–459. doi:10.1002/jts.20052

Perrone, K. M., & Sedlacek, W. E. (2000). A comparison of group cohesiveness and client satisfaction in homogenous and heterogenous groups. *Journal for Specialists in Group Work, 25*, 243–251. doi:10.1080/01933920008411465

Pianta, R., Egeland, B., & Adam, E. (1996). Adult attachment classification and self-reported psychiatric symptomatology as assessed by the Minnesota Multiphasic Personality Inventory—2. *Journal of Consulting and Clinical Psychology, 64*, 273–281.

Pietromonaco, P. R., Laurenceau, J., & Barrett, L. F. (2002). Change in relationship knowledge representations. In A. L. Vangelisti, H. T. Reis, & M. A. Fitzpatrick (Eds.), *Stability and change in relationships* (pp. 5–34). *Advances in personal relationships* New York, NY: Cambridge University Press. doi:10.1017/CBO9780511499876.003

Piper, W. E. (2008). Underutilization of short-term group therapy: Enigmatic or understandable? *Psychotherapy Research, 18*, 127–138. doi:10.1080/10503300701867512

Piper, W. E., Azim, H. F. A., Joyce, A. S., McCallum, M., Nixon, G. W. H., & Segal, P. S. (1991). Quality of object relations vs. interpersonal functioning as predictors of therapeutic alliance and psychotherapy outcome. *Journal of Nervous and Mental Disease, 179,* 432–438. doi:10.1097/00005053-199107000-00008

Piper, W. E., & Ogrodniczuk, J. S. (2004). Brief group therapy. In J. Delucia-Waack, D. A. Gerrity, C. R. Kolodner, & M. T. Riva (Eds.), *Handbook of group counseling and psychotherapy* (pp. 641–650). Beverly Hills, CA: Sage.

Piper, W. E., Ogrodniczuk, J. S., Joyce, A. S., & Weideman, R. (2011). Effects of group composition on therapeutic outcome. In *Short-term group therapies for complicated grief: Two research-based models* (pp. 159–173). Washington, DC: American Psychological Association. doi:10.1037/12344-006

Piper, W. E., Ogrodniczuk, J. S., Joyce, A. S., Weideman, R., & Rosie, J. S. (2007). Group composition and group therapy for complicated grief. *Journal of Consulting and Clinical Psychology, 75*(1), 116–125. doi:10.1037/0022-006X.75.1.116

Piper, W. E., & Perrault, E. L. (1989). Pretherapy preparation for group members. *International Journal of Group Psychotherapy, 39,* 17–34.

Pistole, M. C. (1989). Attachment: Implications for counselors. *Journal of Counseling & Development, 68,* 190–193. doi:10.1002/j.1556-6676.1989.tb01355.x

Pistole, M. C. (1997). Attachment theory: Contributions to group work. *Journal for Specialists in Group Work, 22,* 7–21. doi:10.1080/01933929708415519

Pistole, M. C. (1999). Caregiving in attachment relationships: A perspective for counselors. *Journal of Counseling & Development, 77,* 437–446. doi:10.1002/j.1556-6676.1999.tb02471.x

Plasky, P., & Lorion, R. P. (1984). Demographic parameters of self-disclosure to psychotherapists and others. *Psychotherapy: Theory, Research, Practice, Training, 21,* 483–490. doi:10.1037/h0085993

Polansky, M., Lauterbach, W., Litzke, C., Coulter, B., & Sommers, L. (2006). A qualitative study of an attachment-based parenting group for mothers with drug addictions: On being and having a mother. *Journal of Social Work Practice, 20,* 115–131. doi:10.1080/02650530600776673

Prenn, N. (2011). Mind the gap: AEDP interventions translating attachment theory into clinical practice. *Journal of Psychotherapy Integration, 21,* 308–329. doi:10.1037/a0025491

Rando, T. A. (1993). *Treatment of complicated mourning.* Champaign, IL: Research Press.

Rice, C. (1992). Contributions of object relations theory. In R. H. Klein, H. S. Bernard, & D. L. Singer (Eds.), *Handbook of contemporary group psychotherapy: Contributions from object relations, self-psychology, and social systems theories* (pp. 27–55). Madison, CT: International Universities Press.

Riva, M., Wachtel, M., & Lasky, G. (2004). Effective leadership in group counseling and psychotherapy. In J. DeLucia-Waack, D. Gerrity, C. Kalodner, & M. T. Riva (Eds.), *Handbook of group counseling and psychotherapy* (pp. 37–48). Thousand Oaks, CA: Sage.

Rom, E., & Mikulincer, M. (2003). Attachment theory and group processes: The association between attachment style and group-related representations, goals, memories, and functioning. *Journal of Personality and Social Psychology, 84,* 1220–1235. doi:10.1037/0022-3514.84.6.1220

Romano, V., Fitzpatrick, M., & Janzen, J. (2008). The secure-base hypothesis: Global attachment, attachment to counselor, and session exploration in psychotherapy. *Journal of Counseling Psychology, 55*(4), 495–504. doi:10.1037/a0013721

Rothbaum, F., Weisz, J., Pott, M., Miyake, K., & Morelli, G. (2000). Attachment and culture: Security in the United States and Japan. *American Psychologist, 55,* 1093–1104. doi:10.1037/0003-066X.55.10.1093

Rowe, C. E., & MacIsaac, D. S. (1991). *Empathic attunement: The technique of psychoanalytic self psychology.* Northvale, NJ: Jason Aronson.

Rutan, J. S., & Stone, W. N. (1993). *Psychodynamic group psychotherapy* (2nd ed.). New York, NY: Guilford Press.

Rutan, J. S., & Stone, W. N. (2001). *Psychodynamic group psychotherapy* (3rd ed.). New York, NY: Guilford Press.

Sable, P. (2001). *Attachment and adult psychotherapy.* Lanham, MD: Jason Aronson.

Sachse, J., & Strauss, B. (2002). Bindungscharakteristika und Behandlungserfolg nach stationarer psychodynamischer Gruppentherapie [Attachment characteristic and psychotherapy outcome following inpatient psychodynamic group treatment]. *Psychotherapie Psychosomatik Medizinische Psychologie, 52,* 134–140. doi:10.1055/s-2002-24959

Safran, J. D., Muran, J. C., Samstag, L. W., & Stevens, C. (2002). Repairing alliance ruptures. *Psychotherapy: Theory, Research, Practice, Training, 38,* 406–412. doi:10.1037/0033-3204.38.4.406

Sagi, A., van IJzendoorn, M., Scharf, M., Koren-Karie, N., Joels, T., & Mayseless, O. (1994). Stability and discriminant validity of the Adult Attachment Interview: A psychometric study in young Israeli adults. *Developmental Psychology, 30,* 771–777.

Satterfield, W. A., & Lyddon, W. J. (1995). Client attachment and perceptions of the working alliance with counselor trainees. *Journal of Counseling Psychology, 42,* 187–189. doi:10.1037/0022-0167.42.2.187

Sauer, E. M., Lopez, F. G., & Gormley, B. (2003). Respective contributions of therapist and client adult attachment orientations to the development of the early working alliance: A preliminary growth modeling study. *Psychotherapy Research, 13,* 371–382. doi:10.1093/ptr/kpg027

Saunders, E. A., & Edelson, J. A. (1999). Attachment style, traumatic bonding, and developing relational capacities in a long-term trauma group for women. *International Journal of Group Psychotherapy, 49,* 465–485.

Scharfe, E., & Bartholomew, K. (1994). Reliability and stability of adult attachment patterns. *Personal Relationships, 1,* 23–43. doi:10.1111/j.1475-6811.1994.tb00053.x

Schermer, V. L., & Pines, F. (1994). *Ring of fire: Primitive affects and object relations in group psychotherapy.* London, England: Routledge.

Schmitt, D. P., Alcalay, L., Allensworth, M., Allik, J., Ault, L., Austers, I., . . . Herrera, D. (2004). Patterns and universals of adult romantic attachment across 62 cultural regions: Are models of self and of other pancultural constructs? *Journal of Cross-Cultural Psychology, 35*, 367–402. doi:10.1177/0022022104266105

Schnurr, P. P., Friedman, M., Foy, D., Shea, T., Hsieh, F., Lavori, P., . . . Bernardy, M. (2003). Randomized trial of trauma-focused group therapy for posttraumatic stress disorder. *Archives of General Psychiatry, 60*, 481–489. doi:10.1001/archpsyc.60.5.481

Schore, A. N. (1994). *Affect regulation and the origin of the self: The neurobiology of emotional development.* Mahwah, NJ: Erlbaum.

Schore, A. N. (2002). Advances in neuropsychoanalysis, attachment theory, and trauma research: Implications for self psychology. *Psychoanalytic Inquiry, 22*, 433–484. doi:10.1080/07351692209348996

Schore, A. N. (2003). *Affect regulation and the repair of the self.* New York, NY: Norton.

Segalla, R. (1998). Motivational systems and group-object theory: Implications for group therapy. In I. Harwood & M. Pines (Eds.), *Self experiences in group: Intersubjective and self psychological pathways to human understanding* (pp. 141–153). London, England: Jessica Kinglsey.

Segalla, R., Wine, B., & Silvers, D. (2000). Response to DiNunno's "Long-term group psychotherapy for women who are survivors of childhood abuse." *Psychoanalytic Inquiry, 20*, 350–358. doi:10.1080/07351692009348892

Shaver, P., & Hazan, C. (1993). Adult romantic attachment: Theory and evidence. *Advances in personal relationships, 4*, 29–70.

Shaver, P. R., Belsky, J., & Brennan, K. A. (2000). The Adult Attachment Interview and self-reports of romantic attachment: Associations across domains and methods. *Personal Relationships, 7*, 25–43. doi:10.1111/j.1475-6811.2000.tb00002.x

Shaver, P. R., & Clark, C. L. (1994). The psychodynamics of adult romantic attachment. In J. M. Masling & R. F. Bornstein (Eds.), *Empirical perspectives on object relations theories* (pp. 105–156). Washington, DC: American Psychological Association.

Shaver, P. R., & Tancredy, C. M. (2001). Emotion, attachment and bereavement: A conceptual commentary. In M. S. Stroebe, O. Hansson, & H. Schut (Eds.), *Handbook of bereavement: Consequences, coping, and care* (pp. 63–88). Washington, DC: American Psychological Association. doi:10.1037/10436-003

Shear, K., Monk, T., Houck, P., Melhem, N., Frank, E., Reynolds, C., & Silowash, R. (2007). An attachment-based model of complicated grief including the role of avoidance. *European Archives of Psychiatry and Clinical Neuroscience, 257*, 453–461. doi:10.1007/s00406-007-0745-z

Shechtman, Z., & Dvir, V. (2006). Attachment style as a predictor of behavior in group counseling with preadolescents. *Group Dynamics: Theory, Research, and Practice, 10*, 29–42. doi:10.1037/1089-2699.10.1.29

Shechtman, Z., & Rybko, J. (2004). Attachment style and observed initial self-disclosure as explanatory variables of group functioning. *Group Dynamics: Theory, Research, and Practice, 8,* 207–220. doi:10.1037/1089-2699.8.3.207

Sherwood, V. R., & Cohen, C. P. (1994). *Psychotherapy of the quiet borderline patient: The as-if personality revisited.* Lanham, MD: Jason Aronson.

Shulman, S. (1999). Termination of short-term and long-term psychotherapy: Clients' and therapists' affective reactions and therapists' technical management. *Dissertation Abstracts International. B, The Sciences and Engineering, 60,* 2961.

Siegel, D. J. (2007). *The mindful brain: Reflection and attunement in the cultivation of well-being.* New York, NY: Norton.

Silvers, D. L. (1998). A multiple selfobject and traumatizing experiences: co-therapy model at work. In I. Harwood & M. Pines (Eds.), *Self experiences in group: Intersubjective and self psychological pathways to human understanding* (pp. 123–141). London, England: Jessica Kingsley.

Simpson, J. A. (1990). Influence of attachment styles on romantic relationships. *Journal of Personality and Social Psychology, 59,* 971–980. doi:10.1037/0022-3514.59.5.971

Simpson, J. A., Ickes, W., & Grich, J. (1999). When accuracy hurts: Reactions of anxious-ambivalent dating partners to a relationship-threatening situation. *Journal of Personality and Social Psychology, 76,* 754–769. doi:10.1037/0022-3514.76.5.754

Simpson, J. A., Rholes, W. S., & Nelligan, J. S. (1992). Support seeking and support giving within couples in an anxiety-provoking situation: The role of attachment styles. *Journal of Personality and Social Psychology, 62,* 434–446. doi:10.1037/0022-3514.62.3.434

Smith, E. R., Murphy, J., & Coats, S. (1999). Attachment to groups: Theory and measurement. *Journal of Personality and Social Psychology, 77,* 94–110. doi:10.1037/0022-3514.77.1.94

Sperling, M. B., Foelsch, P., & Grace, C. (1996). Measuring adult attachment: Are self-report instruments congruent? *Journal of Personality Assessment, 67,* 37–51.

Sperling, M. B., & Lyons, L. S. (1994). Representations of attachment and psychotherapeutic change. In M. B. Sperling & W. H. Berman (Eds.), *Attachment in adults: Clinical and developmental perspectives* (pp. 331–347). New York, NY: Guilford Press.

Sroufe, L. A. (1996). *Emotional development: The organization of emotional life in the early years: Cambridge studies in social and emotional development.* New York, NY: Cambridge University Press. doi:10.1017/CBO9780511527661

Sroufe, L. A. (2005). Attachment and development: A prospective, longitudinal study from birth to adulthood. *Attachment & Human Development, 7,* 349–367. doi:10.1080/14616730500365928

Sroufe, L. A., Egeland, B., Carlson, E., & Collins, W. A. (2005). *The development of the person: The Minnesota Study of Risk and Adaptation From Birth to Adulthood.* New York, NY: Guilford Press.

Sroufe, L. A., Fox, N., & Pancake, V. (1983). Attachment and dependency in developmental perspective. *Child Development, 54*, 1615–1627. doi:10.2307/1129825

Sroufe, L. A., & Waters, E. (1977). Heart rate as a convergent measure in clinical and developmental perspective. *Child Development, 61*, 1363–1373. doi:10.2307/1130748

Steele, H. (Ed.). (2002). The psychodynamics of adult attachments—Bridging the gap between disparate research traditions [Special issue]. *Attachment & Human Development, 4*(2).

Stein, H., Jacobs, N., Ferguson, K., Allen, J., & Fonagy, P. (1998). What do adult attachment scales measure? *Bulletin of the Menninger Clinic, 62*, 33–82.

Stein, H., Koontz, A. D., Fonagy, P., Allen, J. G., Fultz, J., Brethour, J. J. R., . . . Evans, R. B. (2002). Adult attachment: What are the underlying dimensions? *Psychology and Psychotherapy: Theory, Research and Practice, 75*, 77–91.

Stern, D. (1985). *The interpersonal world of the infant.* New York, NY: Basic Books.

Stern, J. (2000). Parent training. In J. R. White & A. Freeman (Eds.), *Cognitive-behavioral group therapy for specific problems and populations* (pp. 331–360). Washington, DC: American Psychological Association. doi:10.1037/10352-000

Stiwne, D. (1994). Group psychotherapy with borderline patients—Contrasting remainers and dropouts. *Group, 18*, 37–45. doi:10.1007/BF01459717

Stone, W. (1992). The clinical application of self psychology theory. In R. H. Klein, H. S. Bernard, & D. L. Singer (Eds.), *Handbook of contemporary group psychotherapy: Contributions from object relations, self-psychology, and social systems theories* (pp. 177–208). Madison, CT: International Universities Press.

Stone, W. N., & Gustafson, L. P. (1982). Technique in group psychotherapy of narcissistic and borderline patients. *International Journal of Group Psychotherapy, 32*, 29–56.

Strauss, B., Kirchmann, H., Eckert, J., Lobo-Drost, A., Marquet, A., Papenhausen, R., . . . Höger, D. (2006). Attachment characteristics and treatment outcome following inpatient psychotherapy: Results of a multisite study. *Psychotherapy Research, 16*, 579–594. doi:10.1080/10503300600608322

Strauss, B., Lobo-Drost, A., & Pilkonis, P. A. (1999). Einschatzung von Bindungsstilen bei Erwachsenen [Assessment of adult attachment styles]. *Zeitschrift für Klinische Psychologie, Psychiatrie und Psychotherapie, 47*, 347–364.

Stroebe, M. (2002). Paving the way: From early attachment theory to contemporary bereavement research. *Mortality, 7*, 127–138. doi:10.1080/13576270220136267

Sue, D., Ino, S., & Sue, D. M. (1983). Nonassertiveness of Asian Americans: An inaccurate assumption? *Journal of Counseling Psychology, 30*, 581–588. doi:10.1037/0022-0167.30.4.581

Sue, D. W., & Sue, D. (2003). *Counseling the culturally diverse: Theory and practice* (4th ed.). New York, NY: Wiley.

Sullivan, H. S. (1953). *The interpersonal theory of psychiatry.* New York, NY: W. W. Norton.

Tasca, G. A., Balfour, L., Ritchie, K., & Bissada, H. (2006). Developmental changes in group climate in two types of group therapy for binge eating disorder: A growth curve analysis. *Psychotherapy Research, 16*, 499–514.

Tasca, G. A., Balfour, L., Ritchie, K., & Bissada, H. (2007a). Change in attachment anxiety is associated with improved depression among women with binge eating disorder. *Psychotherapy: Theory, Research, Practice, Training, 44*, 423–433.

Tasca, G. A., Balfour, L., Ritchie, K., & Bissada, H. (2007b). The relationship between attachment scales and group therapy alliance growth differs by treatment type for women with binge-eating disorder. *Group Dynamics Theory, Research, and Practice, 11*, 1–14. doi:10.1037/1089-2699.11.1.1

Tasca, G. A., Foot, M., Leite, C., Maxwell, H., Balfour, L., & Bissada, H. (2011). Interpersonal processes in psychodynamic-interpersonal and cognitive behavioral group therapy: A systematic case study of two groups. *Psychotherapy, 48*, 260–273. doi:10.1037/a0023928

Tasca, G. A., Illing, V., Lybanon-Daigle, V., Bissada, H., & Balfour, L. (2003). Psychometric properties of the Eating Disorders Inventory—2 among women seeking treatment for binge eating disorder. *Assessment, 10*, 228–236. doi:10.1177/1073191103255001

Tasca, G. A., Ritchie, K., & Balfour, L. (2011). Implications of attachment theory and research for the assessment and treatment of eating disorders. *Psychotherapy, 48*, 249–259.

Tasca, G. A., Ritchie, K., Conrad, G., Balfour, L., Gayton, J., Lybanon, V., & Bissada, H. (2006). Attachment scales predict outcome in a randomized controlled trial of two group therapies for binge eating disorder: An aptitude by treatment interaction. *Psychotherapy Research, 16*, 106–121. doi:10.1080/10503300500090928

Tasca, G. A., Szadkowski, L., Illing, V., Trinneer, A., Grenon, R., Demidenko, N., . . . Bissada, H. (2009). Adult attachment, depression, and eating disorder symptoms: The mediating role of affect regulation strategies. *Personality and Individual Differences, 47*, 662–667. doi:10.1016/j.paid.2009.06.006

Tasca, G. A., Taylor, D., Bissada, H., Ritchie, K., & Balfour, L. (2004). Attachment predicts treatment completion in an eating disorders partial hospital program among women with Anorexia Nervosa. *Journal of Personality Assessment, 83*, 201–212. doi:10.1207/s15327752jpa8303_04

Terrell, F., & Terrell, S. L. (1981). An inventory to measure cultural mistrust among Blacks. *The Western Journal of Black Studies, 5*, 180–184.

Travis, L., Bliwise, N., Binder, J., & Horne Moyer, H. (2001). Changes in clients' attachment styles over the course of time-limited dynamic psychotherapy. *Psychotherapy: Theory, Research, & Practice, 38*, 149–159. doi:10.1037/0033-3204.38.2.149

Tronick, E. Z. (1989). Emotions and emotional communication in infants. *American Psychologist, 44*, 112–119. doi:10.1037/0003-066X.44.2.112

Tsai, J. L., & Levenson, R. W. (1997). Cultural influences of emotional responding: Chinese Americans and European American dating couples during interpersonal conflict. *Journal of Cross-Cultural Psychology, 28*, 600–625. doi:10.1177/0022022197285006

Tschuschke, V., & Dies, R. R. (1994). Intensive analysis of therapeutic factors and outcome in long-term inpatient groups. *International Journal of Group Psychotherapy, 44*, 185–208.

Twaite, J. A., & Rodriguez-Srednicki, O. (2004). Childhood sexual and physical abuse and adult vulnerability to PTSD: The mediating effects of attachment and dissociation. *Journal of Child Sexual Abuse, 13*, 17–38. doi:10.1300/J070v13n01_02

van Andel, P., Erdman, R. A., Karsdorp, P. A., Appels, A., & Trijsburg, R. W. (2003). Group cohesion and working alliance: Prediction of treatment outcome in cardiac patients receiving cognitive behavioral group psychotherapy. *Psychotherapy and Psychosomatics, 72*, 141–149. doi:10.1159/000069733

van der Kolk, B. A., Roth, S., Pelcovitz, D., Sunday, S., & Spinazzola, J. (2005). Disorders of extreme stress: The empirical foundation of a complex adaptation to trauma. *Journal of Traumatic Stress, 18*, 389–399. doi:10.1002/jts.20047

Vogel, D. L., Wade, N. G., & Hackler, A. H. (2007). Perceived public stigma and the willingness to seek counseling: The mediating roles of self stigma and attitudes toward counseling. *Journal of Counseling Psychology, 54*, 40–50. doi:10.1037/0022-0167.54.1.40

Wallin, D. J. (2007). *Attachment in psychotherapy*. New York, NY: Guilford Press.

Wang, C., & Mallinckrodt, B. (2006). Acculturation, attachment, and psychosocial adjustment of Chinese/Taiwanese international students. *Journal of Counseling Psychology, 53*, 422–433. doi:10.1037/0022-0167.53.4.422

Waters, E., Hamilton, C. E., & Weinfeld, N. S. (2000). The stability of attachment security from infancy to adolescence and early adulthood: General introduction. *Child Development, 71*, 678–683. doi:10.1111/1467-8624.00175

Wayment, H., & Vierthaler, J. (2002). Attachment style and bereavement reactions. *Journal of Loss and Trauma, 7*, 129–149. doi:10.1080/153250202753472291

Wei, M., Russell, D. W., Mallinckrodt, B., & Zakalik, R. (2004). Cultural equivalence of adult attachment across four ethnic groups: Factor structure, structured means, and associations with negative mood. *Journal of Counseling Psychology, 51*, 408–417. doi:10.1037/0022-0167.51.4.408

Wei, M., Vogel, D. L., Ku, T.-Y., & Zakalik, R. A. (2005). Adult attachment, affect regulation, negative mood, and interpersonal problems: The mediating role of emotional reactivity and emotional cutoff. *Journal of Counseling Psychology, 52*, 14–24. doi:10.1037/0022-0167.52.1.14

Wessler, R. L., & Hankin-Wessler, S. W. R. (1986). Cognitive appraisal therapy. *Cognitive-behavioral approaches to psychotherapy*. London, England: Harper & Row.

West, M., & George, C. (2002). Attachment and dysthymia: The contribution of preoccupied attachment and agency of self to depression in women. *Attachment & Human Development, 4*, 278–293. doi:10.1080/14616730210167258

West, M., Sheldon, A., & Reiffer, L. (1987). An approach to the delineation of adult attachment: Scale development and reliability. *Journal of Nervous and Mental Disease, 175*, 738–741. doi:10.1097/00005053-198712000-00006

West, M. L., & Sheldon-Keller, A. E. (1994). *Patterns of relating: An adult attachment perspective.* New York, NY: Guilford Press.

White, J. R. (2000). Introduction. In J. R. White & A. Freeman (Eds.), *Cognitive-behavioral group therapy for specific problems and populations* (pp. 3–28). Washington, DC: American Psychological Association. doi:10.1037/10352-000

White, J. R., & Freeman, A. (Eds.). (2000). *Cognitive-behavioral group therapy for specific problems and populations.* Washington, DC: American Psychological Association. doi:10.1037/10352-000

Wilberg, T., & Karterud, S. (2001). The place of group psychotherapy in the treatment of personality disorders. *Current Opinion in Psychiatry, 14,* 125–129.

Wilberg, T., Karterud, S., Pedersen, G., Urnes, O., Irion, T., Brabrand, J., . . . Stubbhaug, B. (2003). Outpatient group psychotherapy following day treatment for patients with personality disorders. *Journal of Personality Disorders, 17,* 510–521. doi:10.1521/pedi.17.6.510.25357

Wilson, J.S., & Costanzo, P.R. (1996). A preliminary study of attachment, attention, and schizotypy in early adulthood. *Journal of Social and Clinical Psychology, 15,* 231–260.

Winnicott, D. W. (1971). *Playing and reality.* London, England: Tavistock.

Woodhouse, S., Schlosser, L., Crook, R., Ligiéro, D., & Gelso, C. J. (2003). Patient attachment to therapist: Relations to transference and patient recollections of parental caregiving. *Journal of Counseling Psychology, 50,* 395–408. doi:10.1037/0022-0167.50.4.395

Wortman, C. B., & Silver, R. C. (1989). The myths of coping with loss. *Journal of Consulting and Clinical Psychology, 57,* 349–357. doi:10.1037/0022-006X.57.3.349

Yalom, I. D. (1995). *The theory and practice of group psychotherapy.* New York, NY: Basic Books.

Yalom, I. D., & Gadban, P. P. (1990). *Understanding group therapy: Vol. 1. Outpatient groups.* Pacific Grove, CA: Brooks Cole.

Yalom, I. D., & Leszcz, M. (2005). *The theory and practice of group psychotherapy* (5th ed.). New York, NY: Basic Books.

You, H. S., & Malley-Morrison, K. (2000). Young adult attachment styles and intimate relationships with close friends: A cross-cultural study of Koreans and Caucasian Americans. *Journal of Cross-Cultural Psychology, 31,* 528–534. doi:10.1177/0022022100031004006

Yutrzenka, D., Whittingham, M., & Greening, K. (2012, August). *Assessing change patterns for the socially inhibited subtype within focused brief group therapy: A mixed-methods approach.* Poster presented at the American Psychological Association Annual Convention, Orlando, FL.

INDEX

Bissada, H., 80, 126, 235
Blehar, M. C., 8–9
Bliwise, N., 57
Blum, H. M., 88
Body cues, in clinical interview, 70
Bonanno, G. A., 214
Borderline personality disorder (BPD), 28
    dialectical behavior therapy for
            treatment of, 79, 80
    and fearful-avoidant attachment
            style, 162–163
    mentalization-based treatment of, 80
    premature dropout by patients with,
            88
Boundaries, pregroup preparation about,
        94
Bowden, M., 57
Bowlby, J., 17–21, 27, 29, 30, 34, 120,
        130, 211–213, 249
Boyer, S. P., 217
BPD. See Borderline personality disorder
Brennan, K. A., 8–9, 158
Briere, J., 164
Burlingame, G. M., 68–69, 90, 99, 119

Caregivers. See also Mothers
    bonds with, 4
    children's attachment to, 18–21, 162
    discipline by, 196
    group attachment vs. attachment
            to, 193
    mentalization by, 26–27
    multiple, 202–203
    primary, 4, 20
    as secure bases, 20
    suboptimal responses by, 23–25
Cassidy, J., 20–21
CATS (Client Attachment to Therapist
        Scale), 48
Caucasians, 190, 191, 195, 203, 204
CBT groups. See Cognitive behavioral
        therapy groups
Chae, M., 201–202
Change
    in adult attachment patterns, 56
    and attachment to therapist, 22–23
    fostering, 246–247
    in group therapy, 34–35
Chen, E. C., 60, 118, 119

Cheng, W. D., 201–202
Children
    attachment to caregivers by, 18–21,
            162
    complex trauma experienced by, 185
    coping behaviors of, 23–25
    development of attachment
            insecurity in, 19–20
    development of attachment security
            in, 18–19
    disorganized attachment style of, 162
    internal models of self for, 18
    mentalization by, 167
    proximity seeking and exploration
            by, 20–21
    reflective capacity of mothers and
            attachments of, 167–168
Clark, C. L., 8–9, 13
Clarkin, J. F., 57
Client Attachment to Therapist Scale
        (CATS), 48
Climate, group, 182, 246
Clinical interview, for screening, 69–72
Clinical Outcome Results Standardized
        Measures (CORE) battery, 68
Closeness, 125
Close relationships
    attachment style in therapy and, 56
    racial–ethnic differences in
            attachment in, 190–191
Coble, H., 48, 54
Cognitive approach to pregroup
        preparation, 92–94
Cognitive behavioral therapy, 33
Cognitive behavioral therapy (CBT)
        groups
    dismissing-avoidant members in,
            80, 81
    interpersonal psychodynamic vs., 245
    for treatment of trauma, 187
Cognitive maps, 32–33
Cohen, C. P., 163
Coherence of mind, 180
Cohesion, group
    as attachment-based process, 98
    and dismissing-avoidant group
            members, 145
    facilitating, 118–121
    and fearful-avoidant group members,
            164

Proximity seeking, *continued*
    and hyperactivation, 24–25
    and infant/child attachment, 20–21
    traumatic emotion associated with,
        25
Psychiatric problems, infant attachment
    and, 21
Psychodynamic group therapy
    dismissing-avoidant members in,
        80, 81
    for eating disorder treatment,
        182–183
    for substance abuse treatment, 184
    for treatment of trauma, 186
Psychodynamic treatment, 56
Psychopathology, 27–28
PTSD (posttraumatic stress disorder),
    185, 186
Punamaki, R. L., 54
Punitive emotional socialization, 196

Quality of object relations (QOR),
    87–88
Quiet borderline, BPD, 163

Racial–ethnic groups, 189–209
    African Americans, 195–203
    Asian Americans, 203–207
    dyadic attachment in, 190–191
    group attachment in, 190–191
    Hispanic and Latino Americans,
        191–195
    multiculturally competent group
        leaders, 208
Racial identity, 208
Racism
    addressing, 201–202
    and attachment avoidance, 196,
        197
Raging borderline, BPD, 162–163
Readiness for group, 69–72
Red signal affects, 130–131
Reflection. *See also* Mentalization
    on emotional experiences, 127–128
    on feelings, 186–187
    self-, 32
Reflective capacity, 27
    and mentalization, 110
    of mothers, 167–168
    of preoccupied group members, 79

Reflective functioning
    assessment of, 75–76
    of preoccupied group members,
        135–136
    of secure group members, 76
Regulation. *See* Affect regulation;
        Emotion regulation
Rejection
    and deactivation, 23–24
    fear of, 131, 132
Relational goals, 71
Relational group therapy, 186
Relational patterns, 113–114
Relationship-focused group therapy, 33
Relationship Questionnaire, 44
Relationships
    close, 56, 190–191
    group member–leader, 59–60
    infant attachment and adult, 26–29
    positive bonding, 99
    therapy, 53–56
Relationship Scale Questionnaire, 45
Repairs, of therapeutic ruptures
    case study, 237–241
    empathic attunement and, 105–107
    at termination of therapy, 223
Repetition, in pregroup preparation,
        94
Repression, of core affect, 152
Research. *See* Empirical research on
        attachment
Resilience, 167
Resilient pattern, 214
Resistant/ambivalent attachment style,
        9
Revised Adult Attachment Scale, 42
Ritchie, K., 80, 126, 182, 235
Riva, M., 121
Rom, E., 120, 132, 145
Romantic attachment, 8–9
Romantic Partner Attachment measure,
        40
Rosenkranz, S., 185
Roth, T., 54
Rules, therapy group, 93–94
Ruptures of therapeutic alliance. *See*
        Therapeutic ruptures
Russell, D. W., 190–191
Rutan, J. S., 113, 117, 146
Rybko, J., 59

by fearful-avoidant group members,
169–171
by preoccupied group members,
127–128
Verbal specificity, 70–71
Vierthaler, J., 215
Wachtel, M., 121
Wall, S., 8–9
Wallin, D. J., 79, 105, 108, 111, 114,
130, 144, 147, 167
Wang, C., 208
Waters, E., 8–9
Wayment, H., 215
Wei, M., 190–191, 204
Weinberger, J., 54
Western cultures, 203, 206, 207

"When the Therapist Says Goodbye"
(Fieldsteel), 225
Whipple, R., 92, 94
Wilberg, T., 175–176
Window of tolerance, 114–116
Wine, B., 235
Winnicott, D. W., 30
Woodhouse, S., 55

Yalom, I. D., 31–33, 35, 58, 60, 90,
92–94, 98, 111–113, 117, 118,
121, 127, 145–146, 148, 209,
215, 217, 219
"You" statements, 70

Zakalik, R., 190–191

ABOUT THE AUTHORS

Cheri L. Marmarosh, PhD, is a full-time associate professor of professional psychology at the George Washington University and a licensed psychologist. She has published numerous empirical and theoretical articles that focus on how group and individual therapy facilitate change. She has supervised the research and clinical work of many doctoral students in the DC area. She is also an associate editor of *Group Dynamics: Theory, Research, and Practice* and on the editorial boards of the *International Journal of Group Psychotherapy* and *Psychotherapy: Theory, Research, Practice, Training*. Dr. Marmarosh is a faculty member in the Advanced Training Program in the Institute of Contemporary Psychotherapy and Psychoanalysis and on the steering committee of the Couple Program at the Washington Center for Psychoanalysis. She is a Fellow of Division 29 (Psychotherapy) of the American Psychological Association. Dr. Marmarosh has a private practice in Washington, DC.

Rayna D. Markin, PhD, is an assistant professor of counseling at Villanova University and a licensed psychologist. She has published numerous empirical and theoretical articles on the group therapy process and outcome, with special attention on how attachment and transference impact group member relationships and the group therapy process. She is interested in studying relationship-based psychotherapies, in general, and the curative factors in individual and group therapies. She is also interested in designing attachment-based interventions that use a group format for at-risk mothers. Dr. Markin has practiced in numerous settings, from counseling centers and hospitals to private practice. She is involved in several professional organizations, such as the Society for Psychotherapy Research and Division 29 of the American Psychological Association. However, she derives the most joy from spending time with her two most precious attachment objects, her husband and young daughter.

Eric B. Spiegel, PhD, is a licensed psychologist in private practice in Philadelphia and Bryn Mawr, Pennsylvania. He enjoys working across therapeutic modalities, offering individual, couples, and group psychotherapy in his practice. Dr. Spiegel specializes in anxiety and mood disorders, attachment and relationship issues, clinical hypnosis, mind–body psychology, and trauma. He is involved in several professional organizations, including the American Society of Clinical Hypnosis (ASCH). In 2012, he was honored by ASCH with the Early Career Achievement Award. He currently serves as the moderator of the Board of Governors and as a member of the Executive Committee for ASCH. He received his doctorate in counseling psychology from the University of Maryland in 2005.